War Damage
in
Western Europe

Other titles in the *Societies at War* series include

War Damage
in
Western Europe

The Destruction of Historic Monuments
During the Second World War

Nicola Lambourne

Edinburgh University Press

© Nicola Lambourne, 2001

Edinburgh University Press Ltd
22 George Square, Edinburgh

Typeset in Melior
by Pioneer Associates, Perthshire, and
printed and bound in Great Britain by
The Cromwell Press, Trowbridge, Wilts

A CIP Record for this book is available from the British Library

ISBN 0 7486 1285 8 (paperback)

Contents

List of illustrations

Acknowledgements

For their help in the researching and illustrating of this book I would like to thank in particular Janice Day of the Courtauld Institute Book Library, the staff of the Conway Library at the Courtauld Institute of Art, staff in the Department of Printed Books, Art Department and Photograph Archive at the Imperial War Museum, the staff of the National Monuments Record, and Jens Boel and Mahmoud Ghander of the Unesco Archives in Paris. For help in funding the research, many thanks to the Arts Faculty of the Open University and thank you also to Cheryl Beasley and Richard Tuffs of the Open University Study Centre in Brussels for 'technical assistance' and general encouragement. I would like to dedicate this book to Christopher Todd, who is indirectly responsible for it being written at all.

Note on the map, place names and translations

Many historic monuments and cities across western Europe are referred to in this book and to orientate the reader I have included a map of the main countries featured: Great Britain, Germany, France, Italy, The Netherlands, Belgium and Luxembourg. The towns marked on the map are those mentioned in the text, that is, the principal locations of cultural war damage during the Second World War plus some other important sites. Sites of First World War damage to historic monuments are also marked.

As place names in different languages make a regular appearance throughout the text, I have adopted the following system: if there is a common anglicised version of the place name, I have used that – Munich instead of München, for example – but have otherwise used the 'local' spelling. In the case of Belgian towns, which fall either north or south of the current Dutch/French 'language line' in that country, place names are given first in the geographically correct language, with the alternative following in brackets, for instance Mechelen (Malines). I have made an exception for Louvain, which should be Leuven, but the notorious war damage that occurred there is associated historically with the French name for the town.

Translations from French and German sources are my own unless otherwise stated.

Introduction

The destruction of architecture during the Second World War had its apologists: 'The Bomber Saves Civilisation' was the optimistic first chapter title of a 1944 book on the bombing of German cities, J. M. Spaight's *Bombing Vindicated*.[1] This book will present a less positive view of the effects of Second World War air raids on historic city centres, although the aim here is not just to add to the many existing criticisms and justifications of the activities of Bomber Command but rather to examine a particular effect of the wartime bombardment of towns carried out by both sides in the conflict. The effect under examination here is that of the destruction of historic monuments and buildings of cultural interest in western Europe, architecture which was a manifestation of the very civilisation that the bombers were supposed to have saved.

The Second World War cultural damage under examination here is primarily that which took place in Britain, Germany and France, with some mention of events in Belgium, The Netherlands and also Italy, all of which fall within the broad category of western Europe for reasons of shared cultural history as well as geography. The focus is on western European cultural damage, despite the fact that extensive damage of this kind was also carried out in the countries of eastern Europe, for two principal reasons, the first being that cultural hostility had accompanied military conflict in western Europe in both the Franco-Prussian War of 1870–1 and the First World War, with the bombardment of the historic monuments and cities of the enemy a feature of both military and propaganda campaigns. The cultural destruction of the Second World War was not an innovation in itself; the novelty lay in its greatly increased extent and in the technology used to cause such damage. The second reason for a western focus is that Nazi treatment of cultural property in eastern and western Europe differed: in eastern Europe, the policy was simply to destroy and many historic monuments in Poland and the invaded areas of Russia were summarily burned after any objects of value had been pillaged. In western Europe the attitude was more one of respect for the cultural history of those countries regarded as members of the same European cultural club, particularly in the case of France. Admiration of French culture was a German tradition and an additional motivation to preserve rather than to destroy the architectural heritage of the invaded France was that the country, with all its historic monuments, was intended as part of Greater Germany. Between Germany and Britain there was less cultural respect on either side, with destructive consequences, but both maintained an apparent faith in the idea that the bombing of historic monuments was 'barbaric', at least in propaganda on the subject.

In place of the single country, single city or single building studies of cultural war damage that constitute the majority of accounts of the destruction, here a comparative approach will be taken, not only with the intention of showing how x happened in country A, while y happened in country B, although this in itself is useful as there is currently no existing overall history of the Second World War from this point of view. The intention is also to examine the phenomenon of cultural war damage as an aspect of modern warfare that was developed to a particularly extensive degree in the Second World War in all countries involved in the conflict, asking why it occurred, whether it was a deliberate policy on the part of either side and how it was used by propagandists and explained by commentators.

War damage to architecture is a relatively under-studied feature of the Second World War for a number of reasons which demonstrate deeply held, if unexamined, attitudes towards both the buildings themselves and this aspect of war – the view that historic monuments are ultimately expendable, for example, whatever the value ascribed to them in peacetime. The destruction of historic monuments in wartime has often been regarded as a 'natural' aspect of conflict, an unfortunate but inevitable consequence of modern forms of warfare which is essentially unproblematic and therefore not in need of historical attention. It is the aim here to problematise the subject thoroughly, to demonstrate that cultural war damage should not be 'taken for granted' by historians of the Second World War and to recover the significance and resonance of what was an emotive and highly visible issue at the time. The bombing of historic city centres and monuments has been subject more to a process of mythologisation than to historical analysis, with the result that for most it recalls only Coventry, Dresden and perhaps the figure of 'Bomber' Harris.

The subject falls into a gap between military, art historical and social history studies of the period. For military historians architectural damage is of peripheral interest, a background to the essential military events and issues, and their studies have focused on particular military campaigns, strategy, weaponry, military intelligence, and the personalities of those in command, in addition to analyses of the political origins of particular conflicts, with little space being found for the wartime fate of the cultural property of the belligerents. The official British history of the activities of Bomber Command during the Second World War, *The Strategic Air Offensive Against Germany 1939–1945* (by Charles Webster and Noble Frankland, published in 1961), typically includes few mentions of the effects on historic town centres and monuments.[2] These targets occasionally appear through the sights of the historian, but only from a safe military distance and not at all in sharp focus. Information from military sources can quantify the damage caused – one source supplies the figure of a total of 207 raids on Berlin, for example, involving 23,407 aircraft and causing damage to 125,775 buildings – but the specific effect on historic monuments, and the significance of this type of damage is hidden within the statistics.[3]

Art historians have tended to prioritise the production rather than the destruction of art during wartime, charting the emergence of new styles in painting and sculpture or the continuation of pre-war artistic concerns, an approach which affirms the survival of the activity under adverse circumstances.[4] Similarly, studies of the history of architecture focus on the 'normal' life of buildings, telling the story of their continued existence, instead of abnormal episodes of their ruin and disappearance. It is significant that one of the best known English-language surveys of architectural history, Nikolaus Pevsner's *An Outline of European Architecture*, takes just this approach, despite being first published in 1942, in the middle of one of the more energetic periods of architectural destruction in western Europe's history. Very little mention is made of the destructions of the war occurring as Pevsner was writing the book – only a discrete caption to a photograph of a still intact pre-war Coventry Cathedral acknowledges that the church had been ruined during an air raid in November 1940.[5] A second edition of Pevsner's book was published in 1945, then a third in 1948, with only the

addition of a brief commemorative reference to the ruin of historic
monuments in Cologne: 'Cologne, until five years ago, possessed an
unrivalled number of churches dating back to the tenth, eleventh,
twelfth and early thirteenth centuries. Their loss is one of the
most grievous casualties of the war'.[6] In the 1960 edition the war is
referred to as a temporary 'barrier' to architectural progress, a dis-
turbance in the smooth narrative of architectural history. Pevsner's
book is an account of the gradual stylistic development of buildings
in western Europe over the centuries, as though the abruptly
negative effects of air raids were of little importance in the overall
history of architecture. One of the purposes of the present book is to
acknowledge the significance of the architectural destruction of the
Second World War and more generally to argue that the destruction
of architecture has a history too, one that can complement more
traditional studies.

   The theft of works of art during World War Two has attracted
more art historical attention than the destruction of architecture.
This aspect of culture in wartime is the subject of a relatively large
literature, in recent years as well as immediately after the events,
reflecting the fact that not all works of art that went missing during
the war have been recovered – the story is as yet unfinished. The
Nazi theft of art has been thoroughly researched, in publications
ranging in emphasis from the documentary to the accusatory. Both
types appeared just after the war, for instance the 1946 report of
the British Committee on the Preservation and Restitution of Works
of Art, Archives and Other Material in Enemy Hands, entitled
Works of Art in Germany. Losses and Survivals in the War, and J. J.
Rorimer's *Survival. The Salvage and Protection of Art in War* (1950).
The French, the victims of art theft on a large scale, produced their
own documentation of the wartime fate of mobile works of art, for
example Rose Valland's *Le Front de l'Art* (1961). A more recent
English language publication in this area is the thorough survey
by Lynn H. Nicholas, *The Rape of Europa. The Fate of Europe's
Treasures in the Third Reich* (1994).[7] The subject lends itself to
exciting titles and lively narratives, the continuing saga of the
recovery of paintings stolen by the Nazis proving popular enough
to become a recurrent story in the newspapers, particularly in the
British and French press.[8] Ruined historic monuments perhaps
lack the glamour and optimism of such tales of loss and recovery,
with pillaged paintings hidden in salt mines repatriated and
restored by heroic (Allied) rescuers to their owners, thus providing
a succession of happy endings that a tale of a bombed cathedral

cannot so easily supply. Curiously, the positive connotations of monument reconstruction have not been exploited to the same extent, just occasionally alluded to in the titles of books on rebuilding, for instance *Ruined and Rebuilt, Phoenix at Coventry* and *Exeter Phoenix*.[9]

Social histories of the Second World War have focused on the human damage and disruption of everyday civilian life caused by RAF and Luftwaffe bombardment.[10] An issue which should be addressed at the start of this book is the appropriateness of studying war damage to historic monuments when the same air raids caused loss of life. The problem is not that of whether to attribute an equally problematic ethical status to the destruction of historic monuments and human life.[11] It is not a question of prioritising buildings over people with a perverse degree of academic distance, but rather an historical look at another aspect of the Second World War, an aspect which was of concern at the time in all the countries involved. The bombs themselves did not discriminate – as one contemporary commentator noted on viewing the results of an air raid:

This has been a day in my life. To have seen the destruction of war, what guns and bombs do to houses and people in them, to towns, cities, bridges, railroad stations and tracks and trains, to universities and ancient noble buildings, to enemy soldiers, trucks, tanks and horses caught along the way.[12]

For most, human damage was naturally regarded as being worse than architectural damage, but the latter was also a wartime issue, part of the experience of this war for all sides in the conflict and a consequence of modern methods of warfare to be debated, criticised, justified and defended. To ignore the phenomenon would therefore be to neglect a feature of the Second World War of much contemporary importance. Uncertainty about the correctness of demonstrating a concern for cultural property when more fundamental humanitarian principles have been compromised was recently demonstrated by a degree of embarrassment over showing a practical interest in the cultural destruction caused during the 1991–5 conflict in Bosnia. Although the war in the former Yugoslavia itself was very different in scale, style and origin to the Second World War, attitudes towards cultural war damage provide an illuminating parallel. This type of damage was monitored throughout the war by the Council of Europe and reports from Bosnia insisted that: '*Our* view is that *people* suffering is of first priority, never mind the monuments. But that is not *their* view. They take global destruction of their monuments very seriously indeed. It is time that their attitude about what is happening to their cultural heritage should be taken seriously by us'.[13] It is an assumption of this book that this argument should also be applied retrospectively to the damaged historic monuments of the Second World War and beyond.

One important reaction, then and now, to the destruction of historic monuments is that it was and is thought of as being in some sense wrong. There is a commonly held assumption that it is contrary to military concepts of honour or, more generally, morally wrong to mistreat works of art and architecture during a military conflict by destroying or stealing them. Employed here is the idea of the 'sanctity of art' and an invocation of the 'loss to all mankind' caused by the bombardment of architecture and the disappearance of paintings. An appeal is made to a supposed commonly, internationally held ideal of the fundamental importance of art and a corresponding instinctive appreciation of the evil inherent in destroying it. These sentiments appeared regularly during the Second World War, in official government statements on cultural war damage – from both sides – and in government-approved propaganda, while large quantities of 'enemy' historic monuments were at the same time being destroyed as part of the bombardment of cities. This gap between what governments of nations at war say about art and what they do to it is the underlying theme of this book.

The assumption of immorality has ensured that such actions have been forbidden under International Law since the early twentieth century by successive Hague Conventions governing conduct during armed conflict. Although the legal provisions established often failed to fulfil the moral intention behind them, alleged German guilt for damage to and theft of the cultural property of France during the First World War was punished by articles in the Treaty of Versailles. It is not the aim here to determine whether it is indeed 'wrong' or 'bad' to bombard a cathedral in wartime, as this is a question for philosophical rather than historical analysis. The relevant questions here are: who expressed the belief that these acts were morally wrong?, when and under what circumstances? and, most importantly, did this belief have any effect on the conduct of either side in the conflict? Although a convincing attitude of sincere belief in the special status of art and architecture has been *de rigueur* for governments during the conflicts of the twentieth

century, this claimed high-mindedness has not always been con-
verted into positive action to avoid their mistreatment in wartime and
has often remained on the level of rhetorical flourish in denunciations of this mistreatment. An opposition between realism and
idealism has characterised the debate on the moral status of
wartime damage to cultural property, and the rights of art and
architecture to special consideration during armed conflict have
frequently been downgraded in the interests of pragmatism. Thus a
failure to prevent such damage has been excused with the argument
that the falling of bombs on cathedrals is regrettable but ultimately
inevitable and unavoidable in wartime. As one commentator on
the bombing of Cologne put it, 'It may be a crime to attack a cathedral, but it is only war to miss a railway station'.[14] In Cologne the
cathedral is next to the main station.

This was the military attitude most commonly adopted during
the Second World War, avoiding the ethical question by assuming
that war is an amoral zone, where conventional morality does not
apply. The 'area bombing' of cities – the indiscriminate bombing
of entire towns with the consequent killing of civilians and devastation of buildings – was regarded as a natural consequence of the
type of war where distinctions between military and non-military
targets are blurred, rather than an act which is morally wrong.
Webster and Frankland expressed the military view as follows: 'It
might appear . . . that a great moral issue was involved in this situation, but the moral issue was not really an operative factor. The
choice between precision and area bombing was not conditioned
by abstract theories of right and wrong, nor by interpretations of
international law. It was ruled by operational possibilities and
strategic intentions'.[15] That there was a gulf between the military and
civilian attitude towards such bombing can be seen from official
government attempts to justify the practice, as a means to destroy
enemy morale and thus shorten the war, for instance. From a
military perspective, the prevarications of politicians and civil
servants over 'air frightfulness' were an unnecessary veneer on a
legitimate military strategy.[16]

Dissenting civilian voices were a rarity during the war, branded
as unpatriotic when permitted. In Britain, a letter to *The Times* in
July 1943 condemned damage to Cologne Cathedral caused by
Allied bombing as 'deplorable', on the grounds that 'Medieval
cathedrals . . . are the heritage of the whole world, wherever they
may happen to be', earning the author the accusation of being a
supporter of Hitler.[17] Public figures such as George Bernard Shaw

and George Bell, Bishop of Chichester consistently resisted the
official line on the bombing of German cities and their historic
monuments, to little effect. In a speech to the House of Lords made
on 9 February 1944, Bell protested at the apparent indifference to
the destructive effects of area bombing:

In the fifth year of the war it must surely be apparent to any but the most
complacent and reckless how far the destruction of European culture
has already gone. We ought to think once, twice, and three times before
destroying the rest. . . . How can the War Cabinet fail to see that this
progressive devastation of cities is threatening the roots of civilisation?[18]

He called for the few remaining intact historic German cities,
including the as yet unbombed Dresden, to be respected, but the
War Cabinet were unmoved by the threat to civilisation and the
honour of the nation. Meanwhile in Germany, where dissent was
even less possible, the perception that cultural damage was 'wrong'
was expressed in other ways: it was acknowledged in a Goebbels
directive of June 1942 on the correct way to refer to air raids having
this effect, the term 'terror raid' (*Terrorangriff*) being prescribed for
descriptions of RAF raids on Germany, while Luftwaffe attacks on
British cultural targets were to be known as 'retaliation raids'
(*Vergeltungsangriffe*), in a different moral category altogether, as the
other side had started it.[19] Just as one manifestation of Hitler's
barbarism for British propagandists was his bombardment of British
historic monuments, Churchill features in Goebbels' propaganda as
the prime war damage criminal, a 'culture gangster' and a menace
to the world of art, with a lust for the destruction of 'cities of
culture above all', who had personally ordered the destruction of
German historic monuments such as Bismarck's mausoleum in
Friedrichsruh and Goethe's house in Weimar.[20]
    The book is structured as follows: Chapter 1 provides historical
context for later chapters by examining pre-Second World War
precedents of cultural war damage and attempts to establish legal
protection for art and architecture in treaties of International Law
governing conduct in war. Chapter 2 surveys the damage done to
historic monuments during the Second World War, when, where,
how and by whom, establishing a chronology of cultural war
damage across western Europe. Chapter 3 deals with contemporary
reaction to the destruction of historic monuments, the use of the
events by propagandists and the intended effect on civilian
morale. In Chapter 4 the questions are those of why and with what

justification large scale air raids were carried out on historic city centres by both sides in the conflict; also considered is the issue of whether there was a deliberate policy on either the Allied or German side to destroy the cultural property of the enemy, or whether historic monuments simply 'got in the way' of air raids on military targets. The literally ruinous state of many European cities at the end of the war is the subject of Chapter 5, together with plans for their reconstruction in the various affected countries and attempts to justify the destructions of the war after the event, especially on the part of the Allies, by telling a particular story of what happened and why.

Finally a note on terminology: the cultural targets for the bombs can be referred to in various ways, as 'architecture', as 'historic monuments', or the more legal 'cultural property', or the currently popular 'cultural heritage'. The expression 'historic monument' will be the most frequently used term here, as shorthand for the more specific 'buildings of historic and/or cultural interest'. Included in the idea of an 'historic monument' are cathedrals, other churches, museum buildings (as opposed to their contents), public buildings such as townhalls and libraries, buildings of political significance such as ministries and private houses of architectural importance. The definition 'cultural and/or historic' interest is intended to include structures used for, say, commercial or industrial purposes which also happen to be architecturally significant. The more general expression 'historic town centres' will also occur, some-times in the guise of 'architectural ensembles', as these rather than particular buildings were frequently the targets for air raids, with the result that entire streets of historic buildings were destroyed, along with road plans surviving sometimes from the medieval period. The entire architectural profile of cities and towns that had been gradually established over centuries, with combinations of buildings from different periods, was vulnerable to indiscriminate air raids.

Notes

1. Spaight (d. 1944) was Principal Assistant Secretary in the Air Ministry and had published several books on the subject of air warfare, listed in the bibliography. His approval of the Strategic Air Offensive – the official title for Allied air operations in Germany – was not unqualified and might well have been revised in the light of later events in the war, such as the bombing of Dresden in February 1945.

2. The authors represent very much the traditional wing of Second World War history, Sir Charles Webster being a military historian and Noble Frankland a former director of the Imperial War Museum in London.

3. Figures – from a British source – quoted in Beseler and Gutschow, *Kriegsschicksale deutscher Architektur*, p. 135.

4. General studies of the destruction of art do exist, although they do not focus on the specifically wartime destruction which is the focus of this book. See for example Briggs, *Goths and Vandals. A Study of the Destruction, Neglect and Preservation of Historical Buildings in England*, Réau, *Histoire du Vandalisme. Les monuments détruits de l'art français* and Gamboni, *The Destruction of Art.*

5. Pevsner, *An Outline of European Architecture*, 1942 edition, published in paperback format. Pevsner was one of many German academics who left Nazi Germany for Britain.

6. Pevsner, *An Outline of European Architecture*, 1948 edition, p. 27.

7. Nicholas provides a bibliography for Second World War art theft. One important primary source for Nazi art theft in France is Jean Cassou's *Le Pillage par les Allemands des oeuvres d'art appartenant à des Juifs en France* (1947). See also the more recent book by Hector Feliciano, *Le musée disparu* (1995). Two German treatments of the subject are Wilhelm Treue's *Kunstraub – Über die Schicksale von Kunstwerken in Krieg, Revolution und Frieden* (1957) and the collection of essays edited by Martin Warnke, *Bildersturm. Die Zerstörung des Kunstwerks* (1977). Both deal with the theft and destruction of paintings in various periods and in various circumstances, not just during war or by German soldiers. Dealing with theft on the other side of Europe is *Beautiful Loot: the Soviet Plunder of Europe's Art Treasures*, by Konstantin Akinsha and Grigorii Kozlov, also the authors of *Stolen Treasure: the Hunt for the World's Lost Masterpieces* (both 1995).

8. An article in *The Independent* of 18 November 1998 had a typically sensational title: 'The last Nazi art scandal. Will the return of the looted art treasures of Europe, after 50 years, mark the final chapter of the Holocaust?'. The most recent book on the subject is *The Lost Masters: the Looting of Europe's Treasurehouses*, by Peter Harclerode and Brendan Pittaway (Gollancz 1999).

9. By Richard Thomas Howard (1962), Basil Spence (1962) and Thomas Sharp (1946) respectively.

10. There are too many to mention here, but for interesting perspectives see Calder, *The Myth of the Blitz* (1991) and Iklé, *The Social Impact of Bomb Destruction* (1958).

11. On the ethical problem of the killing of civilians, see Garrett, *Ethics and Air Power in World War II. The British Bombing of German Cities.* Also controversial was the high number of casualties among aircrew: in the case of Bomber Command alone the figure was 55,573 (quoted in Frankland, *The Bombing Offensive against Germany*, p. 91).

12. Shirer, *Berlin Diary 1934–1941*, p. 274, entry for 20 May 1940. The author was then the Berlin correspondent for the American broadcaster CBS.

13. The view of Roger Shrimplin, the then Chairman of the East Europe Committee, Royal Institute of British Architects, quoted in Council of Europe, Doc. 6904, *Third Information Report on war damage to the cultural heritage in Croatia and Bosnia-Herzegovina, presented by the Committee on Culture and Education*, Strasbourg 20 September 1993, p. 26.

14. Webster and Frankland, *The Strategic Air Offensive Against Germany 1939–1945*, Vol. II, pp. 22–3.

15. Ibid.

16. The expression 'air frightfulness' was common in the literature and even appears in Arthur Harris' – Commander-in-Chief of Bomber Command – book *Bomber Offensive*, p. 176–7.

17. Letter to the Editor from Sydney Cockerell in *The Times* of 13 July 1943.

18. The speech is reprinted in Bell's collection of essays *The Church and Humanity (1939–1946)*, pp. 129–41. See also the article by Best, 'The Bishop and the Bomber' in *History Today*, September 1983, pp. 28–32. For George Bernard Shaw's view, see for instance a letter to the editor of *The Times* of 28 April 1941.

19. Quoted in Boelcke, *Wollt Ihr den totalen Krieg?*, entry for 2 June 1942, p. 247.

20. Churchill was regularly characterised as such in Goebbels' speeches and articles, for instance in the *Völkischer Beobachter* of 30 April 1942 and in 'So etwas wie eine zweite Front', 1 May 1942, and 'Der Luft- und Nervenkrieg', 14 June 1942, both in Goebbels, *Das Eherne Herz*, pp. 302–8 and 344–50 respectively.

1

Precedents and Laws –
War Damage to
Historic Monuments 1870–1939

PRECEDENTS

War damage to architecture was not a new phenomenon in 1939, waiting to be inaugurated during the Second World War. By this time the bombardment of historic monuments during wars in western Europe had a history of its own, as the practice had been a controversial feature of the First World War and of the Franco-Prussian War before that. In 1940 France was invaded by Germany for the third time in seventy years, causing a third round of cultural damage, and cities in Germany and the south of England were bombarded from the air for a second time in the Second World War, having already been damaged in this way in 1914–18, albeit on a much lesser scale. For this reason, although the principal subject of this book is war damage to historic monuments during the Second World War, it is appropriate to begin with a short survey of the earlier history of such destruction. The war years 1870–1, 1914–18 and 1939–45 are the natural focus of this survey, but this particular aspect of war history cannot be confined to such a narrow periodisation, as the interwar years saw much debate on the significance and threat of cultural war damage, as well as the agreement of international legislation to prevent it. The years 1870–1945, and beyond to the immediate post-Second World War years, form a continuous period of war damage, payment of indemnities for this damage, followed by reconstruction and restoration, then a repeat of the damage. When the first bombs fell on historic city centres in

May 1940, the official reopening of the cathedral of Reims, damaged in World War One, had taken place only two years earlier in July 1938, after twenty interwar years of restoration. Cologne Cathedral, damaged during the bombardments of 1942–5, had only been completed as the German 'national cathedral' in 1880. City of London churches such as St Paul's Cathedral were threatened by bombs in both 1914–18 and 1939–45. The modern history of some of the most important historic monuments in western Europe is inseparable from their wartime fate, as a result of events which rarely feature in architectural histories.

The destruction of churches, castles and other cultural targets had always been part of war but by the time of the Franco-Prussian War attitudes towards historic monuments had changed, as had methods with which to bombard them. Throughout the nineteenth century an interest in the preservation of architecture had developed, along with a concept of cultural heritage belonging to a nation, a connection encouraged by the emergence of new nation states such as Germany. Contemporary histories and press commentary on the 1870–1 conflict showed a heightened awareness of the threat to historic monuments represented by modern techniques of warfare, and of the significance of this threat to the cultural property of the nation. This aspect of warfare was also attractive to propagandists, who focused on episodes such as the German bombardment of Strasbourg and the consequent damage to the city's cathedral and museums, the threat to the art and architecture of Paris during the winter siege of the capital and the German occupation of Versailles.

The French were the sole victims of cultural war damage in this conflict, having been invaded so swiftly by the enemy – France had declared war on Prussia in July 1870, Napoleon III had surrendered and been taken prisoner at Sedan on 2 September, the siege of Paris was well under way in October, and the peace agreement was signed by Bismarck and Thiers on 21 February 1871.[1] By way of revenge the French took the propaganda offensive, portraying the invaders as 'barbarians', as opposed to the 'civilised' French, a contrast which was still flourishing during the First World War. Any instances of cultural war damage were reported in this light, as resulting directly from a character fault of the enemy, rather than as an unfortunate consequence of war. During the siege of Strasbourg from 18 August 1870 until the city's surrender on 27 September, shells fired from long-range guns caused damage to the cathedral and several other churches; the principal art museum, the Musée de l'Aubette was burnt down with its contents, including paintings by Perugino, Memling, Schongauer and Vouet. These events were described in French publications as typical of the uncivilised destructive methods of the Prussian army, an indisputable 'act of monstrous barbarity and appalling vandalism'.[2] The German 'race' was portrayed as having put down their philosophy books and picked up their guns, abandoning themselves to a long-repressed desire to destroy and damage:

This is the way the sons of noble and philosophical Germany, in the grip of an uncontrollable frenzy, carry out the promise, made solemnly and before the whole of Europe on their entry into Alsace, to respect religion, humanity and civilisation.[3]

Engravings such as Figure 1.1, published in *Le Monde illustré*, represented the apocalyptic scenes, showing clouds of smoke, shells shooting through the night sky towards Strasbourg Cathedral and flames spreading fast.[4] In this way French commentators made the best of their military humiliation: in French accounts and histories of the 1870–1 war, military inferiority was at least partly excused by cultural superiority – precisely the weak point of the Prussians, the argument went.

Once formulated, this characterisation of Prussian-style cultural war damage was applied to all instances of threatened or actual destruction. Paris was perceived as a natural target for the jealous Germans and protection measures were taken for historic monuments and museums there: the stained glass of the Sainte-Chapelle was covered with an elaborate scaffold of sandbags, as was the Arc de Triomphe, while the contents of the Louvre were removed for safety to Brest from 1 September 1870, ready to be shipped abroad in the event of the Prussian army taking the capital.[5] Shells from Prussian long-range guns did fall on Paris, launched from vantage points on high ground in the suburbs, and the church of St Sulpice and the dome of the Panthéon were hit (see Figure 1.2). Damage was sporadic and not serious, however, as the French surrendered before a full-scale invasion of Paris became necessary. Considerably more architectural damage was caused during the Commune, when the Hôtel de Ville and the Palais des Tuileries were completely burnt out and many other buildings affected, including the Gobelins tapestry manufactory and the Bibliothèque du Louvre. Even the church of Notre-Dame was threatened in this civil war: in May 1871 piles of wood were arranged inside the church, but the insurgents were persuaded not to apply torches to them.[6] This self-inflicted

FIGURE 1.1 Strasbourg Cathedral under bombardment on the
night of 24 August 1870. The cathedral was not as badly
damaged as the image suggests, as the right-hand tower was
never actually built. Engraving published in *Le Monde illustré*
and in Armand Dayot (1901), *L'Invasion, le Siège 1870, la
Commune 1871*, p. 51.

destruction was more extensive than anything caused by the Prussian
invasion and occupation and was condemned by commentators as
home-grown barbarism.

The perceived Prussian cultural threat culminated in the enemy

FIGURE 1.2 The Prussian position in the Parc de Saint-Cloud. St Sulpice
and the Panthéon can be seen to the right of the central tower.
Engraving published in *Le Monde illustré* and in Armand Dayot (1901),
L'Invasion, le Siège 1870, la Commune 1871, p. 135.

use of the palace at Versailles from October 1870 as Prussian
military headquarters, although there was no actual physical damage to this most symbolic of French historic monuments. The
damage done was that to cultural and historical pride, particularly
when the occupied palace was chosen as the venue for the proclamation of the German Empire and the crowning of the Prussian
King Wilhelm I as Emperor of a unified Germany on 18 January
1871. For the French this constituted a most humiliating political
and cultural invasion. The ceremony took place in the Salle des
Glaces, decorated with Charles Le Brun's scenes of a golden age of
French military triumphs over her European neighbours under
Louis XIV, including the subjugation of parts of what was about to
become Germany. In 1871 the famous room saw the establishment
of a German nation which threatened to dominate France and
Europe in its turn.[7] As one French historian of the Franco-Prussian
war expressed it: 'This triumphalist ceremony at the gateway to
Paris in a palace so symbolic of the glory of our nation, and this

threatening proclamation, are perhaps the two most cruelly humiliating insults to our national pride of the entire campaign'.[8] The appropriation of French history and architecture for German political ends at a moment when the two countries were still at war was another type of cultural aggression, destructive in other, perhaps more durable ways. The damage done here was not as easily repaired as a burnt out building and a symbolic use of Versailles was to feature again at the end of the First World War.

Although the extent of actual, rather than perceived, war damage to historic monuments was relatively limited during the Franco-Prussian War, a change in the status of this particular effect of conflict had occurred. This aspect of war was established as something worth commenting on and as something which could and ought to be avoided – if it was not avoided, it attracted censure, singled out for particular attention as a feature of modern warfare especially repugnant to all civilised persons. Precedents of action and reaction were established that would later be followed assiduously in both the First and Second World Wars.

There were many similarities in the damage to architecture occurring in both the Franco-Prussian and the First World Wars, not least on the level of how the damage was caused. Although air raids were a feature of the war in, or over, France, Germany and southern England, most damage to historic monuments during the Franco-Prussian and the First World Wars was inflicted by shells fired from long range cannon, during the employment of siege tactics. In both conflicts, towns in northern France were wholly or partly surrounded by the German army and bombarded with exploding shells from long range guns. By 1870 the German manufacturer Krupp had developed the heavy artillery guns which were tried out during the sieges of Strasbourg and Paris; by 1914 the guns had grown in size and range: the largest was the 42cm Mörser (mortar), nicknamed 'Dicke Berta', or 'Big Bertha', which was capable of firing shells weighing 1,800lb a distance of approximately six miles. This was a rarity, however, and smaller but equally effective artillery guns, such as the 21cm howitzer with its range of just over 10,000 yards, were in more common usage.[9] High explosive shells were found to be particularly effective when fired at buildings. There are of course more details of contemporary weaponry of interest to the war historian, but these are the elements of contemporary warfare that are of primary interest to the historian of cultural war damage, as these were the techniques that enabled shells to be aimed at cathedrals. More precisely, they made possible the deliberate targeting of specific buildings and also, by extension, lent support to the frequent accusations of this activity. As will become apparent in later chapters, the more general destructive effect of the area bombing carried out during the Second World War made allegations of the targeting of particular historic monuments less convincing, as it was more commonly whole historic city centres which were affected.

Another element of continuity between the two earlier wars was the way in which damage to historic monuments and cultural targets was characterised: the character of the Germanic 'barbarian' survived, indeed flourished, in French commentary during the interwar years to begin the First World War in healthy form. An opposition was maintained between 'Latin' French *civilisation* versus Teutonic, northern European *Kultur*, and parallels were drawn between the 1914 invasion of France and previous barbarian invasions of Gaul, for instance in 406, when the Vandals crossed the Rhine, sacking Reims, Arras and Amiens, and the later fifth-century invasion of the same area by Attila the Hun, when Reims was destroyed again, along with Metz and Troyes, on the route to Paris. St Nicaise, bishop of Reims, was decapitated by invading Vandals on the steps of his church; the martyred saint appears in sculptural form on the facade of the Gothic cathedral of Reims and, when this figure was damaged by German shellfire in 1914, it appeared to French commentators that the Vandals had returned to repeat the barbarous massacre.[10] These 'historical' comparisons invited analogies between the temperament of the fifth and twentieth century invaders.

Continuity of characterisation of war damage was ensured partly by the fact that some commentators who had reported on such events during the Franco-Prussian War were still writing on this subject in 1914–18. Marius Vachon, for example, published books detailing the 'barbarian' nature of cultural damage inflicted on France by Germany during both wars, using the same themes in the First World War as he had developed in 1870–1. His best known publication on the destructions of 1914–18 was *Les Villes martyres de France et de Belgique* (1915), and the expression *ville martyre* (martyred town), with all its Christian connotations, became the standard phrase used to describe a war damaged town. The 1914–18 war saw the publication of a large French literature on the subject of damage to historic monuments – while German shells fell on the buildings of besieged northern French towns, French propagandists fought back with accusations of vandalism in books and pamphlets with inflammatory titles.[11] Although the association between the Germans and barbarism in this cultural sense had not diminished by the time of the Second World War – the physical 'proof' had remained very visible throughout the interwar years in the form of war-damaged cathedrals and historic towns in the process of gradual restoration – in this war the French were not free to reiterate the judgement as the press and all publications were under the control of the occupying army.[12]

The most famous case of a First World War *ville martyre* was Reims. This town was one of many invaded during the German advance across north-eastern France at the start of the war. The western front, once established, remained largely static for the duration of the war and parts of north-eastern France were under German occupation from September 1914 until October 1918. As a result, the general pattern of war damage to historic monuments in this area was that of an intense period of bombardment at the start of the war, followed by a lull during the war, then another period of shelling towards the end of the conflict, accompanying the German retreat from the occupied towns. Reims was an exception, however, as the French army succeeded in regaining the town soon after its invasion, forcing a rather earlier German retreat in early September 1914. The danger to the citizens and historic monuments of Reims was not alleviated, as German troops set up their guns on nearby hills and began what was to become a four-year bombardment. Much damage, both human and architectural, was caused but it was the damage to the cathedral of Reims which attracted most reaction, becaming a cause célèbre for the propagandists. The church was first hit by German shells on 19 September 1914, when the wooden roof was burnt, the stained glass shattered and the west front damaged by shell splinters and the heat of the fire. Later bombardment caused further damage of a structural nature, to the stone vault in February 1915 and to flying buttresses around the apse in early 1918 (see Figures 1.3 and 1.4).

This instance of war damage supplied the commentators with a particularly strong combination of historical, ecclesiastical and architectural significance. Reims Cathedral was the coronation church of France (the equivalent of Westminster Abbey), a site associated with the mythical origins of the French nation, as Clovis, the first King of Gaul and a convert to Christianity, was said to have been baptised there in 496.[13] The present building had been the site of all coronations of French kings from the thirteenth century until the Revolution and once again in 1825 for the crowning of Charles X.

FIGURE 1.3 Shells exploding on Reims Cathedral in April 1917.
Photograph reproduced in Maurice Landrieux (1919), *La Cathédrale de
Reims. Un crime Allemand.*

FIGURE 1.4 Aerial view of the damaged Reims Cathedral. The roofless
structure to the right of the church is the ruined Archbishop's Palace.
Photograph reproduced in Maurice Landrieux (1919), *La Cathédrale de
Reims. Un crime Allemand.*

Figures from both the political and religious history of France appear in the form of statuary on the facades. From an architectural perspective, Reims Cathedral is an important example of the Gothic style, a thirteenth-century 'High Gothic' structure, with external and internal facades decorated with nearly three thousand statues, many dating from the mid-thirteenth century. The national and cultural significance of Reims Cathedral made the war damage to this building all the more shocking to French commentators, who added a layer of significance of their own: if the physical damage to the fabric of the building was the work of German shells, the rich wartime meaning acquired by Reims Cathedral was a product of French propagandists.

The propagandists presented the damage to Reims in the most inflammatory manner. The following quotation is typical of the general tone and content of their characterisation of the events – this was the official response of the French government to the shelling of Reims Cathedral, issued by the Sous-Secrétariat d'Etat des Beaux-Arts on 27 September 1914:

Without the excuse of even a semblance of military necessity, for the pure pleasure of destruction, German troops have systematically and furiously bombarded the cathedral in Reims. The famous basilica is now no more than a heap of ruins. It is the duty of the Government of the Republic to denounce this revolting act of vandalism, which in committing this monument to our history to the flames, robs the whole of humanity of an irreplaceable piece of its artistic heritage.[14]

Apart from the exaggeration of the extent of the damage – the cathedral was not the complete ruin suggested here – the key point is the assertion that the shelling of the church was deliberate, systematic, entirely without military justification and a source of gratuitous pleasure to the 'barbaric' enemy. The standard German account of the damage to Reims was rather different:

Our enemies knew that we did not want to do it, and that is why they created this military necessity. I would even dare to suggest that they had an interest in the bombardment of Reims Cathedral: they wanted it to happen.[15]

The alternative story here was that the cathedral had been shelled only very reluctantly, as a result of the provocative French use of their own historic monument as a signal station and a weapons store, which made its bombardment necessary and legitimate. As for the allegation that the French were secretly delighted at this German gaffe, the subsequent extensive use of the events as a propaganda stick with which to beat the enemy seemed to support this analysis.[16]

The French allegation of a systematic programme of cultural destruction, although unverifiable and unlikely, was difficult for German counter-propaganda to dispel. Reims Cathedral was only one of several French cathedrals to be shelled by German artillery: September 1914 also saw damage to the cathedrals of Noyon, Soissons and Senlis during German bombardment of these towns. The churches are all Gothic in style, another factor which suggested some element of planning to the propagandists, as did the regular and apparently revengeful pattern of the attacks, all of which took place after the forced retreat of German troops from a town.[17] A French Inspector of Historic Monuments recorded on a visit to Soissons in November 1914 that most of the damage caused during the shelling there on 13 and 24–5 September was to buildings of architectural importance. He concluded that all the evidence pointed to a German plan.[18] The French were naturally looking for plots and were more inclined to see the damage done to individual historic monuments as parts of a pattern of destruction than as unconnected and isolated military accidents. A deliberate policy of destroying French historic monuments was attributed to the Germans, along with the now traditional 'vandal' tag. The unfortunate location of many French cathedral towns in the area of the Western Front was seen as an enemy objective, rather than a military coincidence.

The accusation of a systematic programme of cultural destruction was countered with the German claim that they had in fact carried out a systematic programme of art protection. The architectural historian Paul Clemen headed a campaign to publicise these activities, in articles with titles such as 'Unser Schutz der Kunstdenkmäler im Kriege' ('Our Protection of Historic Monuments in Wartime') and in books such as *Kunstschutz im Kriege* ('Art Protection in Wartime'), a two-volume survey of First World War German protection measures for works of art and architecture on both the western and eastern fronts.[19] Any German safeguarding or repairs took place, it should be remembered, behind the western front in occupied territory and was therefore difficult to verify. Another German propaganda strategy was to list historic monuments on French territory that had been damaged by Allied bombardment, usually while attempting to force a German retreat from an occupied town. From the perverse point of view of wartime cultural propaganda, it was unfortunate for the Germans that the list included no cathedrals, and the nearest equivalent to the shelling of Reims was the Allied bombardment of the *collégiale*, or 'collegiate church' (known as the cathedral), in Saint-Quentin in 1917.[20]

A great deal of ambiguity still attaches to these events, as most of the existing information on damage to historic monuments during the First World War is cultural propaganda, produced by the interested parties. Although we know in most cases what damage was done and which side did it, the reasons and motivations for the destruction remain obscured behind rival French and German propaganda narratives. As will be discussed in later chapters, there was less ambiguity of this kind in the case of Second World War bombing of historic town centres, although there was a considerable gap between the stated aim of extensive area bombing raids – to reduce military production capacity on enemy territory – and the number of historical and cultural centres affected. On the evidence of all three wars under consideration here, cultural war damage has regularly been accompanied by particularly large measures of ambiguity and controversy.

The case of one war-damaged historic monument illustrates particularly clearly the continuities in action, ambiguity and interpretation between the First and Second World Wars: that of the University Library in Louvain (Leuven), Belgium. At the beginning of the First World War, during the German progress across Belgium in August 1914, the University Library (completed in 1725 in late Baroque style) was burnt with all its contents, including many medieval manuscripts and incunabula. The Belgians, the French and the British attributed sole responsibility for this destruction to German forces and accused them of having done it deliberately, in books with titles such as *Le crime de Reims après le crime de Louvain* and *Les Barbares en Belgique*.[21] The Germans maintained that damage to this and other historic buildings in Louvain was the result of a fire accidentally started while they were defending themselves from Belgian *franc-tireurs* (civilian snipers). The Allied explanation of events prevailed, however, and Article 247 of the Treaty of Versailles required the German nation to make reparations in the form of printed books and manuscripts.[22] The Library was rebuilt in the interwar period, funded with American donations and stocked with books from the Allied countries as well as the German contributions, and eventually reopened in July 1928, with a commemorative plaque declaring in Latin 'Destroyed by German fury; rebuilt by American generosity'. Thus the destruction of the Library retained its symbolic value, as did the shelling of Reims Cathedral.

On the night of 16–17 May 1940, during the German progress across Belgium as the Second World War began in earnest in western Europe, the new University Library in Louvain was burnt

FIGURE 1.5 Leuven (Louvain), Belgium: reading room of the University Library, photograph taken 16 November 1944 (Macmillan Committee photograph).
The Conway Library, Courtauld Institute of Art.

down, leaving only the outer walls standing (see Figure 1.5). The circumstances gave rise to a controversy similar to the First World War version: some British soldiers had not yet left the town on 16 May and the Germans claimed that the fire had been started by them, deliberately and with the intention of discrediting the invading German troops.[23] Traces of petrol had been found in the ruined building, it was claimed during a much-publicised German inquiry into the damage. The British denied this version of events, counterclaiming that the fire in the Library had been caused by the deliberate German bombardment of the building with 'Stuka' dive bombers. One piece of evidence which seemed to contradict this claim was the fact that the windows of nearby buildings were not broken, which might have been expected in the course of an air raid – an ambiguity noted by the American (and therefore still in theory neutral) journalist William Shirer, on a visit to Louvain soon after the events.[24] Further ambiguities were recorded by Lord Methuen in *Normandy Diary* (1952):

The fire is said to have broken out during the night of 16/17 May, between the withdrawal of the British about 23.00 hours and the entry of the Germans early next morning, but not much is known precisely, since practically all civilians had been evacuated from the town. Its origin is very mysterious ... The fire seems to have spread from the bottom, since the entire basement was burnt out ... The Germans would not allow the Belgians to have access to the ruins for a year after the disaster and themselves held two commissions of enquiry. The first attributed the fire to the British Secret Service. This convinced no one in Belgium, and apparently a second commission sat ... The findings of this commission were never published.[25]

Despite these elements of uncertainty as to who was responsible for the burning of the library, the Allied account was the one popularly accepted, as during the First World War. This postwar remark from a Unesco publication expresses a typical attitude: 'In August 1914 the Germans devastated the Library of the University of Louvain. In May 1940 they returned to do it again'.[26] The truth of the matter being obscured, the attitude itself is nevertheless historically interesting, as it demonstrates the continuing exclusive association between cultural barbarism and the methods of the German armed forces – a particularly tenacious association which had survived from the Franco-Prussian War through the First World War and into the post-Second World War period, apparently unaffected by the very different circumstances of the latter conflict. The damage to historic monuments in western Europe which occurred between 1939 and 1945 did not happen on neutral historic territory or in an attitude-free zone, but was informed by, reacted to and characterised according to already existing conceptions of this aspect of war.

LAWS

One important link between all three wars was the gradually increasing threat to non-military targets from the Franco-Prussian War onwards, with obvious consequences for historic monuments as well as for civilians. This threat had grown progressively over the period, to such a proportion that the Second World War was referred to as 'total war' – a war in which everything was a target, whether military or civilian, the result of the available military technology and an accompanying change in attitudes. The increased scope of possible military action was, at least in theory, limited by legislation, by means of treaties constituting the international law on this area of human activity, developed in an attempt to keep up with the technical possibilities of modern warfare. How effective these limitations were in practice in the wartime protection of historic monuments is the subject of this section.

For one commentator – Arsène Alexandre, 'Inspecteur Général des Musées' during the First World War, and author of the propagandist catalogue of war damage *Les Monuments français détruits par l'Allemagne* (1918) – the wartime bombing of art and architecture was immoral, as well as illegal:

It is neither in the name of the Hague Convention, nor in the name of the Geneva Convention, that the scholars and artists of France and of all the civilised world have cried out in protest. The laws in the name of which they protest have no date, since they are not written in ephemeral words, these laws of beauty, goodness and justice, but rather in the hearts of men and in the conscience of nations.[27]

This assumption that it is morally wrong to destroy historic monuments, even in this most extreme of situations, was common to much of the propaganda produced on the subject during and after the 1914–18 war. The moral tone of such publications was high, with a correspondingly low moral status attributed to the destructive activities of the enemy. Unfortunately, the existing legal protection for art and architecture in wartime did not entirely support these moral judgements – armies were, strictly speaking, allowed to do in practice that which conventional morality would prohibit. It was this gap between legal and moral action which the World War One propagandists exploited to such effect.

Outraged French propaganda and protests on the subject of aesthetic atrocities allegedly committed by the Germans frequently employed the idea that works of art should be protected from such acts by a kind of artistic immunity. The German counter-propaganda contained similar sentiments – a convincingly sincere belief in the inviolability of art was required for both sides. These stated beliefs were rarely reflected in action and supplied material for propagandists rather than for army personnel on the ground. An opposition developed between realism and idealism with regard to the 'rights' of works of art to special consideration during armed conflict which ran through the war-long debate on the immorality of cultural war damage. The status of any proposed rights was claimed to be either legal or generally understood on some less positivist, more abstract level. Occasionally both types of rights were invoked at once, but in practice both were ignored by both sides in the fighting.

At the outbreak of World War One, legal protection for works of art in wartime was contained in articles of the 1907 Hague Convention on Land Warfare, a treaty intended to regulate all aspects of the correct conduct of hostile armies. The Convention had been signed then ratified by most European countries, including France, Germany, Britain and Belgium, and should in theory have proved sufficient to prevent such events as the bombardment of Reims Cathedral. At this point, however, it seems that the concept of an international law of wartime conduct was too recently developed to have been regarded as entirely binding on the contracting parties and arguments as to whether the law had actually been broken at all, including in the area of cultural war damage, continued long after the end of the First World War. Before the second half of the nineteenth century, no written laws of war existed. There had been loosely acknowledged codes of conduct, generally observed by hostile armies, but these were in no sense legally binding and no penalties were imposed on those breaking them. Honourable behaviour was maintained as an ideal, and sometimes adhered to in practice.[28] These codes certainly did not include provisions for the protection of works of art and architecture, which were traditionally considered 'fair game' in time of war. Neither was protection for historic monuments and paintings a priority in the first attempts to codify the conventions of war into a widely recognised set of rules. The first European written rules were those established at the Geneva Convention of 1864, but their purpose was protect the wounded and to give wartime immunity to doctors, hospitals and ambulances. The 1868 Declaration of St Petersburg forbade the use of certain kinds of weapons and continued the humanitarian trend of the Geneva Convention in laying down principles for the protection of civilians.

The first reference to a ban on destroying or stealing works of art in wartime appeared in the text of the Brussels Conference of 1874. This conference, attended by all the European powers, was organised in the wake of the 1870–1 Franco-Prussian War, during which allegations of illegal conduct were made by both sides with no means of settling the claims. The text of the conference was not a treaty but rather a set of guidelines for future use in drafting a more solid body of international laws of war, and some of its articles were incorporated into the later Hague Conventions (see below). The article most relevant to the protection of historic monuments is in Section 1, Chapter IV on 'Sieges and bombardment':

Article 16: The commander of a besieging army, when bombarding a fortified town, must take all measures in his power to spare, as far as possible, churches and buildings used for artistic, scientific and charitable purposes.[29]

In this form it is a clear and strong directive, containing only the qualifying phrase 'as far as possible', a pragmatic recognition that the protection of historic monuments cannot always be a priority during a war. The force of the article was weakened considerably, however, by a later change made to the wording: at the end was added the phrase 'on the condition that they are not being used at that time for military purposes'. This in effect removed any prescriptive power the article may have had in its previous form by supplying an infinitely flexible excuse for bombardment of cultural targets, as it was always possible to claim that they were thought to be in military use – a church tower as an observation post, for example, or a museum as a weapons store. This qualifying phrase was included in all subsequent treaties on the rules and regulations of wartime conduct and was symptomatic of the inadequacy of the law, which stopped short of forbidding the use of cathedrals for military purposes and which could not, therefore, condemn the bombardment of cathedrals in supposed self-defence.

The customary laws of war were finally codified in the Hague Conventions on Land Warfare of 1899 and 1907, where the guidelines established at the Brussels Conference were developed and given the status of international law.[30] Their content formed the body of international law governing wartime conduct during the First World War. The legal provisions for safeguarding historic monuments had not, however, changed since 1874 and the relevant article in the text of the Hague Convention was simply a reworded version of that agreed at the Brussels Conference:

Article 27: In sieges and bombardments all necessary steps must be taken to spare, as far as possible, buildings dedicated to religion, art, science, or charitable purposes, historic monuments, hospitals and places where the sick and wounded are collected, provided they are not being used at the time for military purposes. It is the duty of the besieged to indicate the presence of such buildings or places by distinctive and visible signs, which shall be notified to the enemy beforehand.[31]

The 'except in case of military necessity' let-out clause was once again included. It was precisely this clause which was later used to justify the bombardment of Reims Cathedral. The essential weakness of Article 27 was identified at the time by Ferdinand Vetter, a professor at the University of Bern who in 1915 proposed the establishment of La Croix d'or, or 'Gold Cross', conceived as a neutral organisation equivalent to the Red Cross but charged specifically with the prevention and repair of damage to historic monuments in wartime.[32] Vetter suggested an addition to Article 27 of the Hague Convention:

An historic monument falling under the protection of the treaty should not, wherever possible, be a target for military action, either on the part of the defending or the attacking side, nor should it be subject to a military action by the defending side, taking place so close to the historic monument that it cannot be carried out without endangering the monument.[33]

Here responsibility for the safety of historic monuments is placed equally on the attacking side and on the 'owner' of cultural property, as the latter is required not to abuse it by using it for military purposes, thus provoking a legitimate attack from the enemy.[34] In the event neither the changes to international law nor the 'Gold Cross' were realised and what might be called the pragmatic approach to the treatment of historic monuments in wartime prevailed.

The pragmatic approach prevailed to such an extent that, despite having failed noticeably to prevent actual damage during the 1914–18 conflict, the same Hague Convention article still constituted the only legal protection for cultural targets in wartime during the Second World War. On the evidence of the First World War, the body of international law relating to the protection of art and architecture was largely ineffective, serving only to produce source material for cultural propagandists. Even the most simple elements of Article 27 had had a tendency to backfire: the requirement that buildings to be protected should be marked clearly (usually with the Red Cross symbol) had the unfortunate extra function of enabling the enemy to target them all the more accurately. The legal situation, however, remained the same until after World War Two – between the wars only one new treaty governing this area appeared and that was an agreement between the governments of North and South America, the 'Treaty on the Protection of Artistic and Scientific Institutions and Historic Monuments', also known as the 'Roerich Pact', signed in Washington DC in 1935. Although it had no legal application in Europe, this treaty is an interesting indication of how little the thinking had changed on the matter of wartime legal protection for art and architecture. Article 1 ruled that historic monuments, museums and cultural institutions should be considered 'neutral' during a war – a new word, but hardly a new protection measure. Article 5 contained the now-familiar loophole: 'The monuments and institutions mentioned in Article 1 shall cease to enjoy the privileges recognized in the present Treaty in case they are made use of for military purposes'.[35] In post-1918 Europe the investigation of measures for the wartime protection of art and architecture became the responsibility of the International Museums Office and the International Commission on Intellectual Co-operation, both divisions of the League of Nations. No further legislation was developed, however, until the establishment of Unesco after World War Two.[36]

One further important distinction from the point of view of the legitimacy of bombardment was that between fortified and open cities. A fortified, or defended city, was traditionally and according to the law a legitimate target for the enemy, while a city declared open, or undefended, was not. In the First World War, part of the German propaganda defence following the bombardment of Reims, with the consequent damage to historic monumnts, was that it had been declared a fortress town by the French (Senlis and Beauvais were also given this dangerous status), thus making it a legitimate target according to international law. In the Second World War

Paris was declared an open city just before the arrival of the German army in June 1940, as was Rome in August 1943, during the Allied invasion of Italy, with the aim of removing at least the justification for damage to these cities and their many historic monuments.

One method of war damage not covered at all – as opposed to inadequately covered – by the law was aerial bombardment. The 1907 Hague Convention did not anticipate the wartime destruction of historic monuments as a result of the indiscriminate area bombing of city centres from the air. The negotiators had in mind the more sedate, if often extremely effective, process of destruction by means of artillery bombardment during a long siege. With the development of aircraft which could carry and drop bombs, a new kind of warfare seemed to present an even greater threat to the security of historic city centres and monuments. The First World War provided evidence of the effect of bombing from the air as opposed to land based artillery fire as Britain, Germany and France all experimented with the potential of air power. German Zeppelin airships, developed and improved since the turn of the century, were the main threat to London in 1915–16, causing loss of life and architectural damage to the centre of the city and the southern suburbs. The City of London was hit, for instance, in September 1915, then the Aldwych area including the Lyceum Theatre in October. The south London suburbs of Streatham, Brixton and Kennington were raided in September 1916.[37] Zeppelins proved most effective for such urban raids, attacking at night and approaching noiselessly, giving little warning. The airships were also capable of long distances and reached as far as the Midlands and the north-eastern coast of England, where the (already-ruined) thirteenth-century Whitby Abbey was hit. The primary disadvantage was that airship attacks were indiscriminate, with no real possibility of accurate targeting.

Aeroplanes provided an alternative means of attack, although they were scarcely more accurate, despite their carrying out of raids during daylight hours. Germany first dropped bombs from aeroplanes on the centre of Paris as early as 30 August 1914, but this exercise was not repeated until 1918, when nearly 400 bombs were dropped, including one which the French claimed hit the roof of Notre-Dame. The north-eastern French town of Nancy was also attacked in this way.[38] By this stage of the war new aircraft were available – the German Gotha, in operation from 1917, was capable of flying higher and further. The proportion of Zeppelin to aeroplane attacks evened out, with fifty-one airship to fifty-two aeroplane attacks on Britain in 1917.[39] The Gothas took off from bases in German-occupied Belgium and so were able to reach south-eastern England.

The air war was not just a German affair – Britain and France, meanwhile, were carrying out aeroplane attacks on towns within range in northern and western Germany: Düsseldorf was hit in September 1914, then Cologne in November of the same year, followed by Freiburg im Bresgau and the Saarland area later in 1917. By 1918 approximately 300 Allied raids on Germany had taken place.[40] As accurate targeting of particular buildings from aeroplanes was a matter of accident rather than design at this time, it is difficult to argue that the destruction of specific buildings was deliberate, although there seems to have been an Allied attempt to hit railway lines and stations in Metz (then in Germany), Trier and Karlsruhe in 1918. The destructive effect of the raids on buildings of cultural significance was emphasised and illustrated in the German propaganda publication *Kunstschutz im Kriege*.

The dropping of bombs from Zeppelins and aircraft was not explicitly regulated by either the 1899 or the 1907 Hague Conventions. The 1899 conference had discussed and prohibited the use of balloons for bombardment purposes, which might seem faintly ludicrous now but was the only type of 'airpower' available at the time. Balloons had thus far only been used for observation of the enemy but by the time of the second Hague Conference of 1907 bombing trials had been conducted in France (1905) and in Germany Count Zeppelin had already developed the third version of his airship. Further legislation was debated, although more in the interests of legitimising bombardment from the air than in restricting it – having developed new means of warfare, the signatories to the Hague laws wished to be allowed to use them.[41] Even so, Article 25 of the 1907 Hague Convention specified that 'The attack or bombardment, by whatever means, of towns, villages, dwellings or buildings which are undefended is prohibited' – it is the phrase 'by whatever means' which seems to protect non-military targets such as historic monuments from air raids. When added to the articles forbidding attacks on cultural targets, this article would seem to provide adequate legal protection against the air bombardment of churches and museums. This did not, however, prevent the experiments of the First World War over London, northern France and Germany.

The new methods of bombing introduced during World War One suggested a need for new laws of conduct in warfare to keep pace with developing technology and to cover the new threat to civilians and other non-military targets. For this reason the issue was discussed at the Washington Conference of 1922 and raised again at a meeting of the 'Commission of Jurists' at The Hague in the winter of 1922–3, with France, Britain, Italy, the Netherlands, Japan and the USA taking part (Germany, not yet readmitted to the international stage, was not included). Their conclusions, published in 1923 with the title *Report of the Commission of Jurists*, included more explicit limitations on the use of aerial bombardment than those contained in the Hague Convention. It is worth quoting them at length, since the proposed restrictions fully anticipate the later transgressions of the Second World War:

Article 22: Aerial bombardment for the purpose of terrorising the civilian population, of destroying or damaging private property not of military character, or of injuring non-combatants is prohibited.

Article 24: (1) Aerial bombardment is legitimate only when directed at a military objective, that is to say, an object of which the destruction or injury would constitute a distinct military advantage to the belligerent.

(2) Such bombardment is legitimate only when directed exclusively at the following objectives: military forces; military works; military establishments or depots; factories constituting important and well known centres engaged in the manufacture of arms, ammunition or distinctively military supplies; lines of communication or transportation used for military purposes.

(3) The bombardment of cities, towns, villages, dwellings or buildings not in the immediate neighbourhood of the operations of land forces is prohibited. In cases where the objectives specified in paragraph 2 are so situated that they cannot be bombarded without the indiscriminate bombardment of the civilian population, the aircraft must abstain from bombardment.

(4) In the immediate neighbourhood of the operations of land forces, the bombardment of cities, towns, villages, dwellings or buildings is legitimate provided that there exists a reasonable presumption that the military concentration is sufficiently important to justify such bombardment, having regard to the danger thus caused to the civilian population.

(5) A belligerent State is liable to pay compensation for injuries to person or to property caused by the violation by any of its officers or forces of the provisions of this article.[42]

If followed to the letter, the restrictions here would provide some effective protection from aerial bombardment for all non-military targets, from civilians to historic monuments, particularly given the very specific definition of what precisely constituted a military target (this had been left more open to interpretation in the Hague Convention) and the legitimisation of the bombing of cities and towns only if enemy land forces were in the vicinity. Unfortunately there was no compulsion to follow these rules, even seventeen years later when the bombardment of cities began in the Second World War, as these articles were never incorporated into the existing Hague Convention and never became part of International Law regulating the conduct of war. The so-called Hague Rules were, however, generally accepted by the participating nations, albeit informally. It has even been suggested that they were followed at the beginning of the Second World War, in western Europe at least prior to May 1940 during the *drôle de guerre*, as the available air-power remained unused until then.[43] Whether this was a demonstration of adherence to the articles of the 1923 *Report* or a restraint caused by other factors during the *drôle de guerre* is unclear, particularly as no restraint at all was exercised on the eastern front in Poland. Sir Arthur Harris, the head of Bomber Command, recognised no such rules in his 1947 account of their activities, maintaining that 'International law can always be argued pro and con, but in this matter of the use of aircraft in warfare there is . . . no international law at all'.[44]

Apart from this official attempt at legislation, the potential problems of air warfare were much discussed elsewhere. The prospects for European cities and their populations and historic monuments were not viewed positively. J. M. Spaight's book *Air Power and the Cities* (1930), for instance, dealt with the specific threat to towns, warning that they would all be at risk in the next war, not just those in the line of battle or near to coasts: 'Great modern cities are, allegorically, glass houses, and people who live in them . . . are wiser not to throw bombs'.[45] In an interesting anticipation of later concerns raised about the area bombing of German city centres, Spaight saw no militarily justifiable point in 'smashing the cities', asking 'Why should any sane belligerent waste his bombs on militarily negligible centres of population? . . . Apart from all questions of possible retaliation, the bombing of cities is a gamble, a wild leap in the dark. It is a thing for scare headlines, spectacular, impressive in a crude way, but not war; merely the flashy stroke of the foolish amateur'.[46] A similarly negative view of the threat presented by the new technology was taken by Frank Morison in *War on Great Cities. A Study of the Facts* (1937): 'It follows that amid all this turmoil and confusion, irreparable damage must be done to the

surviving vestiges of our own historic past . . . A gap in the continuity of human culture will be made beyond all mending. And
remember that this is true not only of London, but of Paris,
Brussels, Berlin, Milan or Rome. Nothing that man has wrought in
the field of the creative arts will ultimately be immune from this
mad threat to our great cities'.[47] These innocent and pessimistic
interwar arguments proved to be alarmingly prophetic.

Some prior practical warning of the danger to historic monuments posed by the 'new' method of war damage was provided
during the Spanish Civil War by the bombardment of Guernica on
26 April 1937 (by German aeroplanes). For several hours successive
waves of aircraft dropped a combination of high explosive and
incendiary bombs on the town in an operation which prefigured in
technique and effect Second World War attacks on cities, if on a
much smaller scale.[48] After two decades of debate, anticipation and
actual experience, when widespread aerial bombardment of city
centres became a reality in 1940 the material effects could hardly
have been a surprise.

Notes

1. For a thorough military history of the Franco-Prussian War, see Howard,
   The Franco-Prussian War – the German Invasion of France 1870–1871.
   For a more interdisciplinary account, see Horne, *The Fall of Paris – the
   Siege and the Commune 1870–1871*.
2. An 'oeuvre de barbarie monstrueuse et de vandalisme épouvantable'.
   Vachon, *Strasbourg, les musées, les bibliothèques et la cathédrale*, p. II.
3. Marchand, *Le Siège de Strasbourg 1870 – la bibliothèque – la cathédrale*,
   1871, p. 50. Marchand was the editor of the newspaper *Le Temps* at this
   time. For further contemporary French accounts containing similar sentiments, see Schnéegans, *La Guerre en Alsace – Strasbourg*, 1871 and
   Fischbach, *Le Siège et le bombardement de Strasbourg*, 1871; also an article by E. Müntz, 'Les Monuments d'art détruits à Strasbourg', in *Gazette
   des Beaux-Arts* 1872, pp. 349–60. The proliferation of French accounts
   was understandably not matched by German authors.
4. A collection of images of the Franco-Prussian War and its aftermath
   appeared in 1901: Dayot, *L'Invasion, le Siège 1870, la Commune 1871,
   d'après des peintures, gravures, photographies, sculptures, médailles,
   autographes, objets du temps*.
5. See Darcel, 'Les musées, les arts et les artistes pendant le siège de Paris
   (1er article)', in *Gazette des Beaux-Arts*, 1 October 1871, pp. 285–306. The
   procedures for the evacuation of mobile works of art from Paris were to be
   repeated at the start of the First World War and prior to the start of the
   Second World War.
6. See Darcel's series of five articles, 'Les musées, les arts et les artistes pendant la Commune', in *Gazette des Beaux-Arts*, 1872, pp. 41–65, 140–58,

210–29, 398–418, 479–90. For images of the damage, see Trimm, *Les Ruines de Paris, chronique de Paris brulé* (1871).

7. The scene was commemorated in huge history paintings by Anton von Werner (and described by the artist in his memoirs *Erlebnisse und Eindrücke 1870–1890*, p. 32). Two of the paintings were later destroyed during the Second World War bombardment of the Schloß and the Zeughaus in Berlin. A third version of his 'Proclamation of the German Empire' can be seen in the Bismarck museum in Friedrichsruh. For a general history of the events leading up to German unification in 1871, see Craig, *Germany 1866–1945*, Chapter 1, which includes an extensive bibliography.

8. Dayot, *L'Invasion, le Siège 1870, la Commune 1871*, p. 164.

9. For more detail on German weapons of this period, see D. B. Nash, *Imperial German Army Handbook 1914–1918*, particularly pp. 79–112.

10. The column figure of St Nicaise is located beside the centre portal of the north transept.

11. For example *Les Allemands destructeurs de cathédrales et de trésors du passé* (issued by the Sous-Secrétariat d'Etat des Beaux-Arts) and *La Cathédrale de Reims. Un crime Allemand* (by Maurice Landrieux, a clergyman at Reims during the war).

12. On the Second World War employment of the concept of the cultural barbarian, see Chapter 3.

13. For an indication of the continuing importance of this event in the late twentieth century, it is interesting to note that the 1,500th anniversary of the baptism of Clovis was celebrated in Reims in 1996 with a visit by the Pope.

14. This was widely quoted in many propaganda publications on the subject, for example by Alexandre in *Les Monuments français détruits par l'Allemagne*, p. 55.

15. This formulation of the German defense is from the art historian Wilhelm Worringer, from the article 'Die Kathedrale in Reims' in *Kunst und Künstler*, November 1914, pp. 85–90.

16. For more detail on the extensive propaganda campaign on the subject of Reims Cathedral, see my article 'Production versus Destruction: Art, World War I and Art History' in *Art History*, Vol. 22, no. 3, September 1999, pp. 347–63.

17. More such allegations first appeared in the official account by the Sous-Secrétariat d'Etat des Beaux-Arts, *Les Allemands destructeurs de cathédrales et de trésors du passé*, 1915. For less obviously biased accounts (although still from an Allied point of view), see the Michelin series on the battles that took place in northern France, including *The Marne Battlefields 1914. An Illustrated History and Guide* and *Soissons Before and During the War* (both 1919, published in both English and French language editions).

18. Letter from Paul Boeswilwald to the Sous-Secrétariat d'Etat des Beaux-Arts, Albert Dalimier, dated 4 November 1914, in Archives de la Bibliothèque du Patrimoine, dossier 103, Soissons.

19. The article appeared in *Internationale Monatsschrift für Wissenschaft, Kunst und Technik*, Band IX, Heft 5, 1 December 1914, pp. 303–16. The book was published in 1919 with the full title *Kunstschutz im Kriege. Berichte über den Zustand der Kunstdenkmäler auf den verschiedenen Kriegsschauplätzen und über die deutschen und österreichischen Maßnahmen zu ihrer Erhaltung, Rettung, Erforschung*.

20. The list of Allied-damaged churches was published in a variety of propaganda articles and books. See for instance Grautoff, *Die Kunstverwaltung in Frankreich und Deutschland*, 1915. On the bombardment of Saint-Quentin there are more German than French publications (for once), for example *Die Zerstörung der Kathedrale von St. Quentin* (im Amtlichen Auftrage zusammengestellt), 1917. The church in question was not a cathedral, as it was not the seat of a bishop.

21. By Pierre Anthony-Thouret and Pierre Nothomb respectively. An English language version of events in Belgium was also published: L. Chambry's *The Truth about Louvain*.

22. Article 247 stated that 'Germany undertakes to furnish to the University of Louvain, within three months after a request made by it and transmitted through the intervention of the Reparation Commission, manuscripts, incunabula, printed books, maps and objects of collection corresponding in number and value to those destroyed in the burning by Germany of the Library of Louvain'. The text of the Treaty of Versailles exists in many editions, for example the English version published by HMSO in 1919 (unpaginated).

23. This version of events was promoted in various German or German-controlled newspapers, for instance the Belgian *Le Soir* of 4 July 1940.

24. Shirer, *Berlin Diary 1934–1941*, entries for 20 May and 26 June 1940. All the details, claims and counter-claims are reproduced in a book published by the Belgian Ministère de la Justice, Commission des crimes de guerre, *Les Crimes de guerre commis lors de l'invasion du territoire national – Mai 1940 – La destruction de la Bibliothèque de Louvain*, 1946. This commission was established in 1944 to collect documentation on possible war crimes, with a view to eventual prosecution.

25. Methuen, *Normandy Diary*, entry for 28 February 1945, pp. 159–61.

26. From Barry, *Libraries in Need*, Unesco 1949, p. 18.

27. Alexandre, *Les Monuments français détruits par l'Allemagne*, pp. 31–2.

28. The status and limits of 'the Law of Nations' as opposed to the law of individual states, was the subject of many publications during and after the First World War. See for instance Carpentier, *Les Lois de la guerre continentale*, 1916, and an account of the legal situation published in 1920 by Garner, *International Law and the World War*, particularly Chapter XVIII, 'Destruction of Historic Monuments, Buildings and Institutions especially protected by the Law of Nations', p. 435 ff.

29. From *Actes de la Conférence de Bruxelles*, 1874. The final agreed text is dated 27 July 1874.

30. The text of the 1907 treaty contained some changes, but was substantially the same as the 1899 version, and there was no change at all in the sections relating to the protection of art and architecture.

31. From Section II, Hostilities, Chapter I, Means of injuring the enemy, sieges and bombardments. The English version of the text of the 1907 Hague Convention has recently been published by the International Committee of the Red Cross, *International Law Concerning the Conduct of Hostilities. Collection of Hague Conventions and some other Treaties*, Geneva 1989.

32. The Red Cross Organisation was founded in Geneva in 1863 with the purpose of supplying medical aid to the victims of war. Vetter's proposals were published in the *Journal de Genève* of 11 May 1915 under the title 'La Croix d'or. Protection des monuments artistiques et historiques en temps de guerre'.

33. Article 4 of a detailed constitution for 'La Croix d'or', first published in the proceedings of the conference *Kriegestagung für Denkmalpflege* [typescript], Berlin: Verlag der Zeitschrift 'Die Denkmalpflege', 1915, p. 80 ff. They appeared later in book form, in Vetter, *Friede dem Kunstwerk! Zwischenstaatliche Sicherung der Kunstdenkmäler im Kriege als Weg zum künftigen dauerhaften Frieden*, Olten 1917.
34. This measure would be included in the much later 1954 Hague Convention for the Protection of Cultural Property in the Event of Armed Conflict – see the Conclusion for discussion of this treaty.
35. The text of the Roerich Pact is included in the International Committee of the Red Cross publication *International Law Concerning the Conduct of Hostilities. Collection of Hague Conventions and some other Treaties*.
36. For details of post-1945 legislation in this area, see the discussion in the Conclusion.
37. An account of the raids is given in the wartime diary of *The Times* journalist Michael MacDonagh, *In London during the Great War*. MacDonagh repeatedly pointed out that newspapers were not entirely free to report the death and damage caused, so as not to lower morale – see pp. 82–6 for instance, on the Aldwych raid of 13 October 1915.
38. See J. Bouret-Aubertot's 1923 account, *Les Bombardements Aériens*, p. 84.
39. The figure is quoted in Royse, *Aerial Bombardment and the International Regulation of Warfare*, p. 181.
40. Ibid.
41. This was argued by Royse, ibid., p. 100.
42. From *Report of the Commission of Jurists*, The Hague 1923.
43. See Watt, 'Restraints on War in the Air before 1945', in Howard, *Restraints on War. Studies in the Limitation of Armed Conflict*, pp. 74–5.
44. Harris, *Bomber Offensive*, p. 177.
45. Spaight, *Air Power and the Cities*, p. 166. Spaight was also the author of *Air Power and War Rights* (1924), *The Battle of Britain, 1940* (1941) and *Bombing Vindicated* (1944).
46. Spaight, *Air Power and the Cities*, p. 233.
47. Morison, *War on Great Cities. A Study of the Facts*, p. 206.
48. On the attack on Guernica (a symbol of Basque separatism), the German bombing of the centre of Madrid in August 1936 and the Italian attacks on Barcelona in March 1938, see Thomas, *The Spanish Civil War*.

2

A Short Second World War History of Architecture

This account of Second World War damage to historic monuments – what happened, where, when, how and who it was caused by – will take the form of a chronology of events, plotting the occurrence of cultural destruction across western Europe from September 1939 to May 1945. This event-by-event approach is more suited to a comparative study of cultural war damage than a country-by-country survey, as it places the emphasis on the overall effect of the war upon historic monuments rather than on the individual experience of particular countries. The surveys of this type of war damage produced immediately after the war were organised by country, as the information they contained was gathered by Allied officers following the progress of the Allied armies through France, Belgium and The Netherlands and into Germany, as well as through Italy.[1] Their purpose was to record quickly and comprehensively the condition of historic monuments at that point in time, a documentary methodology which the present historical and comparative account need not follow. Another type of account produced shortly after the war was the monument-by-monument survey – La Farge's *Lost Treasures of Europe* (1946), for example, which focused on the condition of war-damaged buildings in 1945, without giving details on when and how the damage occurred. This approach would also be inappropriate for this study, as the intention is to examine war damage to historic monuments in the context of the Second World War as a whole, rather than to present this type of destruction simply as a fait accompli, isolated from the circumstances in which it occurred.

This chapter will instead follow the chronology and progress of the war itself, detailing instances of damage and campaigns which represented a particular threat to historic monuments in Britain, France and Germany, with some mention of such events in the Benelux countries and Italy. The intention is not to provide a comprehensive survey, which – even if possible – would be a very long book indeed.[2] What follows is an overview of the extent and cause of cultural war damage in western Europe during the Second World War, focusing on examples identified as especially significant during the conflict. It should also be noted that, although much of this variety of destruction was caused during air raids, this is not just a history of air bombardment during this war – air raids and the effects of area bombing will feature in so far as they relate to the wartime history of architecture, as will other types of military activity.

Before beginning the account of the damage, first some remarks on what was a common problem for all countries in western Europe immediately prior to the war, that of how to protect historic monuments from the effects of the approaching conflict. The protection of mobile works of art was relatively straightforward and effective: paintings and other non-fixed objects were removed to safe havens in areas thought unlikely to be affected by the fighting. In France, evacuation of the contents of the Louvre to the Loire Valley château of Chambord began as early as September 1938, followed by the contents of other Parisian museums after the war began; further evacuations southwards were necessitated by the unexpected progress of the German army in June 1940.[3] In Germany and Austria salt mines and remote castles became wartime art depots, and in Britain underground shelter was found in Wales. Protection measures for the museum buildings, and for other historic monuments, were more of a challenge and often consisted of attempts at damage limitation rather than positive protection. Some lessons had been learned from the experience of the First World War: the buildings themselves, particularly those with massive stone walls or buttresses, were to a certain extent resistant to bombardment, and protection measures were concentrated on the weak spots of roof, statuary and glass.[4] Whereas in 1914–18 stained glass was removed during the fighting, sometimes under fire (at Reims, for instance), much stained glass was taken down from cathedrals and churches in Britain and France before 1939; the medieval glass of Chartres Cathedral was packed away in the autumn of 1938, for example, followed by the rose windows of Notre-Dame in Paris. The stained glass of Cologne Cathedral had also been removed by August 1940, although relatively few monument protection measures were taken in Germany until 1942, when increasing numbers of German cities became the targets for Allied bombardment.

On a less progressive note, many of the protection methods of the earlier war were still the only methods available during the Second World War. Fragile sculptures attached to buildings, such as column figures on church portals or tombs inside, were still covered with layers of sandbags, while free-standing statues in open spaces were still walled-in with non-flammable brick or concrete. Buildings themselves were sometimes partly filled with earth, to lessen the impact of bombardment – the nave of Canterbury Cathedral received this treatment. One new preventive measure for the roofs of large historic monuments was a non-reflective coating that could be painted on to reduce their visibility from the air in moonlight. The most basic protection measure, however, had not changed at all, that is the storing of water close to endangered monuments and the posting of night fire-watchers to raise the alarm. This was the unpromising technology with which historic monuments were armed to confront the Second World War.

1939, 1940

The first serious instances of cultural damage of the Second World War occurred in eastern Europe, during the German invasion of Poland from 1 September 1939 onwards. The bombardment of Gdansk (then Danzig) on 1 September was the initial act of destruction in this war, a city distant both geographically and culturally from the countries of western Europe whose importance to them had only recently been questioned in France in an article entitled 'Why die for Danzig?'.[5] The Polish army resisted for five weeks, until 5 October, during which time much damage was inflicted on the country's historic monuments. Although the enormous cultural damage caused in eastern Europe is outside the scope of this book, it is important to note that the character of the damage there was in contrast to that which occurred later in the West: the destruction of buildings of cultural and historic interest in Poland has been described as deliberate and systematic, rather than accidental in the course of action, and it has been estimated that 43 per cent of this type of building in the country as a whole were destroyed during the Second World War.[6] The historic town centre of Warsaw was entirely destroyed during the Luftwaffe's first substantial air attack involving approximately 400 aircraft on 25 September. Buildings damaged included the market square, St John's Cathedral and the castle, with 782 out of a pre-war total of 987 historic monuments disappearing, and 141 partly damaged, figures which seem to support the accusation of a deliberate intention to remove all traces of Polish cultural identity.[7] Such an overt policy of cultural destruction was not adopted in western Europe, although a Warsaw-style decimation of historic cities remained for all sides an extreme and troubling example of the threat to their cultural heritage.

In the west of Europe active fighting, bombardment and the possibility of destruction began in May 1940 with the German invasion of The Netherlands, Belgium and Luxembourg, then France. The invasion began on 10 May and progress was rapid, with a combination of ground forces and air attacks sweeping across the region. German propaganda persistently maintained that British aeroplanes had carried out the first air raid in the west, with an attack on Freiburg im Bresgau on 10 May 1940 which became the focus for much 'you started it first' accusation from both sides.[8] British raids were made on more obviously industrial targets in the Ruhr throughout May, and the cities of Cologne, Hamburg and Munich received the first of many and more extensive air raids on 13 May, 18 May and 5 June respectively. At this stage of the war, air raids were still small in scale, with relatively minor effects on mostly industrial targets.

The first thorough bombardment from the air of a western European city centre was the German attack on Rotterdam of 14 May, causing massive fires which damaged the fifteenth-century Grote Kerk among many other buildings. The immediate result was the surrender of the Dutch armed forces the next day, an outcome which could only have encouraged further extensive air raids on cities. The destruction of Middelburg followed on 17 May, including the abbey and town hall. Cities and historic monuments in Belgium were affected at the same time, as towns on the initial front running from Antwerp down through Leuven (Louvain) to Wavre were defended and bombarded – Leuven suffered some damage, notably to the University Library on the night of 16 May, while in Wavre the Hôtel de Ville and many houses in the centre were destroyed.[9] Tongeren (Tongres) was also badly damaged in this wave of attacks. Brussels was spared, having been declared an open city, but most of the centre of nearby Nivelles was destroyed during air raids, with the partly tenth-century collegiate church Ste Gertrude affected. As the German army pushed through further lines of defence in Belgium, buildings in Mons were damaged, including the late

Gothic church Ste Waudru. Kortrijk (Courtrai) was bombarded and most of the Grand-Place in Tournai was destroyed, along with the Halle aux Draps (1611) and the eighteenth-century Hôtel de Ville.

German attacks on Belgian towns ceased on the surrender by King Leopold III on 28 May, although coastal towns such as Oostende and Zeebrugge were still subject to RAF raids. By then the first attacks on north-eastern France had already taken place, beginning on 13 May. In the old town of Calais churches and the old lighthouse were destroyed. There was some cultural damage in Lille, where the seventeenth-century Citadelle was set alight, in Valenciennes, where the main square was burnt, and in the Somme Valley where Abbeville was badly damaged, with the church of St Wulfran half destroyed. On 19 May an air raid on Amiens caused extensive fire damage in the historic town centre and some structural damage to the Gothic cathedral. Another French cathedral town affected was Beauvais, where the Gothic cathedral itself survived the destruction of the surrounding old town in early June, including houses dating from the sixteenth and seventeenth centuries and buildings on the Place de l'Hôtel de Ville. The German bombardment of Rouen in early June caused an extensive fire in the *quartier pittoresque* surrounding the cathedral, burning old streets of half-timbered houses. The fire spread to the cathedral itself, damaging the north-west tower. The cathedrals of Evreux and Toul were also damaged, suffering destroyed bell-towers and steeples, burnt roofs and chipped masonry. Dunkirk, a town more commonly associated with the British evacuation in late May-early June, was also partly destroyed during the fighting.

The taking of Paris itself caused no significant cultural damage, despite an air raid on the capital on 3 June. Paris was undefended by the time German troops arrived there on 14 June – it had been declared an open city on 11 June, when plans for an 1870-style siege resistance were abandoned in the face of approaching enemy tanks and with the precedents of Warsaw and Rotterdam in mind. This part of the invasion at least did not fulfil expectations of destruction. German air raids on French towns continued, now south of Paris, along the line of the Loire river. From 14 to 19 June communications targets such as railway lines and stations were bombed in Orléans, Châteauneuf-sur-Loire and other towns along the river, but the historic town centres were bombarded too. As Pétain, the newly appointed Prime Minister, was announcing from Bordeaux on 17 June that an armistice with the invading army would be requested, German tanks provided an additional threat, arriving at the Loire on 18 June. In Tours, the Ecole des Beaux-Arts and a library were bombed and burned. Various Loire Valley châteaux were also damaged by shellfire during this part of the campaign, for example at Amboise and Chenonceaux.

By the time the armistice was signed at Compiègne on 22 June, it was estimated that 550 historic monuments had been damaged to varying degrees during the German invasion of France.[10] After France fell under German control, the German threat to such buildings retreated during the four years of occupation, not to return until the 1944 Allied invasion. The Allied threat was however maintained throughout the war, particularly from 1942 onwards, when the bombardment of German military installations in occupied France had occasional repercussions for non-military architectural targets.

France having been secured, German attention then turned to Britain, and London received its first air raid on the night of 24–5 June. While the fighter planes of the RAF and the Luftwaffe fought the Battle of Britain over south-eastern England between 10 July and 31 October, experiments in the other possible military use of aircraft representing a danger to historic monuments – the bombardment of cities from the air – were being conducted by both sides. Throughout August an exchange of air attacks took place: the RAF began the sequence on 1 August with a raid on Hannover, then again on Hamburg on 6 August. Luftwaffe raids on southern England started in earnest on 8 August, continuing throughout the month, while Berlin received its first air raid on 23 August. Although this exchange was maintained during the late summer and autumn (a British attack on Kiel on 19 October, followed by a German raid on Birmingham on 25 October, for example), the most extensive use of this relatively new military technique at this point of the war was the Blitz, the sustained and intensive sequence of German raids on British cities which began in London on 7 September and continued until May 1941. Nightly bombardment of London was carried out for seventy-three successive nights until 18 November and, although the first targets were the dockland areas of East London, the Blitz represented a serious threat to non-military and non-industrial targets too, particularly in the City of London, where the thirteenth/fourteenth-century church of Austin Friars (also known as the Dutch Church and a rare survivor of the great fire of London) was destroyed completely by a direct hit. A further indication of the danger to historic monuments came on 10 October when St Paul's Cathedral received a direct hit, with the outer roof of the choir being pierced by a bomb. The West End of London was also affected, with shops in Regent Street and Bond Street damaged, as well as Buckingham Palace; Figure 2.1 shows the latter being inspected by Churchill and the King and Queen. Various buildings in the London suburbs suffered some damage, from the partly thirteenth-century Eltham Palace to the centre court of the Wimbledon All-England Tennis Club.

From mid-November 1940 until 19 January 1941 the air raids on London became lighter, while other British cities and their historic monuments received correspondingly more attention. The RAF continued to carry out attacks on German cities – Munich on 8 November and Berlin on 12 November for instance – but it was the Luftwaffe which conducted the more sustained programme of bombing during this phase of the war. It is worth listing the pattern of air raids to determine the proportion affecting possible cultural targets: during November and December substantial night raids included those on Southampton (17, 23 and 30 November, 1 December), Birmingham (19, 20 and 22 November, 3 and 4 December), Bristol (24 November, 2 and 6 December), Plymouth (27 November),

FIGURE 2.1 Damage to Buckingham Palace, London, being inspected by
Winston Churchill and the King and Queen.
© Care of National Monuments Record.

Liverpool (28 November), Portsmouth (5 December), Sheffield (12 and 15 December) and Manchester (22 and 23 December).[11] These cities contained military and naval installations, plus the armaments factories and other industrial structures which constituted the primary targets during this stage of the Blitz, but historic buildings and town centres were affected by the same attacks. In Birmingham, for instance, the eighteenth-century English Baroque cathedral, St Philip's, suffered a burnt roof, while in Manchester there was a direct hit to the fifteenth-century cathedral, and damage to nine-teenth and twentieth-century secular monuments such as the Free Trade Hall and the Royal Exchange. The threat of such damage was as constant as the raids, which were by no means limited to the larger attacks listed above.

The air raid on Coventry of 14 November 1940 was the most serious example of this dual targeting. Taking place shortly after British raids on Munich and Berlin, the attack on Coventry was particularly extensive and not just upon the aircraft factories on the outskirts of the town which were ostensibly what made this town a possible target for German bombardment. Incendiary bombs also fell on the city centre, falling most famously on Coventry Cathedral, where a bomb exploded on the roof, melting the lead and causing a fire which lead to the collapse of the upper parts of the church, including the clerestory.[12] An attempt was made to put out the fire, but the water supply failed and everything in the interior burned, from wooden church furnishings and the organ, to the stone pillars which were severely calcinated by the heat. Some of the outer walls survived, as did the tower, but otherwise the cathedral was a ruin, the most seriously damaged historic monument in Britain at this stage in the war and certainly the most damaged church at any stage (Figure 2.2). During the attack, which lasted approximately ten hours, many houses and shops were destroyed too, as were the railway lines leading into the town.[13] Whether or not the 'real' target was the local aircraft industry, all types of building, whether indus-trial, commercial, residential or cultural, were affected in a way which announced the increased danger to architecture and other non-military targets in Britain. The year ended there with what was labelled the 'second fire of London' on 29 December, when heavy bombardment of the City further damaged churches.

Large scale air attacks were not the preserve of the Luftwaffe, however: a similar experiment in air raid style was tried out during an RAF attack on Mannheim on 16 December 1940. Large numbers of aircraft were sent to bomb a large section of the city intensively

FIGURE 2.2 Coventry Cathedral: the ruined church with only the
tower and outer walls still standing.
© Crown Copyright. National Monuments Record.

in a single raid, an early example of the 'area bombing' later developed as the standard method of air attack on enemy cities during the Second World War. It was the industrial areas of Mannheim and its large inland port which were bombed this time, not the residential and historic districts in the city centre. These were avoided, at least at this point in the war.

1941

The new year saw the continuation of the Blitz, with further attacks on previously bombed cities in the south of England, all particularly easily reached from Luftwaffe air bases in northern France: Bristol was first (3 January), followed by Portsmouth (10 January), Plymouth and Devonport (13 January) and Southampton (19 January). Wales was attacked for the first time, with air raids on Cardiff (2 January) and Swansea (17 January, then 19 and 20 February). After a lull in the bombing during February, the provinces were subjected to a new wave of attacks in March, April and May, with many towns receiving their third round of major raids, quite apart from the minor variety, and extending this time to Scotland and Northern Ireland: Glasgow and Clydeside were raided on 12 March, then on 7 April, then again on 5 May, while Belfast was attacked on 15 April and 4 May.[14] Again, throughout this period of bombing, the Luftwaffe emphasis seemed to be on industrial, shipbuilding and armaments targets but, again, cultural and historical buildings were also hit – Llandaff Cathedral, outside Cardiff, lost much of its roof during an air raid on the city, with much damage occurring to the interior and to the stained glass. Liverpool's Anglican Cathedral – begun in 1904 and still incomplete at this point – was damaged during the bombardments of the first week of May, with part of the south transept and the chancel windows affected. Large churches of any period were easy to hit, accidentally or otherwise.

Of the bombarded towns of this period in the war, Plymouth suffered particularly on the level of damage to historic monuments. The most extensive raids took place on 20–3 and 28–9 April (although it was estimated that there were as many as thirty-one raids in total on this town alone).[15] In the case of Plymouth, the old town remained relatively intact while the more recently built districts were thoroughly bombarded, destroying the city centre with all its public buildings and commercial areas and causing damage to forty churches, the best known being the early fifteenth-century St Andrew's (restored in 1874–5 by Gilbert Scott) and Charles Church (completed in 1708). The reminders of Elizabethan naval triumphs and the symbols of Britain's sea power were threatened as much as the modern shipbuilding and naval installation at the adjacent Devonport.

Meanwhile, RAF attacks on German cities had become more sporadic after the December 1940 bombing peak over Mannheim. The raid which caused most concern to German propagandists was that of the night of 9–10 April on Berlin as this was the occasion of the first direct hit on a major historic monument in the German capital: the eighteenth-century neoclassical German State Opera House on Unter den Linden. The Prussian State Library was also damaged. The German response was a heavy attack soon after – on 16 April – on the British capital and this time St Paul's Cathedral received its second direct hit. A bomb fell on the north transept, piercing the dome, exploding inside the church, then falling through the floor into the crypt; the portico surrounding the inside of the north door was also destroyed, along with the carved epitaph to Wren.[16]

London had been an almost continual target for the Luftwaffe since the beginning of the Blitz, but the worst air raid on the city occurred on 10 May. Historic monuments in many central areas were affected: Westminster Abbey was damaged at the crossing, with further damage to the cloister, the deanery and to Westminster School hall. Across the road in the Palace of Westminster the Chamber of the House of Commons was destroyed by an incendiary bomb induced fire. Further east, the Law Courts – the Inns of Court and the Temple Church – were damaged, as was the river wing of Somerset House with its 'Navy staircase', and the Tower of London and the fifteenth-century Guildhall too. All the major museum buildings were hit during this air raid, with the National Gallery, the National Portrait Gallery, the British Museum, the Tate Gallery and the Wallace Collection all suffering some damage to roofs and by now mostly empty exhibition rooms.

The general effect of the Blitz on London's historic monuments might be described as 'a little damage to a lot of monuments' – although the bombardment from the air was widespread, relatively few buildings of this type were completely destroyed. The most extensively damaged buildings were the churches of the City of London, an area which received a high proportion of the bombardment at this early stage of the war and which contained a high concentration of historic churches. The air raids were responsible for damage to nineteen of the area's fifty-one Wren-designed churches, themselves replacements for those burnt during the Great Fire of London.[17] Apart from the destruction of the pre-1666 Austin Friars, the most seriously damaged were St Vedast, on Foster Lane, Christ Church, on Newgate Street, St Mary-le-Bow, on Cheapside, and St Mary Aldermanbury. Outside of the City, St George's Roman Catholic Cathedral in Southwark (designed by Pugin, 1840–8) suffered a burnt roof and gutted interior and further west only the outer walls and tower of St Anne, Soho survived. Wren's St James, Piccadilly was badly damaged and St John, Smith Square was burned out, while the thirteenth/fourteenth-century Chelsea Old Church was completely destroyed.

The raid on London on 10 May 1941 was the last major attack on the city, with the exchange of air raids on capital cities of April–May over and the Blitz officially ending on 19 May. For the remainder of the year the Germans concentrated their air power on the Eastern Front, bombarding cities in the Soviet Union. The RAF carried out occasional raids on German cities, for instance Münster on 8–9 July, causing some damage to the centre of the town including the cathedral and the castle, then Hamburg on 26–27 July, and Kassel on 9 September, when the Landesbibliothek (Regional Library) was hit. There was little air raid damage to historic monuments or indeed buildings of any kind in Britain and Germany in the second half of 1941 and this diminution of destruction seemed to signal a change of strategy for both sides in the war in western Europe and a lifting of the threat to architecture and other non-military targets.

1942

This diminishing trend did not continue the following year, during which the air raid on the city centre was further developed and experimented with as a method of fighting a war, with obvious consequences for architecture. This experimentation was a feature of RAF activity in particular and almost nightly attacks were made on German cities, too many to list – it is the attacks with most effect on historic monuments which will concern us here. Air raids became heavier in 1942, with the use of larger quantities of both aeroplanes and bombs. They also became less discriminate – we have seen so far the danger to all parts of a city that an air attack could represent, but the number of historic town centres targeted increased significantly in 1942.

A British raid on occupied Paris on 3 March hinted at a change in policy. As part of a series of regular raids on targets in northern France such as power stations, air bases and ports, railway stations and bridges, many of which caused damage to nearby historic buildings, the RAF carried out an attack on the Renault factories at Boulogne-Billancourt, to the south-west of the city, but still remarkably close to the centre of Paris. The stated purpose of the raid was

to destroy the industrial installations which were producing armaments for the German army instead of cars, 'the outstanding symbol
of collaboration with Germany', as *The Times* report put it the
following day, also stressing that 'No bombs were dropped on Paris
itself'.[18] Apart from the loss of life caused – Vichy sources gave a
figure of 600 dead – the threat to the historic monuments of the
nearby city centre was extreme if unrealised. This raid marked a
notable increase in willingness on the part of the British air forces
to risk civilian deaths and the destruction of buildings of cultural
and historic interest, even on French territory, details that were
noted enthusiastically in German propaganda.[19]

The risks to historic city centres escalated further with the RAF
raid on Lübeck on the night of 28–9 March (the emotive date of
Palm Sunday that year). Unlike the trial area bombing raid on the
industrial districts of Mannheim of December 1940, this was the
first overt indiscriminate bombing of a town centre with little military or industrial significance. Lübeck, the capital of the Hanseatic
League during the thirteenth and fourteenth centuries, was the site
of Gothic churches and a Town Hall dating from this period,
besides preserved streets of timbered merchants' houses in its
medieval-plan centre. During the RAF raid approximately seventy
aircraft flew over the city, dropping bombs in three waves over a
period of three and a half hours and causing extensive fires – this
effect was exacerbated by the large number of wooden buildings.
The attack caused severe damage to the Gothic churches St Petri
and the Marienkirche, destroying the altarpiece by Hermann Rode
(1494) inside the latter; it had not been removed as such an attack
had not been expected. The more literary monument of Thomas
Mann's family 'Buddenbrook' House was also burnt down. It was
later estimated that eleven per cent of the *Altstadt* (old town centre)
was destroyed as a result of this air raid – far less than the figures
for other cities later in the war – but the initial impression was of
total devastation. New expressions were coined to refer to this new
style of air raid: 'to Lübeck' joined 'koventrieren' (a German verb
version of 'to Coventry') as a description of the area bombing of
town centres.

More strictly military targets such as industrial centres were not
ignored, as the period from March to July saw a series of forty-three
air raids on the Ruhr Valley. But at the same time the RAF continued
to attack the centres of cities perceived or at least presented in
German propaganda as primarily cultural and historical in importance: several raids on Rostock, another Hanseatic town, were carried

out in April using similar numbers of aircraft, particularly during the attacks of 24–7 April. Rostock was a port and the site of a Heinkel aeroplane factory but, as in the case of Lübeck, it was the old houses and public buildings in the historic centre which were most affected, including the town's oldest church, the Nikolaikirche. Choosing to target cities more famous for their history than their industry exposed the RAF to German newspaper headlines such as 'British barbarians: historic monuments in Rostock bombarded', even if similar levels of cultural damage had already been caused in Ruhr Valley towns more associated with industry.[20]

This dangerous precedent having been set by the British in Lübeck and Rostock, the Luftwaffe responded with their own series of attacks on non-military targets of particular historic and cultural interest in Britain. These were the so-called 'Baedeker raids' – named after the guidebooks – which took place in the following locations on the following dates: the first raids were on Exeter on the three nights of 23–5 April (Figure 2.3); Bath was attacked on 25 April, then again the next night (26 April); there were raids on Norwich starting the night after that (27–9 April) and on York on 28 April. Exeter and Norwich received further attacks on 3 May and 8 May respectively. There was then a lull until the raids on Canterbury on the night of 31 May–1 June, followed by one on a smaller scale on 3 June.[21] From the German point of view, the Baedeker raids were a success on the level of material damage and a considerable amount of specifically cultural damage was caused in each town, besides the destruction of residential and commercial areas, as the focus of the raids was in each case the historic town centre. Particular historic monuments affected included Exeter Cathedral, which received a direct hit that destroyed the thirteenth-century Chapel of St James on the south side of the choir. Bath received the heaviest attack and the interior of the Assembly Rooms (1769–71) was gutted by fire, as were two houses in the Royal Crescent (1767–75). Other houses were damaged in Queen Square, Lansdown Crescent and Lansdown Place East. The mid-fifteenth-century Guildhall in York was badly damaged by fire, leaving only the outer walls, and St Martin-le-Grand, a church of the same period, was semi-ruined (Figure 2.4). In Norwich four churches were damaged, as was stained glass and window tracery in the cathedral. Canterbury Cathedral escaped serious damage – some bombs fell on the roof, but these did not explode and were thrown off by fire wardens; bombs also fell in the cathedral precincts, destroying the Cathedral Library (1868) with a direct hit and damaging the Canon's House.

FIGURE 2.3 Exeter in 1942 after the Baedeker raids: the High Street
looking east, with the damaged church of St Lawrence (15th–19th century,
now demolished) on the left.
© Crown Copyright. National Monuments Record.

The gateway of the already ruined monastery of St Augustine was
also damaged (Figure 2.5). Here I have detailed only the damage to
'major' historic monuments but in all five towns the older districts
suffered generally.

The Baedeker raids, occurring so close together, formed a discrete
cluster of attacks with specifically cultural targets. There was,
however, a gap between the raid on Norwich on 8 May and that on
Canterbury on 31 May, a gap filled by another attack with severe
consequences for historic monuments: the most significant RAF air
raid between those two dates was the 'thousand bomber' attack on
Cologne, carried out on the night of 30–1 May, the night before the
Canterbury raid. There had already been many smaller scale raids
on Cologne (this was the 107th), causing damage to various industrial targets but also notably to several churches in the centre: the
'Dekagon' or ten-sided dome of the early thirteenth-century St Gereon
was hit on 8 July 1941 (Figure 2.6), St Kolumba (twelfth–seventeenth

century) was slightly damaged on the same day and the roof of St
Pantaleon (tenth–twelfth century) burnt on 28 April 1942. The
attack of 30–1 May was on an altogether new scale, developing
dramatically the method of area bombing tried out on Lübeck and
Rostock – this time over a thousand aircraft were used (hence the
names 'Operation Millennium' and 'thousand-bomber raid') to
drop approximately 1,500 tons of bombs, an increase in bombing

FIGURE 2.4 York in 1942 after the Baedeker raid, with the damaged
church of St Martin-le-Grand.
© Crown Copyright. National Monuments Record.

FIGURE 2.5 Canterbury in 1942 after the Baedeker raid, showing
damage to the old town centre, with the damaged gateway to
St Augustine's Abbey in the background.
© Crown Copyright. National Monuments Record.

capacity which made the helpless situation of historic city centres
clear to both sides in the conflict. A large proportion of incendiary
bombs were used in this attack, leading to extensive fire damage,
besides the effects of direct hits on buildings. In the case of ecclesiastical architecture alone, the following Cologne churches were
damaged in this attack: the Rhenish-Romanesque churches of St
Aposteln (1192–1230), St Maria im Kapitol (eleventh century) and
St Gereon (1219–27), the Gothic churches Groß St Martin, St Ursula,
St Maria Lyskirchen, St Andreas and the Antoniterkirche, and the
Klosterkirche St Elisabeth (1670) which was completely destroyed.[22]
Cologne Cathedral itself was not affected by this raid but it and
many of these churches would be damaged during many raids later
in the war. Similar numbers of London churches had been damaged
or destroyed during the Blitz, but this destruction had taken place
over a period of eight months, not in one night. Bomber Command
were officially congratulated the next day on the efficiency of the
attack by Churchill:

I congratulate . . . the whole of Bomber Command upon the remarkable feat of organisation which enabled you to dispatch over 1,000 [aircraft] to the Cologne area in a single night, and without confusion to concentrate their action over the target into so short a time as one hour and a half. This proof of the growing power of the British bomber force is also the herald of what Germany will receive, city by city, from now on.[23]

Historic city centres were now, it seems, openly considered as possible targets for military action. As in the case of Coventry, and indeed of most cities, Cologne had a dual industrial/cultural nature, in particularly close conjunction in this case as the main railway station was located in the heart of the historic *Altstadt*, next to the Gothic cathedral. The indiscriminate nature of the attack – an inevitable feature, given the concentration of bombs dropped in a small area – was especially marked in this air raid. On the question of why Cologne was chosen for this attack, its relatively accessible location and favourable weather conditions on the night of the raid were the official reasons, but the city was also famous for its Roman history and Romanesque churches and an element of post-Baedeker

FIGURE 2.6 Cologne, St Gereon with damaged Dekagon.
Photograph taken 7 March 1945 (Macmillan Committee photograph).
The Conway Library, Courtauld Institute of Art.

raid revenge cannot be discounted. With the Luftwaffe attack on Canterbury taking place immediately after, another new period in the war was entered from the perspective of damage to historic monuments.

In recognition of this, more intensive German efforts began to be made to protect historic monuments on their own territory, after two years of observing the efforts of enemy countries to safeguard architecture against German bombardment. Measures taken thus far were manifestly inadequate, but then a long war on the 'home front' had not been expected. Much use was made of techniques learnt during the invasion of France in 1940: the roof timbers of German churches and town halls were in their turn impregnated with anti-inflammatory material and all sculpture that could not be removed was sand-bagged or walled-in. In Berlin the monument to Frederick the Great on Unter den Linden was encased in concrete. Particular attention was paid to German cathedrals: in the partly Carolingian (ninth century) cathedral in Aachen, the *Kaiserstuhl* – Charlemagne's throne – was given a protective mantel, as were the stone figure of the 'Bamberg rider' in the Romanesque/Gothic Bamberg Cathedral and the sculptured portals of the Gothic cathedral in Cologne. Here a concrete bunker – known as the '*Dombunker*' – was constructed on the south side of the church to house precious and flammable church furnishings such as the choir stalls.[24] As for the effectiveness of these measures, early optimism soon evaporated as the new effects of area bombing were observed. Techniques of protection developed in response to levels of damage during World War One were no longer relevant and, in practice, little protection could be given in the face of the extensive destruction methods of World War Two. Even basic damage limitation such as the extinguishing of fires was impossible during large scale raids, when access roads and the water supply would be as badly affected as the burning cathedrals. The survival of historic monuments – in all countries involved in this conflict – was frequently more the result of luck than of planning.

Despite Churchill's threat to repeat the exercise, another raid on the scale of 'Operation Millennium' was not carried out until the following year. The RAF did, however, maintain regular smaller attacks on German cities and August 1942 saw two with particularly strong cultural and historical connotations: on the night of 12–13 August Mainz, a city with a Roman and Holy Roman imperial history to rival that of Cologne, received its first major air raid, damaging the cathedral (begun in 1036, with a twelfth-thirteenth-century nave) and many smaller parish churches. Then Nuremberg was attacked on the night of 28–9 August, affecting parts of the well-preserved fourteenth/fifteenth-century *Altstadt*; this German town had recent, as well as an historical significance, having been the site of the Nazi rallies in the 1930s.

Luftwaffe attacks on Britain also continued, although their scale was considerably smaller than those carried out by the RAF this year and the policy of overtly targeting towns of primarily historic importance was not pursued. British towns on or near the coast were bombed, for instance Ipswich (1 June, 14 August), Weston-super-Mare (27–8 June), Colchester (10 and 26 August). Hull had been attacked on 19 May and was once again on 31 July. These were reported in the German press as purely military targets, as were seaside holiday destinations such as Torquay, Poole and the Isle of Wight.[25] Inland attacks were also maintained, for example on Birmingham on 24 June and 27–30 July. By this stage, though, the air raid threat to British cities was much reduced compared to that presented in previous months and years.

Towards the end of 1942 air raid activities switched to a certain extent to northern Italy, with RAF attacks being carried out on Milan, Turin and Genoa. Italy had joined Germany in the war on 10 June 1940, but by the end of 1942 was proving to be one of the weaker spots on Axis territory. The threat to historic monuments being a well established and well publicised feature of the war by now, the Pope requested that Rome be declared an open city in order to avert the danger of area bombing there.

1943

British area bombing raids upon German cities continued to increase in frequency and scale in 1943, with corresponding consequences for historic monuments. The pattern during the first half of the year changed: instead of regular small attacks with the occasional large-scale 'Operation Millennium'-style raid, regular major raids were carried out. Nuremberg was the target once more on 25–6 February and 8–9 March, then Munich on 9 and 18 March, during which the nineteenth-century area of the city with its many grand public buildings and private houses was most affected, including museums such as the Alte Pinakothek (designed by Klenze) and the Neue Staatsgalerie. Cologne was bombed again heavily on 29 June (after the earlier 26 February raid which destroyed the Wallraf-Richartz

Museum), causing the first damage to the cathedral when bombs exploded on the roof of the north transept and close to the south tower, damaging the vault and the facade. Although it was the effect on the cathedral that attracted most German propaganda outrage, provoking headlines such as 'England's Assassination Attempt on European Culture',[26] there was also further damage to churches affected during the 'thousand-bomber raid' – St Aposteln, St Kolumba, St Maria im Kapitol, St Maria Lyskirchen – as well as damage to buildings previously unaffected: the Rathaus, the fifteenth century 'Gürzenich' municipal hall, plus the churches St Alban, the eleventh-twelfth-century St Georg, the thirteenth-century St Johan Baptist and St Kunibert, and the eighteenth-century St Gregor. Cologne is a particularly good indicator of the cumulative effects of the regular area bombing of historic town centres, with its high concentration of progressively ruined historic monuments.

Attention returned to cities in the Ruhr area in a series of attacks between March and June, known as the 'Battle of the Ruhr', a relatively new use for the word 'battle', as here the combatants were bomber aeroplanes and anti-aircraft fire. The first significant air raid was carried out on Essen on 5 March, the site of the Krupps factory in the city centre providing the main target. In most other Ruhr cities under attack, the industrial and armaments installations were in modern suburbs, but the routine focus of the air raids was the older town centres. The area bombed cities were raided several times, the dates of the major raids being as follows: Essen (12 March, 3 April), Duisburg (26 March, 12 May), Bochum (29 March), Dortmund (24 May), Düsseldorf (12 June), Krefeld (21 June), Wuppertal (24 June) and Remscheid (30 July). Other bombed cities included Mülheim, Mönchengladbach, Oberhausen and Gelsenkirchen. Once again, the large amounts of industrial activity in this part of Germany and the fact that few of these cities were as commonly associated with German culture and history as a Cologne or a Nuremberg, did not ensure that only industrial buildings were damaged. The many raids on Essen, for example, also destroyed the Folkwang Museum, established to encourage local factory workers to appreciate art. Every town contained buildings of historical and cultural interest, a fact sometimes forgotten in the case of other countries' historic monuments – a useful antidote to this attitude is to imagine British reaction to a German report of the November 1940 air raid on Coventry as 'an attack on an industrial target'.

Elsewhere in western Europe, the RAF had attacked the Brittany coastal towns of Lorient and Saint-Nazaire in January and February

1943 with the intention of destroying German U-Boat installations; the U-Boats themselves were however well camouflaged and the town centres were flattened without military gain. These were air raids which Sir Arthur Harris himself disapproved of, judging in his 1947 account of Bomber Command activities that 'We did, in fact, uselessly destroy two perfectly good French towns . . .'.[27] A further raid had been carried out on 4 April on the Renault factory in Paris, this time by the United States Air Force, who had joined what had become known as the Strategic Bombing Offensive at the beginning of 1943. The Luftwaffe continued to be active over British cities throughout 1943, carrying out repeat night raids on many towns already hit during the Blitz of 1940–1. In addition, daylight raids were made by a different type of aircraft with a smaller range, the fighter-bomber; this type of attack focused on coastal towns and seaside resorts in southern England and between 7 March and 6 June the following towns, all with their own variety of cultural and historical significance, received some war damage: Eastbourne, Yarmouth, Hastings, Bournemouth, Brighton, Torquay, Margate and Folkestone.[28]

On the level of the scale and destructive capacity of RAF attacks, what had been shocking in 1942 had become almost routine in 1943. The boundaries were pushed back still further by the series of raids on Hamburg on 24–9 July and 2 August which involved the use of approximately 2,500 aircraft. The attack reached its peak on the night of 27–8 July when the volume of incendiary bombs being dropped created a huge firestorm, causing enormous loss of life (approximately 40,000 people) and destruction of buildings on yet another new scale. In the case of Hamburg it is inappropriate to single out particular affected historic monuments, as the appropriately named 'Operation Gomorrah' damaged or destroyed most buildings in the city regardless of type. Once again the swiftness and comprehensiveness of the destruction was unexpected – the firestorm itself was not planned but such large quantities of aircraft and bombs could not but have had an extreme effect. As following the previous benchmark raid on Cologne, the British threat was of further area bombing on this new increased scale, with the implication that Berlin would be the next victim.

Area bombing of German cities continued steadily throughout the summer and autumn of 1943, if on a less dramatic scale than in Hamburg, with regular cultural consequences. In Nuremberg, the Gothic St Lorenzkirche was hit on 10 August, causing structural damage to the choir and nave vaults. A raid on Mannheim on 5 September affected the area of the town laid out in the eighteenth century. Further damage to Cologne's historic monuments occurred on 25 September, when the twelfth-century church St Cäcilien was hit for the first time. On the night of 2–3 October Munich's classical sculpture museum, the Glyptothek, was damaged, then on 8 October the *Altstadt* of Stuttgart was bombed (the Daimler-Benz factory on the outskirts of the city was later bombed on 26 November). The night after saw an attack on Hannover which destroyed the Leibnitzhaus, a seventeenth-century half-timbered townhouse in German Renaissance style where the philosopher had lived. The centre of Münster and its Romanesque cathedral were hit once again on the night after that, 10 October, in a major attack involving over 250 United States Air Force planes. Frankfurt was bombed on 26 November, causing fire damage to the Goethehaus. The centre of Leipzig was damaged on the night of 3–4 December, with many public buildings, trade fair and exhibition halls affected.

The Commander-in-Chief of Bomber Command, Arthur Harris, had supplied a list of successful area bombing raids on Germany to Churchill on 2 November 1943. The list is worth quoting in full, despite some inaccuracy and exaggeration, as it gives an impression of the general spread of the attacks and of the way in which they were categorised by the RAF:

1. 'Virtually destroyed': Hamburg, Cologne, Essen, Dortmund, Düsseldorf, Hannover, Mannheim, Bochum, Mülheim, Köln Deutz, Barmen, Elberfeld, Mönchengladbach, Rheydt, Krefeld, Aachen, Rostock, Remscheid, Kassel, Emden.
2. 'Seriously damaged': Frankfurt, Stuttgart, Duisburg, Bremen, Hagen, Munich, Nuremberg, Stettin, Kiel, Karlsruhe, Mainz, Wilhelmshaven, Lübeck, Saarbrücken, Osnabrück, Münster, Rüsselsheim, Berlin, Oberhausen.
3. 'Damaged': Brunswick, Darmstadt, Leverkusen, Flensburg, Jena, Augsburg, Leipzig, Friedrichshafen, Wismar.[29]

It is the extent of damage, rather than what was damaged, which is prioritised here. Harris felt no need to differentiate between the destruction of military targets or historic monuments, as a concentration on the former category of building does not appear to have been the primary criterion of 'success' – any damage would do. This was the precarious situation of historic buildings located in the centres of large German towns.

The Allied threat to target Berlin, made after the Hamburg raid, was realised in a series of sixteen area bombing raids between 18

November 1943 and mid-March 1944. Although spaced well apart, these attacks became known collectively as the 'Battle of Berlin'. No individual raid was of the intensity of the earlier attack on Hamburg but damage was caused across the entire city, to industrial, residential and historic districts. The area to the east and south of the Brandenburg Gate was targeted in particular, as this was where the government offices were located – another variety of historic monument. The raid on the night of 22–3 November damaged many Ministry buildings, along with the Reichstag, the Reich Chancellery and the Kaiserhof Hotel where Hitler kept an apartment (Figure 2.7). The Gendarmenmarkt was hit with its neoclassical Garrison and French churches. Potsdamer Platz was also damaged, as was the area around the Zoo, including the Kaiser-Wilhelm-Gedächtnis-Kirche, or 'memorial church', built 1891–5 (Figure 2.8). Further west, the Schloß and park of Charlottenburg were hit, causing damage to the dome of the central building and one wing, while two buildings in

FIGURE 2.7 Berlin, the postwar state of the Reichstag.
Photograph taken 3 June 1945.
Imperial War Museum, London, neg. no. BU 8573.

the gardens – the Belvedere and the Schinkel-Pavilion – were destroyed. The end of 1943 presented a less than encouraging spectacle in the German capital.

Meanwhile, what had already happened to historic monuments in north-western Europe was expected and feared in the Italian theatre of war. The first air raid on Rome was carried out by the American Air Force on 14 July. The stated target was the railway

FIGURE 2.8 Berlin, the ruined Kaiser-Wilhelm-Gedächtnis-Kirche.
Imperial War Museum, London, neg. no. HU 56711.

marshalling yards just outside the city walls; in the course of bombing, one historic monument was damaged, the church of San Lorenzo fuori le Mura, and this remained one of the very few historic buildings in Rome directly affected by air bombardment (Figure 2.9). Elsewhere in Italy growing concerns for the safety of other historic town centres were not calmed by the Italian surrender and signing of an armistice with the Allies on 8 September 1943, as the German army fought on in Italy as an occupying army, signalling its intentions soon after the armistice by seizing Rome on 10 September. The Allied armies had begun their campaign by invading Sicily in July and, as fighting for control of Italy moved northwards, some historic sites and buildings were affected by air and artillery attack from both sides. The archaeological site of Pompeii was slightly damaged by Allied bombardment in September. Naples was taken by the Allies on 1 October, after fighting which had caused some damage to the fourteenth-century church of Santa Chiara. North of Naples, the Allied siege of the German-held hill-top monastery of Montecassino began on 19 December. This was to last for six months, becoming one of the most notorious cases of historic monument destruction in Italy (Figure 2.10).

1944

Throughout 1943 the imbalance between the scale of British/Allied and Luftwaffe air raids had increased to such a degree that the air threat to the cities and architecture of Britain seemed negligible. Luftwaffe efforts revived, however, in early 1944 and a series of raids known as the 'Little Blitz' or 'Baby Blitz' lasted from January to March. London was the most targeted city for this new wave of night attacks, although coastal towns such as Hull and Portsmouth were also hit. Meanwhile there was yet more large scale British bombing of German cities at this stage of the year, causing steadily more destruction of historic monuments as more and more city centres were targeted. In Stuttgart air raids on 21 February and 2 and 15 of March damaged the Neues Schloß and the Stiftskirche, among many other buildings. A heavy attack on Frankfurt on the night of 22–3 March continued the destruction of the already damaged Goethehaus. Aachen was hit on 11 April and Munich on 25 April – this last raid had particularly serious consequences for the *Altstadt*, damaging the Residenz complex (the palace of the Bavarian rulers), including the Nationaltheater, the Altes

Residenztheater and the Hofgarten. Structural damage was severe and interiors were burnt (Figure 2.11). Also affected by this raid were the Alte Pinakothek and Neue Pinakothek buildings.

While the steady accumulation of cultural damage in Germany continued by means of the methods of air bombardment established in earlier years of the war, the Allied invasion of occupied France in June 1944 represented a new threat to the historic monuments of north-western Europe. Since mid-1940, following the German invasion of the Benelux countries and France, air raids and area bombing had constituted the prinicipal means of destruction but now ground fighting and artillery fire joined bombardment from the air. The Allied attempt to dislodge the occupying German army meant also that French towns were subjected to these various types of attack from both sides in the conflict at once, by the Allies on the offensive and by the retreating German troops.

FIGURE 2.9 Rome, San Lorenzo fuori le Mura, looking towards east end, showing damage caused by Allied bombing on 19 July 1943 (Macmillan Committee photograph).
The Conway Library, Courtauld Institute of Art.

FIGURE 2.10 The bombarded monastery of Montecassino,
photograph taken May 1944 from the north-west battleground
(Macmillan Committee photograph).
The Conway Library, Courtauld Institute of Art.

Even before D-Day on 6 June, the Allies had attacked targets in
France: during the first half of 1944 smaller-scale but precise air
raids were carried out on railway lines, stations and German rocket
launching sites in the north of the country. These precision raids
constituted a new role for Bomber Command, that is, preparatory
work in advance of the later invasion, rather than large scale area
attacks intended as an end in themselves. In general their precision
meant less damage for non-military targets, although in north-eastern
France air raids were carried out on the occupied towns of Arras,
Douai, Cambrai and Valenciennes, damaging town centres and
churches – the cathedral in Arras was hit, having only recently
been rebuilt after First World War damage. As early as 19 April air
raids had been carried out on Rouen, then again on 30–1 May
and 1 June. The old town was bombed again on 19 April (the first
damage having been done by German forces in June 1940), including
the Gothic cathedral which was hit by three high explosive bombs,

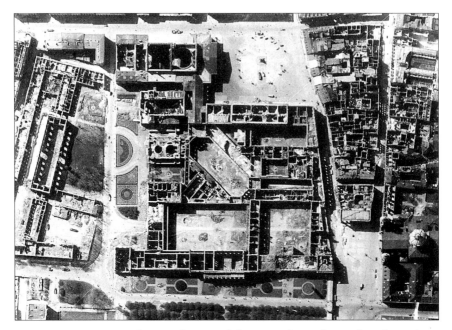

FIGURE 2.11 Munich, aerial view of the ruined Residenz after the area
bombing raid of 24–5 April 1944. The official caption to this
RAF photograph was 'Bomb damage to Nazi Party meeting place'.
Imperial War Museum, London, neg. no. C 4375.

demolishing bays and chapels in the south aisle and south transept,
as well as four flying buttresses (Figure 2.12). On 1 June the bombardment caused a fire inside the Tour St Romain, destroying the
upper parts. One church – St Vincent – was completely destroyed
on 31 May and the destructive week that followed acquired the
name 'la semaine rouge' (the red week), with its connotations of
fire and blood. The week ended with the bombardment of the
fifteenth/sixteenth-century church St Maclou on 6 June, the choir
of which was cut in two by a bomb. Besides the historic town
centre, the more obviously military target of the harbour quays
were also hit. This time most of the bombardment was Allied in
origin, but the retreating German forces also contributed to the
damage, to the Palais de Justice, for instance.

More severe destruction was caused in other Normandy and
Brittany towns from 6 June onwards during Operation Overlord.[30]
Air power was used as a support for the armies on the ground,
destroying and preventing the movement of enemy artillery and

backing up the ground-based besieging of occupied towns, which
suffered greatly from the carpet-bombing contribution of Allied
aeroplanes to the campaign. Caen, bombarded by British and
American aircraft and artillery between 6 June and 15 August, was
an extreme example, eventually liberated with 80 per cent of its
buildings destroyed. All this destruction was caused during these
two months of 1944 as, unlike Rouen, Caen had not been damaged
when taken over by the German army in June 1940. On 6 June 1944
air raids distributed incendiary bombs over the town, causing
massive fires and burning two churches, St Etienne-le-vieux and
St Jean, and many other historic buildings. On 7 June bombardment
on a huge scale occurred, with hundreds of aircraft involved;
approximately twenty bombs hit the Hôtel de Ville, causing the
collapse of the facade. The following day bombardment from the
direction of the sea began, from Allied ships off the Normandy
coast, and this combination of attacking methods continued daily.

FIGURE 2.12 Rouen, view of the cathedral from the south, showing
damage to the south side of the church and to the surrounding old *quartier
pittoresque*. Allied photograph taken after the liberation of the city
(Macmillan Committee photograph).
The Conway Library, Courtauld Institute of Art.

It was a shell fired from a ship which fell upon the Gothic church of St Pierre on 12 June, damaging the spire and the nave roof. The day after that more general damage was caused by more widespread fires in the town and by 15 June two-thirds of it had been burned, the destroyed historic monument count rising steadily. On 7 July the churches St Julien and St Sauveur were hit, the university buildings and library were on fire and the Hôtel de Ville finally collapsed completely (Figure 2.13).

Despite the departure of the majority of occupying German troops by 9 July, some remained to the south of the town, within bombardment range of the centre, and the progressive destruction of Caen continued. From then on it was primarily German aircraft and artillery attacks which caused what little damage there was left to do. Two of the town's most important historic monuments did survive: when the liberation of Caen was complete, the two Romanesque churches, the Abbaye aux Hommes and the Abbaye aux Dames, were almost intact, perhaps as they were located slightly to the west and east of the town centre respectively. Several shells had fallen on the roof of the former but there was no serious damage otherwise, a fact attributed to miraculous causes by Caen residents, a not unreasonable explanation, given the ruinous state of the rest of their town.

During the intense fighting over Caen, other Normandy towns were also being damaged as the invasion progressed throughout July and August, or rather when it progressed least, as it was the towns where the invasion was most resisted where the greatest damage was done. On the coast, Le Havre was generally decimated on 14–15 June, from harbour quays to historic town centre, where the Musée des Beaux-Arts, the municipal museum, the theatre and the Hôtel de Ville were destroyed. Further east, Boulogne was bombarded the same night, mostly around the port but also causing some damage to the old ramparts and gates and to the church of Notre-Dame. For the first two weeks of August Saint-Malo was bombarded by both American and German artillery, leaving very little of the walled citadel standing. Inland in Falaise the Palais de Justice was destroyed, along with two churches (St Gervais and La Trinité) and most of the old town centre. Saint-Lo was similarly decimated, as shown in Figure 2.14; even the relatively intact cathedral of Notre-Dame was more badly damaged than it appears in this photograph, having lost one tower, part of the nave and stone carvings from the main portals. Much of the old town of Lisieux was also destroyed, but the Carmelite convent and basilica

FIGURE 2.13 Caen, the damaged St Pierre and surrounding ruins of
the town (Macmillan Committee photograph).
The Conway Library, Courtauld Institute of Art.

of Ste Thérèse were not damaged. Large towns and communications
centres were not the only targets affected: Allied bombing of a
German airbase between Lisieux and Evreux strayed into the small
nearby town of Beaumont-le-Roger, for instance, damaging the
church of St Nicolas.

Beyond Normandy the Allies moved south and eastwards,
approaching Paris from the west. To the south-west of Paris,
Chartres was in the firing line, suffering damage to the town centre,
not to the cathedral but to the Hôtel de Ville, the Mairie and the
municipal library all three of which were largely destroyed. Further
south Orléans was hit once again, by means of artillery and air
power, continuing the process begun in 1940 and this time partly
destroying the north tower of the cathedral. Damage caused on the
route to the north-west of Paris included that to Claude Monet's
studio in Giverny, near Vernon, where shell fire caused the loss of
three paintings. Meanwhile in the far south of France an Allied
invasion from another direction was taking place: Operation Dragoon

FIGURE 2.14 Saint-Lo, the ruined town centre, with Notre-Dame on the
right. The official SHAEF caption was 'St Lo, wrested from the Nazis by
American forces July 18, 1944' (Macmillan Committee photograph).
The Conway Library, Courtauld Institute of Art.

began on 14 August with the bombardment of the south coast,
particularly the small harbours of Cannes and Saint-Tropez, with
the much larger port of Marseille being hit later on 28 August. In
all three cases the old town centres, the *vieux ports*, close to the
targeted harbours and docks, were destroyed; in Marseille, the
seventeenth-century Hôtel de Ville was also damaged.

Paris was entered by the Allied armies, headed by the French
General Leclerc, on 25 August. Spared bombardment – and spared
also from a German plan to mark their withdrawal from the capital
by blowing up many of the city's power stations, bridges and
monuments – the French capital was almost intact; as one postwar
French account put it, 'To her liberators, Paris resembled a city that
had just survived a close brush with death'.[31] Some damage had
been caused in the centre, however, as a result of the placing of guns
in the Tuileries gardens and along the Champs-Elysées.[32] The Grand
Palais had also suffered a fire during fighting between German
tanks and French Resistance fighters. A combination of Allied and
German damage was caused to other public buildings in this area:
the Senate building, used by the occupiers as the headquarters for

their 'Western Europe Air Command', was damaged by Allied shells and there was a fire in the Chambre des Députés on the day that the city was liberated. As the war was not yet over further to the east of Paris there was still a lingering threat to the capital, realised during German bombing of the centre at the end of August, then again in December 1944, this time near the Louvre. Nevertheless, Paris emerged from the Second World War in infinitely better architectural shape than London or Berlin (Figure 2.15).

After their arrival in Paris the Allied armies, moving eastwards from Paris and northwards from the south coast, continued in the direction of the German border, gradually forcing the retreat of the German army. Lyon was reached on 1 September, Dijon on 11 and Nancy on 15 September; Strasbourg was taken on 24 November – during the Allied bombardment two bombs hit the cathedral and the city's oldest church, St Etienne, was destroyed. Progress was faster in the far north-east of France, meaning less damage for historic town centres as no long destructive sieges were required. The early Gothic cathedral of Laon was slightly damaged, nonetheless, and a Soissons church, St Jean des Vignes, previously almost completely destroyed during the First World War, was hit once again. The armies continued eastwards across the Belgian border early in September, leaving the towns and historic monuments of France in relative safety. One estimate of the number of historic monuments damaged overall in France gave the following figures: as the war moved out of French territory, of 8,000 *monuments classés*, or listed buildings, 68 were completely destroyed and 1,270 were damaged; of these 569 were badly damaged.[33]

In Belgium historic town centres were menaced by the artillery of both the advancing Allies and the retreating Germans, who blew up bridges to slow the Allied progress, in Bruges for instance. Progress was fast, however, with British and Canadian forces operating in the north of the country and the Americans in the south. Brussels, Ghent, Oostende, Bruges and Antwerp were liberated 3–5 September, as were Mons, Charleroi and Namur. Further east, Liège and the city of Luxembourg were reached by 10 September. Despite the swiftness of the Allied progress, the following examples of damage to historic town centres occurred: in Brussels, the Palais de Justice (used as SS headquarters during the occupation) was damaged by the retreating Germans, a fire destroying the cupola; in Kortrijk (Courtrai) the Gothic cloth hall was so extensively damaged that it was later demolished; Allied bombing affected the centre of Mons; in Leuven (Louvain) damage to the old town

FIGURE 2.15 Paris, Notre-Dame intact after the liberation of
the capital on 25 August 1944, with the French flag flying on
the tower (Macmillan Committee photograph).
The Conway Library, Courtauld Institute of Art.

included that to the seventeenth-century Sint Michielskerk;
Mechelen (Malines) was bombed, as was Dinant (for three days). In
Namur and Liège more bridges in the city centres were blown up,
and the churches and monuments of the latter suffered particularly

from bomb and rocket attacks, including the eighteenth-century Hôtel de Ville, the cathedral and the churches of Ste Croix and St Jacques. This 1944 damage, when added to that caused during May 1940, led to a toll of destruction which rather contradicts one British commentator's analysis of February 1945 that 'it is clear that Belgian monuments have suffered little from the war'.[34] This revealed more about the cultural attitudes of the writer than about the extent of the destruction; the more familiar French historic monuments were perhaps more of a priority for the British than those of much-invaded Belgium, across which rival armies had moved in both World Wars.

Further north in the Netherlands, the old centre of Arnhem was destroyed by Allied bombardment in September during Operation Market Garden, while Rotterdam was further damaged by bombing from both sides in the autumn of 1944 (and once again in the spring of 1945). The efficient advance of September was halted in the northern part of Luxembourg over the winter of 1944–5, as German forces fought back in what came to be called the 'Battle of the Bulge'. Another dismissive comment was made on the 'importance' of the damage caused in this area, this time in the Report of the American Commission for the Protection and Salvage of Artistic and Historic Monuments in War Areas: 'The Battle of the Bulge occurred in a region relatively unimportant from the point of view of monuments, so that no major damage was incurred . . .'.[35] This dismissive view notwithstanding, in Echternach the eleventh-century Romanesque abbey church of St Willibrord was destroyed during German bombardment, as was the castle at Clervaux.

Before following the progress of cultural damage into Germany, a brief Italian interlude: on the other front where a common European cultural heritage was assumed and at risk, June and July of 1944 had also seen an intensifying threat to historic monuments, where damage followed the retreating line of the German forces through Italy, but was by no means exclusively caused by them. Some Allied bombardment had taken place before the advance northwards, most notoriously in the case of Padua, where Mantegna frescoes in the Eremitani Church were destroyed on 11 March 1944 (Figure 2.16). Rome was taken by the Allies by 4 June without further destruction, the status of the city as 'open' having been observed by both sides (Venice was also entirely undamaged). Some progress north was then made, to Orvieto on 14 June and to Siena by 3 July. It was towards the end of July, as the Allied advance was halted outside Pisa, that the damage to historic city centres began in earnest

– the battle for Pisa lasted a month, causing much destruction, including in the Campo Santo area. Other cities of particular cultural and historical importance caught in the middle of Allied and German fire were Verona, Vicenza, Mantua, Faenza, Ferrara, Ravenna and Rimini – all were close to large communications centres, such as Bologna. The historic as well as the industrial centres of Milan and Turin were also badly damaged. Florence was largely spared, although bridges over the Arno and some buildings along the river were exploded by the Germans during their retreat.

Meanwhile mutual German and Allied air raids had not stopped during the new concentration of the war in France. As the fighting in Normandy progressed in June and July, 'Doodlebug' flying bombs – or V-1 rockets – were being launched in the direction of London and south-eastern England. What they lacked in range and accuracy, they made up for in destructive effect, and the London suburbs south of the Thames (also Hackney and Westminster) suffered regular rocket attacks for the rest of the year, totalling thousands of direct hits on residential areas in particular.[36] The nineteenth-century Royal Military Chapel in Wellington Barracks, Birdcage Walk was one historic victim. In September 1944, the V-1 rocket was

FIGURE 2.16 Padua, the damaged Eremitani church. Photograph taken in May 1945 (Macmillan Committee photograph).
The Conway Library, Courtauld Institute of Art.

replaced by the even more effective V-2, causing many casualties and much damage.

Allied area bombing of German cities had also continued throughout the invasion of France. Hamburg was attacked once again on 18 June, then in July Munich again (finishing off damage to the Neue Staatsgalerie), Cologne again on the 9 (another hit on St Aposteln) and Stuttgart again from 25–9 July, causing further damage to what was left of the *Altstadt*, including the Altes Schloß; the roof and vault of the fourteenth-sixteenth century Stiftskirche collapsed during the raid on 25 July. More recent architecture was equally vulnerable: modernist houses on the 1927 Weissenhof estate were also damaged, including those designed by Gropius, Poelzig and the Taut brothers.[37] New targets were found to supplement these much-raided cities: Trier was attacked for the first time on 18 August, resulting in some damage to the fourth-century basilica and the Dom and more serious damage to the nearby Gothic Liebfrauenkirche, leaving it close to collapse (Figure 2.17). Another, worse, series of raids between 19–24 December completed the effect, although the fourth-century AD Porta Nigra was not affected.

From September to December further heavy bombing of many German cities was carried out, compounding earlier damage to city centres and causing more. While Allied troops were moving towards Germany on the ground – the first German city to surrender was Aachen on 21 October – the pressure from the air was maintained and even increased at this stage of the war. To give some impression of the regularity and spread of this wave of air raids, the following list gives some of the major attacks of the autumn campaign, month by month:

September: 6 Emden, 8 Mainz, 10 Nuremberg, 11 Darmstadt and Fulda, 12 Münster, 13 Osnabrück, 25 Frankfurt, 27 Cologne, 30 Bielefeld and Münster
October: 5 Münster and Saarbrücken, 6 Bremen, 7 Kleve and Emmerich, 15 Braunschweig, 17 Cologne, 18 Bonn, 22 Geldern, 28 Münster
November: 4 Solingen, 6 Koblenz, 16 Jülich and Düren, 21 Aschaffenburg, 27 Freiburg
December: 3 Saarlouis, 4 Heilbronn, 5 Soest, 6 Giessen, 10 Bingen, 17 Munich and Ulm, 19-24 Trier, 31 Neuss

Much of the targeting was overtly industrial – a synthetic oil plant outside Bonn, for instance – but still historic city centres were severely affected by the indiscriminate nature of the bombing.

FIGURE 2.17 Trier, the damaged west front portal of the
Liebfrauenkirche (1227–43). Photograph taken after the Allied
taking of the town on 2 March 1945 (Macmillan Committee
photograph).
The Conway Library, Courtauld Institute of Art.

Another factor contributing to the increasing levels of architectural
destruction was a change in the type of bombs used for these particular raids: Bomber Command's favoured combination of incendiary
and blast bombs, the first to start fires and the second to damage

intact buildings, was judged inappropriate at this stage as many
targeted cities contained relatively few intact buildings – as Arthur
Harris put it 'the 4,000lb blast bomb . . . was no great use against
already ruined cities in which life was mostly going on in cellars'.[38]
High concentrations of high-explosive bombs took their place, with
the intention of blowing up what remained of the cities.

Some of the more notable instances of damage to historic
monuments during this period of bombing included that to the
cathedrals in Mainz (8 September) and Münster where the nave,
south transept and apse vaults collapsed. The last raid on Frankfurt
of 25 September finished off the *Altstadt*, leaving only the damaged
cathedral standing in this area. A heavy raid on Koblenz on 6 November contributed to the destruction of the *Altstadt* there, and one on
27 November had a similar effect on that of Freiburg im Bresgau. A
third of all buildings in the centre of Ulm were destroyed in the
attack of 17 December, although the Gothic minster was only slightly
affected, creating the curious spectacle of the largely undamaged
church with its high steeple in the centre of the general devastation.

The situation in Germany at the end of 1944 was summed up by
Arthur Harris: 'By December of 1944 we had devastated or very
seriously damaged 80 per cent of all the cities in Germany with a
population – before the war – of more than 100,000; yet more
cities, especially in the east of Germany, were devastated in 1945'.[39]

1945

The account of destruction taking place in western Europe in 1945
is dominated by the results of further Allied air raids in Germany.
Fighting had ceased in France, while in Belgium it continued in the
far south-eastern region of Ardennes, around Arlon and Bastogne
and crossing over into Luxembourg, until the middle of January
when the German army was finally pushed back over its own border.
Air attacks by Germany on Allied territory had all but ceased –
there were some German rocket attacks, most extensively in
Antwerp in February, when the Plantin-Moretus house was damaged.
As for the Luftwaffe threat to British cities, it no longer existed and
what had been a mutual exchange of damaging air raids earlier in
the war had now become a one-way campaign. The Allies carried
out a combination of long-range attacks on cities towards the eastern
border of Germany and shorter-range raids in advance of their
armies, which were gradually moving into western Germany at this

point. Despite the obvious military objective of forcing the German army out of the cities and into surrendering, the targets of the air raids were particularly cultural and historical in nature during this phase of the bombardment.

The first devastation of the new year occurred in Nuremberg which received its most extensive raid of the war on 2 January 1945, involving approximately one thousand aircraft and adding greatly to the effect of earlier raids on the *Altstadt*. The larger Gothic churches of St Lorenz and St Sebald were still standing, albeit in near ruins, but the rest of the historic centre was destroyed, including the Albrecht Dürer house and the nineteenth-century building housing the German National Museum (Figure 2.18). Mannheim, the city with the honour of having received the first RAF area bombing raid in December 1940, was hit once again on 13 January, leaving 80 per cent of the town centre severely damaged. Berlin was the subject of a particularly heavy raid on 3 February, damaging the Berliner Schloß (the former residence of the Prussian kings and Kaisers), completely destroying the applied arts and ethnographic museums (the Kunstgewerbemuseum and the Museum für Volkerkunde), and hitting the German State Opera House once again. This last building was in effect ruined twice in one war, as it had been reconstructed after the damage caused during the raid in April 1941, in time for the bicentenary of its original construction in 1743.

After the Yalta Conference of 4–11 February, where the post-war division of Germany was debated by the Allies and the Russians, more raids on cities in the east of Germany were carried out, suppos-edly as support for the Russian army moving westwards, to create confusion and prevent the movement of German troops towards the eastern front. As ever, the effect of such raids was not as purely military as the military intention would suggest. On 6 February Chemnitz and Magdeburg were attacked, damaging the *Altstadt* and cathedral of the latter in particular. Then on the night of 13–14 February Dresden was raided by the RAF (followed by smaller scale American bombing) in what has become an iconic episode of the Allied Strategic Bombing Offensive, as has the bombardment of Coventry among all the air raids of the Blitz. The area bombing of Dresden was a notorious demonstration of the threat to human life represented by such military methods (estimates of the death toll vary from 35,000 to 100,000, since the city was full of unregis-tered refugees from the eastern front) but seemed also to many commentators to be the zenith – or nadir – of the Second World

FIGURE 2.18 Nuremberg, the devastated historic city centre in 1945.
Imperial War Museum, London, neg. no. CL 3413.

War bombing of historic town centres. It has retained this reputation, remaining the single most famous instance of urban destruction,
at least in English-speaking countries. Dresden was known primarily
as a city of culture, not for industry or commerce, or indeed military installations; with its many Baroque buildings – the Zwinger
art gallery, Georg Bähr's Frauenkirche and Gottfried Semper's
Opera House – the town was known as the 'Baroque Florence' or
'Florence on the Elbe'. Few were left intact by the bombardment
and the spectacle of destruction was completed when the dome of
the damaged-but-still-standing Frauenkirche collapsed two days
after the attack, leaving a ruin that would remain in that condition
for over fifty years; it is only recently that the reconstruction of the
church has begun (Figures 2.19 and 2.20). This long-lasting
reminder of wartime cultural destruction, the occurrence of the
damage in the final stages of the war, together with the evident
embarrassment of the Allies after the event, have all been factors
contributing to the notoriety of this instance of the bombardment of
historic monuments, despite its being one of a great many more
instances of this feature of the Second World War.

Dresden was by no means the last episode of wartime cultural

FIGURE 2.19 Dresden, the Frauenkirche intact with the Neumarkt
in the foreground, photograph taken in 1897.
Bildarchiv Foto Marburg, neg. no. KBB 9747.

and historical destruction, being followed soon after by further
attacks in the west of Germany in support of the Allied advance.[40]
The medieval *Altstadt* of the Rhineland town of Xanten was badly
damaged in a raid on 21 February and the Romanesque cathedral of
Worms (officially the 'Kaiserdom', because of the town's earlier
imperial status) was hit on the same day, resulting in a burned roof,

smashed windows and damage to the stonework. Another cathedral of the same period, with a similarly important place in German history, was hit on 27 February during one last major raid on Mainz, the twenty-minute attack completing the process which left 80 per cent of the town centre damaged (American forces took Mainz three weeks later). Cologne saw its final area bombing attack on 2 March, causing further serious structural damage to the city's Romanesque churches, including St Pantaleon, St Maria-im-Kapitol and St Georg. The Gothic cathedral suffered more collapsing vaults and on 15 March was hit by Allied artillery shells during their advance on the city, followed by German shelling after their retreat; Figures 2.21 and 2.22 show the *Altstadt* around the cathedral before and after the wartime destruction. Würzburg was the target on 16 March, with an air raid causing serious damage to the Baroque Residenz (designed by Balthasar Neumann) and indeed to 90 per cent of all buildings and historic monuments in this city. The *Altstadt* of Worms was revisited by Allied aircraft on 18 March; further east, the early Romanesque church of St Michael's (c.1022) in Hildesheim was gutted by fire and partly ruined on 22 March, in

FIGURE 2.20 Dresden, the Frauenkirche and Neumarkt after the bombing of 13–14 February 1945.
Imperial War Museum, London, neg. no. HU 3318.

FIGURE 2.21 Cologne, the cathedral and surrounding *Altstadt* before area
bombing (Macmillan Committee photograph).
The Conway Library, Courtauld Institute of Art.

a raid which also destroyed the rest of the historic town centre,
including the Gothic cathedral. Paderborn and its Gothic cathedral
were hit on 27 March. The Bavarian town of Rothenburg was hit on
31 March, with Bayreuth, further east, affected on 14 April. Further
north in the direction of Berlin, the Gothic cathedral of Halberstadt
had been badly damaged in a raid on 8 April, while the eighteenth/
nineteenth-century Baroque *Altstadt* of Potsdam was the target on
14 April (the various palaces of Frederick the Great's Sanssouci
park were mostly undamaged). After the taking of Potsdam, Allied
troops were then at the gate of Berlin.

It is in Berlin that this chronology ends, as it was here that the
war was finally lost by the German forces and here that the last war
damage to historic monuments was carried out. The destruction
of such buildings in the German capital had always carried extra
significance and the extent of the damage there was enormous:
hardly a building was left intact on Unter den Linden or in the
surrounding area – even Goebbels' Ministry of Propaganda building

on Wilhelmstraße had been destroyed in a raid on 13 March. The last Allied air raid took place on the night of 20–1 April, with Russian raids and artillery fire taking over the day after as the means of destruction, delivering the coup de grâce to remains of the capital's public, cultural and historic structures. German forces in Berlin surrendered on 8 May 1945, although the official surrender of the German government had taken place the day before in Reims – an appropriate location from the perspective of cultural war damage, Reims having been the site of the most notorious World War One instance of this type of destruction.

If the chronology of cultural damage in western Europe seems to have been dominated overall by events in Germany, that is a reflection of the particularly great extent of this category of damage caused there. But this short history of the Second World War in western Europe from the point of view of historic monuments gives a less than encouraging impression of the chances of architectural survival in any country during modern warfare. A combination of

FIGURE 2.22 Cologne, the cathedral and surrounding *Altstadt* after the Second World War (Macmillan Committee photograph).
The Conway Library, Courtauld Institute of Art.

inadequate protection measures and more than adequate methods of destruction made the situation of fragile architecture and historic ensembles most precarious, regardless of nationality. In this chapter the questions under consideration – what happened, where, when, how and who the damage was caused by – have concerned the material threat to historic monuments; the next chapter will consider the less concrete issues of how such events were used in wartime propaganda and the intended effects on morale.

Notes

1. See for instance Woolley's *A Record of the Work done by the Military Authorities for the Protection of the Treasures of Art and History in War Areas* (1947), Rorimer's *Survival* (1950) and Methuen's *Normandy Diary* (1952).
2. For more complete catalogues of cultural war damage in individual countries, see for example Beseler and Gutschow, *Kriegsschicksale deutscher Architektur*, Richards and Summerson, *The Bombed Buildings of Britain* and Verrier, *Les Monuments historiques atteints par la guerre*. The damage in Germany is the most thoroughly and recently documented.
3. For a detailed account of the protection of mobile works of art in France, see Valland, *Le Front de l'art*.
4. For an interesting example of pre-war thinking on monument protection, see the 1939 report by the Office International des Musées, *La Protection des monuments et oeuvres d'art en temps de guerre*.
5. The question *Mourir pour Dantzig?* was the title of an article by Maurice Déat, leader of the pro-Nazi National Popular Party, published in *L'Oeuvre* on 10 July 1939, asking why France should go to war again for this cause. The city was further destroyed in the final stages of the war in 1945.
6. In the 1949 Unesco publication *Art Museums in Need* (Leymarie), p. 6.
7. On the destruction of Warsaw, see Jankowski, 'Warsaw: Destruction, Secret Town Planning 1939–1944 and Postwar Reconstruction', in Diefendorf, *Rebuilding Europe's Bombed Cities*, pp. 77–93.
8. The British line was that Freiburg had been bombed by the Germans themselves, mistaking it for the city of Mulhouse just over the border in France.
9. The cause of the fire which destroyed the Leuven University Library was once again a source of controversy – see Chapter 1.
10. This is the figure given by Jean Verrier in his survey 'Les Monuments historiques atteints par la guerre', in *Bulletin Monumental*, 1940, tome XCIX, pp. 239–260.
11. For a list of cities affected and dates see Collier, *The Defence of the United Kingdom*, Appendix XXX, 'Notable Night Attacks on United Kingdom Cities 14 November, 1940 – 16 May 1941', pp. 503–5.
12. See Howard, *The Story of the Destruction of Coventry Cathedral, November 14th, 1940* and the more recent Thomas, *Coventry Cathedral* for detailed accounts of the bombardment of the church. Iron girders, added as support for the roof and clerestory in the 1880s, were weakened

by the heat of the fire, causing the collapse of the walls (Thomas, p. 72).

13. 554 people were killed, and 865 injured.
14. Other targeted cities in this period included Birmingham, Liverpool, Portsmouth, Sheffield, Cardiff and Hull. For dates see Collier as in Note 11.
15. See Watson and Abercrombie, *A Plan for Plymouth*, p. iv–v.
16. The epitaph said simply in Latin 'Reader, if you seek his monument, look around you'. On the damage to St Paul's see in particular Kent, *The Lost Treasures of London*.
17. As Pevsner points out in *The Buildings of England, London, I. The Cities of London and Westminster* pp. 66–7, twenty-five city churches had been demolished before the war, having fallen into disuse or inconvenience. Before the 1666 Great Fire, there had been 108 churches in the City.
18. *The Times* 4 March 1942.
19. Goebbels noted the 'usefulness' of such threats to cultural targets in his diary – see Lochner, *The Goebbels Diaries 1942–1943*, entries for 5–6 March 1942.
20. *Völkischer Beobachter*, 26 April 1942.
21. There were further attacks this year on Norwich on 26 June and 13 August, and on Canterbury on 31 October. Collier gives the dates of the major raids in *The Defence of the United Kingdom*, Appendix XXXVII, 'Principal German Night Attacks, 1942', pp. 513–14. For the complete list of all raids, major and minor, see Rothnie, *The Baedeker Blitz*.
22. These were the damaged churches mentioned in Pevsner's *An Outline of European Architecture*.
23. 'A Message to the Air Officer Commanding-in-Chief, Bomber Command, following the first 1,000-bomber raid on Germany', May 31, 1942, in Churchill, *The End of the Beginning. War Speeches 1942*, p. 112.
24. On the progress of protection measures in Germany, see Hampe, *Die Zivile Luftschutz im Zweiten Weltkrieg*, which includes a section on 'Die materiellen Verluste – Die Kulturbauten', pp. 193ff.
25. *Völkischer Beobachter* 1 June 1942.
26. 'Das Attentat Englands auf die europäische Kultur', from the *Völkischer Beobachter* 1 July 1943.
27. Harris, *Bomber Offensive*, p. 137.
28. For all the dates, see Collier, *The Defence of the United Kingdom*, Appendix XXXIX, 'Notable Day Attacks by German Fighter-Bombers 1943', p. 517.
29. The list is quoted in Webster and Frankland, *The Strategic Air Offensive Against Germany 1939–1945*, Vol. II, p. 47.
30. For a military history of the D-Day landings and subsequent battles, see for instance Keegan, *Six Armies in Normandy*.
31. Taittinger, . . . *Et Paris ne fut pas détruit*, avant-propos.
32. For an eye-witness description of the fighting around the Place de la Concorde, the Louvre and the Tuileries on 19 August 1944, see Valland, *Le Front de l'art*, pp. 202–11.
33. Figures from an article by Paul Léon, '1939–1955. Les Monuments', in the journal *Les Monuments historiques de la France*, January–March 1955, pp. 3–8. This was the first edition of the journal since before the war. Léon was a long-established figure in the fields of protection and restoration of historic monuments in France and had written on the subject following the cultural damage of the First World War – see Léon (1917), *Les Monuments historiques, conservation, restauration*.

34. Methuen, *Normandy Diary*, entry for 3 February 1945, pp. 147–8.
35. See p. 100 of the Report.
36. For more precise figures, see Collier, *The Defence of the United Kingdom*, Appendix XLVII, 'Boroughs or Districts in London Civil Defence Region reporting Thirty or more Flying-Bomb Incidents', p. 525.
37. The estate, or 'Weissenhofsiedlung', consisted of show houses constructed for the 1927 Deutsche Werkbund exhibition 'Die Wohnung', directed by Mies van der Rohe.
38. Harris, *Bomber Offensive*, p. 238.
39. Ibid., p. 242.
40. The progress of the Allied armies across Germany from mid-March onwards was as follows: Cologne, Worms, Mainz, Speyer, Bingen, Darmstadt, Giessen, Frankfurt am Main, Heidelberg, Paderborn, arriving in Nuremberg by 16 April.

3

Propaganda on Damaged Monuments – Morale and Guilt

An account of Second World War damage to historic monuments based only on the propaganda produced on this subject would take a very different shape to the short history given in Chapter 2. Propaganda material on cultural war damage was produced by both sides, for consumption both at home and abroad, backing up the air raids themselves as a means to maintain the morale of the home side, while attempting to further demoralise the enemy. While the full extent of the destruction caused by area bombing raids in Germany did not feature in either the Allied or the German press, landmark examples of damage to particularly famous or nationally significant buildings structured the rival propaganda stories, with the overall picture and detail obscured by the need to score a point against the enemy. Buildings of cultural and historic interest became even more 'interesting' than ever, to those who would make symbols of them and to those who had never thought of them before wartime commentary suggested they should.

There are three points to bear in mind in this chapter: firstly, that it is notoriously difficult to measure the effect of propaganda on public morale, although there are some indications of this for both Germany and Britain. A less nebulous object of study is the effect intended by the propagandists and it is primarily the attempts to use wartime damage to historic monuments to manipulate morale which will be discussed below. Secondly, the discussion will focus on German and British/Allied cultural propaganda and symbol-making, as the press in countries occupied by Germany was essentially German in attitude. Thirdly, some distinctions should be made between the nature of the rival German and British propaganda organisations. In Germany, the *Reichsministerium für Volksaufklärung und Propaganda*, or Propaganda Ministry, headed by Joseph Goebbels, took a unified approach to propaganda production and censorship. The extent of Goebbels' power over the representation of events is indicated by his additional roles as Director of the Nazi Party Propaganda Department and President of the Reich Chamber of Culture. All information released to the public via the press and radio was strictly controlled in form and content and, although some Allied propaganda reached German civilians via radio broadcasts and leaflet drops, the German public was only allowed to know a limited range of details about the progress of the war. In Britain, propaganda was the responsibility of the Ministry of Information, which included the Press and Censorship Bureau and attempted to orchestrate the propaganda output of the various government departments. Control here was much looser, and there was no over-all centralised propaganda plan to compare to that controlled by Goebbels – which does not of course mean that the British and Allied public were given entirely straightforward accounts of the progress of the war. While newspapers released reports and commentary for consumption at home and abroad, the two sides also broadcast propaganda to each other, with the BBC's German Service countering Lord Haw-Haw.[1]

CULTURAL DAMAGE AND MORALE

That damage to cities and historic monuments at home was a potentially powerful morale-destroyer was recognised by both sides. The morale of German civilians was even adopted as a specific target by the Allies in the 'Casablanca directive' of 21 January 1943, which included this idea as one justification for the area bombing of enemy city centres.[2] The actual psychological effect of such damage was not known in advance, however – just as the physical effects of bombarding German towns on a large scale were estimated on the basis of the British experience of the Blitz, the damage to enemy morale was guessed at by observing public reaction in towns such as Coventry. These guesses were supported by prejudice concerning the temperament of the enemy, characterised as lacking the specifically British stiff upper lip: Sir Charles Portal, Marshal of the Royal Air Force, recommended strategic city centre bombing to Churchill on the basis that 'the consensus of informed opinion is that German morale is much more vulnerable to bombing than our own'.[3]

In the campaign to destroy enemy morale, threats of damage preceded and supported actual bombardment. Various threats concerning the danger to city centres were broadcast by both Britain and Germany, published in the press or included in political speeches, for consumption both home and abroad. As early as September 1940, as the Blitz began, the German press was suggesting that 'no British stones will be left standing'.[4] Similar British threats were made prior to the first big area bombing raids on Lübeck and Rostock in 1942 – Goebbels judged it unwise to repeat these in the German press 'because there are still dumb-bells among us who fall for such threats'.[5] Following the attacks themselves, Hitler gave a speech in the Reichstag promising *Vergeltungsangriffen*, or 'reprisal raids', while Goebbels ordered leaflets with illustrations of the damage caused to the centres of Lübeck and Rostock to be dropped over the British towns targeted for the Baedeker raids ('I expect quite a psychological effect from this stunt').[6] A further substantial threat featured in Churchill's 'World Broadcast' of 10 May 1942, following the set of Baedeker raids, making specific reference to British plans and capacity for bombing:

We are in a position to carry into Germany many times the tonnage of high explosives which [Hitler] can send here, and this proportion will increase all the summer, all the autumn, all the winter, all the spring, all the summer, and so on, til the end! The accuracy of our bombing has nearly doubled, and, with continued practice, I expect it will improve still more . . . We have a long list of German cities . . . All these it will be our stern duty to deal with, as we have already dealt with Lübeck and Rostock . . .[7]

It was recommended to German civilians that they depart from the cities immediately, to safely 'watch their home fires burning from a distance'.[8] Posters encouraging support for Bomber Command's mission were produced in Britain, for example Figure 3.1, which depicts RAF bombers over the burning skyline of Lübeck, its church towers silhouetted against the flames, with an incitement to 'Back Them Up'. The official German response, communicated by Goebbels' Propaganda Ministry, was to insist that such threats made no impression on the German people and that every British attack on a German city would be repaid with an even more damaging Luftwaffe raid.[9] A few weeks later, soon after the 'thousand-bomber' raid on Cologne on 30 May 1942, the British threat was reiterated in a controversial propaganda broadcast advertised as being made by Arthur Harris and criticised in the House of Lords for the barbarity of its sentiments:

FIGURE 3.1 'Back Them Up', poster from 1942 by Roy
Nockolds.
Imperial War Museum, London.

We in Britain know quite enough about air raids. For ten months your
Luftwaffe bombed us ... They bombed London for ninety-two nights running. They made heavy raids on Coventry, Plymouth, Liverpool, and other
British cities. They did a lot of damage ... Many of our most cherished
historical buildings were destroyed. We are bombing Germany, city by city,

and even more terribly, in order to make it impossible for you to go on with the war.[10]

The episode is interesting as it demonstrates the need to balance effective threats with a certain conception of 'honourable' war, itself a feature of British propaganda material at this stage in the conflict which included 'honourable' concern for historic monuments. As area bombing became more regular and familiar, squeamishness faded and Churchill was not vilified for repeating essentially the same threat in a speech given a year later:

The war industry of Germany has already to some extent been dispersed in the numerous smaller towns. When the cities are disposed of we shall follow it there . . . This is, I can well believe, a sombre prospect for the German people, and one which Dr. Goebbels is certainly justified in painting in the darkest hues.[11]

If the effect of such threats on German civilian morale was impossible to judge, particularly as the Nazis controlled the information released within Germany, the effect at home was not always the desired one. Threats made to the enemy did not always have a correspondingly comforting effect on home morale: Churchill's speech to the House of Commons of 2 June 1942, for instance, referring to the 'thousand-bomber' raid on Cologne as typical of the treatment that Germany could expect from then on, only served to cause anxiety about further reprisal raids on the Baedeker raid towns.[12]

While attempting to gauge the possible effects on morale abroad, attention also had to be paid to morale at home. The struggle to control public reaction to bombardment at home, while not revealing sensitive information to the enemy, was a common concern on both sides. British and German propaganda encouraged an attitude of defiant resistance and resiliance, insisting that the determination of the people to win the war was only strengthened by the damage to the cities. The arrival of the experience of war on the home front was accompanied by Churchillian declarations such as 'we would rather see London laid in ruins and ashes than that it should be tamely and abjectly enslaved'.[13] The Baedeker raids inspired the following verse published in the *Daily Mail*:

'We keep our history, Though buildings fall –
Mansion or Minster, Monument or hall'.[14]

Accounts of the martyrdom of the Baedeker towns were published – one illustrated book on the raid on Bath stated its purpose as 'We do it to help steel the heart of all those who will fight to the end to destroy utterly this monstrous regime'.[15] A similar stoicism was incited by the German propagandists, and indeed reported by sources such as Albert Speer, who noted a new resolve in the damaged cities he visited.[16]

One on-the-spot morale raising technique for bombed towns was a swiftly-arranged visit by a suitably reassuring politician or even royalty. Churchill visited the ruined centre and monuments of Plymouth on 2 May 1941, the week after the air raids there, reporting to the nation that 'Their houses may be low, but their hearts are high'.[17] The King and Queen toured the damage in Bath a week after the raids of 25–6 April 1942, and the Duke of Kent was on duty in devastated Canterbury on 4 June 1942. In Germany, Hitler himself did not visit the ruined cities, leaving this work to his ministers.[18] Goebbels, as Propaganda Minister, made many such trips, to show a supporting Party presence, as well as to inspect the real extent of the damage, to both buildings and morale.[19]

Rapid repairs to damaged architecture were another possible aid to recuperating local morale, a link exploited by Goebbels, whose propaganda responsibilities were expanded to include the organisation of repair and relief work in bombed towns after the raid on Lübeck in March 1942, the efforts of the Ministry of the Interior to manipulate morale having been judged inadequate. This raid marked the beginning of a new extent to bomb damage within Germany and so required a new level of response – prior to this, it had been possible to repair damaged buildings quickly and relatively completely, with any potentially depressing sights kept to a minimum behind rapidly-erected hoardings at street level. Compensation claims were paid by the War Damage Office.[20] Buildings of cultural and historical interest also received such attention at this stage of the war, not just essential industrial structures and housing. It has been estimated that historic monuments continued to receive attention until December 1942, when Goebbels himself recorded in a diary entry on the occasion of a visit to Hannover that the city 'looked almost as it did in peacetime. Almost no trace is left of past air raids'.[21] But it was not possible to mask the extent of the devastation following the area bombing of Lübeck, so a new policy of makeshift repairs was introduced – something should be seen to be done, however incomplete, so that the local population feel that the situation was under the control of a capable and benevolent government, contrasting with the apocalyptic and chaotic scenes during the raids. As the frequency and intensity of the area bombing of Germany increased, the non-essential morale-building category of repairs decreased, due to growing shortages of building materials and available workers.[22]

Devastation on the scale of that inflicted during the massive raids on Cologne (1942) and Hamburg (1943) could be neither hidden nor quickly patched and the best the Propaganda Ministry could do for morale was to promise the building of new cities, better than before. An optimistic article in the *Völkischer Beobachter* of 21 December 1942, entitled 'How long will the rebuilding last?', insisted that none of the damage was irreversible.[23] Expectations were fuelled by news of new town plans for Hamburg, Mainz, Mannheim and Lübeck, among others. In some cases, urban redevelopment plans had been made before the war on the order of the architecturally ambitious Führer – for Berlin, Nuremberg, Munich, Dresden and Cologne, for instance – and were pressed into wartime morale-boosting service, particularly from mid-1943 onwards, when the replacement of the ruins became a regular theme for Goebbels.[24] The Christmas promise published on the front page of the *Völkischer Beobachter* on 25–6 December 1943 was 'Immediate preparations for the rebuilding of bombed cities'. Similar sentiments were still being broadcast in Hitler's New Year radio speech for 1945:

Our cities will become more beautiful than ever before . . . Nevertheless, we will no longer possess many immortal artistic and cultural features of these cities, and will not be able to rebuild these either.[25]

Despite the propaganda line of optimism for the architectural future, even Hitler could not deny the irreplaceability of cultural and historic monuments at this stage of the damage.

In occupied France thoughts of reconstruction followed on immediately after the invasion of 1940, permitted by the occupying Germans as a possible morale booster-cum-pacifying device. Although little actual reconstruction of damaged historic town centres took place during the occupation, optimistic plans for affected cities such as Orléans were formulated and published in architectural journals such as *Urbanisme*, which continued to be published throughout most of the war.[26] In France too, much emphasis was placed on the opportunity for the development of new styles of architecture and town planning afforded by the war's destructions. Le Corbusier's modernist manifesto *La Charte d'Athènes* was even published during the occupation, in 1941.[27]

The emphasis on rebuilding and replacing the ruins of the past with new, better buildings was mirrored in Britain, with an optimism expressed in this verse of A. A. Milne's 1940 poem 'London', on the Blitz damage to the City:

> 'What if the splendour of the past
> Is shattered into dust, we raise
> A monument that shall outlast
> Even the Abbey's span of days'.[28]

Radical plans were shown to the public in the 'Rebuilding Britain' exhibition held at the National Gallery in 1943. In the same year the Royal Institute of British Architects published proposals in *Towards a New Britain*. There were also voices in favour of faithful reconstruction in the case of some historic monuments in particular: Churchill himself made a plea for the swift rebuilding of the damaged House of Commons, emphasising the morale-boosting effect the reconstruction of such a symbolic site would have, claiming it to be 'at least as important as a fortification or a battleship, even in time of war'.[29] His interest in the faithfulness of the proposed reconstruction extended to the preservation of the traditional opposing benches – the conversion to a continental-style semi-circle model would not, presumably, have been appropriate at this point in history.

Minimum Damage, Maximum Damage

When dealing with the subject of damage to city centres and historic monuments propagandists had to decide between a policy of either minimising or maximising the extent of the damage in their material. This choice had to be made for propaganda produced for consumption both at home and abroad and concerned damage caused by air raids both at home and abroad. Various permutations of these attitudes were adopted at the same time, depending on the audience. The approach to damage caused to enemy towns was the most straightforward: both British and German propagandists naturally tended to exaggerate the extent of bomb damage inflicted by their own aircraft, and also the negative effect on enemy morale, to create an impression of military success for the home audience. The same incidents would receive a very different treatment in the enemy press, with wide discrepancies in estimates of destruction. This was an area in which the propagandists were particularly powerful, since in practice verification of the extent of damage on enemy territory was difficult even for those carrying out the raids. The kind of machinations performed by the propagandists were neatly summarised by Goebbels in connection with the major RAF raid on Berlin of 22 November 1943:

The British are greatly overestimating the damage done to Berlin. Naturally it is terrible, but there is no question of 25 per cent of the capital no longer existing. The English naturally want to furnish their public a propaganda morsel. I have every reason to want them to believe this and therefore forbid any denial. The sooner London is convinced that there is nothing left of Berlin, the sooner will they stop their air offensive against the Reich capital . . .[30]

London was unlikely to have been convinced of this, as the Ministry of Information there had itself exercised its powers of censorship in reports of damage caused in order to avoid advertising the facts to the Germans.

As for the home audience, Goebbels' original policy on the propaganda treatment of air raid damage in German cities was to under-report and minimise the physical effects of the raids. Early on in the war, the American press, still officially 'neutral', had publicised the discrepancy between exaggerated British claims of serious damage caused to cities such as Berlin and Hamburg, and what could actually be seen by foreign correspondents still in Germany (a *Herald Tribune* article, 'No Trace of British Raids in Berlin', appeared on 29 August 1940, for instance). This perception suited the Germans, who attempted to maintain this impression by very selective reporting, even after the damage caused became more extensive. From October 1940 the press was not permitted to give details of air raid damage which might depress morale and alert the British to their successes.[31] The practice of taking foreign journalists on propaganda tours of bombarded towns ceased at the end of September 1940. When raids too large to conceal commenced in 1942, under-reporting of the damage continued, albeit less convincingly. The actual number of aircraft used in the 'thousand-bomber' raid on Cologne was much disputed, with both the propagandists and the Luftwaffe having an interest in reducing the reported figure. Goebbels' control sometimes slipped: he was incensed that the Foreign Office, who 'have no faculty whatsoever for calculating psychological effects in advance', had arranged a visit to the damaged Lübeck for Countess Ciano, wife of the Italian Foreign Minister and Mussolini's daughter – he feared that the extent of the destruction would soon be the talk of Rome, then of the world.[32] Public expression of fear of raids and destruction was also discouraged: the painter Gerhardinger, reluctant to hang his works in the Munich Art Exhibition of 1943 for fear that they might be destroyed in an air raid, was punished on Hitler's orders.[33]

The inhabitants of the damaged towns themselves did not appreciate this playing down of their suffering. Early stirrings of discontent with the propaganda were noted by foreign correspondents in Berlin after the first substantial air raid there on 25 August 1940: even the local press was not allowed to report what the inhabitants of the city could see with their own eyes. Noting the adverse reaction of the Berliners after further raids and continued silence, Goebbels permitted some commentary in general terms on British brutality a few days later.[34] Similarly, the minimalist treatment of the March 1942 raid on Lübeck in the *Oberkommando der Wehrmacht* reports risked destroying any trust that German citizens had in official accounts of the war.[35] After the large-scale raids of 1942, the strategy changed: following a tour of bomb-damaged Rhineland towns in the summer of 1942, Goebbels concluded that a better 'psychological' effect could be obtained by acknowledging the damage and the suffering caused. He decided to emulate the British treatment of Blitz-induced damage: 'We could learn a good lesson from the English who, during the heavy raids on London, hailed as heroic the behaviour of the people there and mythologised the city'.[36] An article distributed to the German press shortly after demonstrated this new approach:

We have just returned from a trip to the Rhineland; we went to Cologne, Düsseldorf and other cities . . . and [saw] the same sights everywhere. That air raids are no fun needs no further confirmation. The heart contracts when one stands before the ruins of a venerable monument of culture or history . . . But everyone in the areas menaced from the air knows that we would lose much more if we gave the English the satisfaction of making us bow before their terrorism.[37]

The heroism of the home front was reiterated in later speeches and articles, with inspirational titles such as 'Berlin unbowed after the British terror-raid of 23–4 August' and uplifting quotes such as 'Out of the fires which flame up after terror raids in the . . . raided cities there arises an unconquerable national strength . . .'.[38] Encouraging signs were hung on damaged buildings: 'Our walls may break, our hearts never!'. The British had in fact adopted this propaganda strategy only after trying to censor many details of air raid damage around the country themselves. Information on the larger raids was not suppressed and Coventry for instance was hailed as a 'Martyred City', while the reporting of less substantial attacks was limited to the formula 'a town in the south of England was bombed on the night of x; seven enemy aeroplanes were shot down'.[39] In March 1941 a recommendation was made by the Ministry of Information to the BBC on how best to report on the raids, stressing that 'Damage should never be minimised' and that the emphasis should be on reconstruction to 'shift attention from the present to the future'.[40]

Damage to historic monuments played a special role in propaganda concerning air raids generally, as details of this category of destruction were judged safe for release to both the local population and the enemy. By only publishing information about damage to churches and buildings of cultural interest, the enemy was given the message that their attack had not been particularly successful, as only buildings of non-military importance had been hit. Thus a *Times* account of the heavy raid on London of 10 May 1941 did not list residential and industrial damage caused but reported that 'It was an indiscriminate raid and damage was done to the following buildings of national and historic importance . . .'.[41] In Germany this practice was adopted immediately after the Lübeck raid, when Goebbels dispatched a party of art experts to gather information about the cultural damage, the better to 'inform' the foreign press.[42] Following a Goebbels directive to the press of March 1943, the reported cultural damage far outweighed that inflicted on industrial military targets.[43] The impression of Germany created was that of burning historic city centres, with ancient churches, town halls and museums in ruins, while otherwise industrial, commercial and military life continued as normal. Even after the policy changed to include references to the suffering of the inhabitants of the raided towns, reports of war on the home front routinely focused on cultural damage, for fear of alerting the enemy to their success. It was only in reporting the destructive effects of Allied bombing of Italian towns that the German press was free to evoke the lack of gas, electricity, water, fire services and hospitals that followed area bombing raids, in addition to the consequences for 'palaces, churches and museums'.[44]

There were dangers in this approach, however, both from the point of view of home morale and giving information to the enemy – as the population of targeted cities became increasingly, as it were, battle-hardened as the war continued, the sentimentality of the cultural damage reporting became less effective, and Goebbels himself noted a tendency to blame war in general for such destruction, rather than blaming the British in particular.[45] It was also recognised that, just as the Germans had calculated the probable level of industrial damage in British towns from the reported cultural destruction, so the British might do the same – the percentage of damaged churches, for instance, could indicate the effect of an air raid on railways and industrial structures in the vicinity, thus rendering the 'cultural smokescreen' approach to reporting the damage rather less impenetrable for enemy propaganda analysts.[46]

The Baedeker raids themselves sent an ambiguous propaganda message, despite striking where it was assumed would hurt British morale most. Goebbels ordered that the success of the raids be emphasised in the German press but was unsure of the conclusions that would be drawn from them in Britain: he expressed a concern that the small scale of the 1942 raids, by comparison with those carried out at the height of the Blitz, would in itself indicate to the British a decline in German aircraft production, just at a time when the scale of British raids on German cities was increasing.[47] An article in *The Times* of 1 May 1942 did indeed publish a football match result-style comparison of Luftwaffe versus RAF activity during the Baedeker raid period: 'Tonnage of Bombs in Six Nights: Luftwaffe 225, RAF 1,300'. Success in the bombing of cultural targets could not guarantee an image of air power.

The actual effect of these propaganda machinations and manipulations on the morale of civilians is difficult to judge, the views and feelings of 'the public' being an elusive category of information. The study of the effects of Allied area bombing on morale by the United States Strategic Bombing Survey gives some indication of the psychological results of the raids in general, concluding that if morale were the sole target, lighter and less destructive raids would have achieved this goal.[48] It does not, however, focus on the effects of damage to historic monuments in particular. There are few indications of civilian reaction to specifically cultural damage, beyond what we can assume by applying common sense assumptions. The first assumption must be that, while the destruction of a local church would be upsetting, people had more pressing concerns, such as the risk of death and the destruction of their own houses, not to mention the complete disruption of normal life in the aftermath of a raid with no telephone, food supplies or medicine. These are the concerns most often recorded in *Dokumente deutscher Kriegsschäden* ('Documents on war damage in Germany'), a collection of documents relating to civilian experience of the air raids in Germany.[49] The reports of local officials, personal memoirs, diary entries and even poems and sections of a novel, *Nie war die Nacht so hell* ('Never before was the night so bright', by one Michael von Soltikov), focus on the human rather than the architectural damage. The contrast between their content and that of Goebbels' historic monument-based propaganda is striking.

It should also be recognised that, despite their usefulness as symbols for the propagandist, historic monuments were not of central interest to the lives of the majority of the population. As the cartoonist Osbert Lancaster put it:

It must be admitted that for 99.9 per cent of the public the grief felt for any individual architectural casualty is largely esoteric; such losses fall into the same category as the death of poor Aunt Agatha, whom the family had always referred to with deepest affection, but no-one had ever actually seen.[50]

A ruined church was more likely to be the object of simple curiosity, rather than grief – in the south of England a certain amount of 'Baedeker tourism' was noted after the raids of 1942, while in Berlin Goebbels ordered damaged city centre buildings to be roped off after an attack: 'They are not to be exhibitions for the public out for a stroll'.[51] As for the hoped-for effect of city centre raids on the morale of the German workers, in reality the German worker was not afforded the luxury of not working due to low morale – downing tools due to discontent was not an option in Nazi Germany. If anything, more work was done following a raid, in order to re-establish pre-damage levels of production, and a ruined cathedral would not stand in the way of that.

BARBARIANS

Despite a possible relative absence of civilian interest, the destruction of so many historic monuments in Germany supplied Allied and German propaganda producers with a rich source of mutual accusation and insult. Each side encouraged hatred of the enemy by characterising the other as barbarians, not destroying architecture thoughtlessly and accidentally but rather intentionally and systematically. While British newspapers reminded their readers of the German bombardment of French cathedrals during the First World

War, with references to the 'characteristic barbarism' of the enemy, a Goebbels directive to the press of March 1943 ordered more emphasis on the 'barbarity of the British terror raids which, unique in world history, are clearly aimed at . . . the most valuable cultural centres of Europe'.[52] The destruction was invariably characterised as gratuitous, with no end but itself and certainly no military function: 'Irreplaceable historic monuments fall victim to the senseless destructive fury of the enemy'.[53] These ideas will be familiar from Chapter 1 above, as there was a revival of the tradition of commentary on cultural war damage established in earlier wars.

The British propaganda message attributed barbarism and wanton destructiveness exclusively to the other side; destruction caused by the enemy was always 'wanton' and never the supposed military necessity of that caused by the home side. This *Times* editorial on the heavy raid on London of 10 May 1941, is typical in tone and content:

But let the world note . . . what manner of men these enemies are who, on a night of brilliant moonlight, when there could be no question of mistaking targets, deliberately sought to destroy things which by any criterion must rank among the architectural treasures of the world. Let it be remembered that these are the same men who battered to pieces in France similar treasures in the last War.[54]

Another recurrent theme was the point that the Germans were the first to bomb cities and destroy architecture, from which it was concluded that the British were not the barbarians: Herbert Morrison, the Minister of Home Security responded to German denunciations of British barbarism in Lübeck and Rostock by denouncing the 'Nazi crocodile tears over the destruction of certain old German buildings in British raids'.[55] This 'you did it first, so we were forced to follow' argument persisted throughout the war, beyond the point where the cause and effect reasoning was entirely convincing, as the scale of the Strategic Bombing Offensive later massively outstripped the achievements of the Luftwaffe.

German cultural war damage propaganda began in earnest in April 1942, in response to the British bombardment of Lübeck and Rostock. The headline in the *Völkischer Beobachter* of 1 April 1942 was: 'This concentration of beautiful historic monuments has been the target of a British attack on the old town centre of Lübeck. Why?'. The answer was not difficult to find and was restated in connection with further area bombing raids that month: 'British barbarism: historic monuments bombed in Rostock'.[56] Although it was Lübeck which suffered most of the cultural damage, Rostock too was included under the new heading of 'cultural target' and it was this result of the air raids which was chosen to embarrass the enemy. With examples of two towns targeted for this non-military reason, German propagandists could argue that a deliberate programme of cultural destruction had begun. The 'thousand-bomber' raid on Cologne provided the next piece in the pattern.

Cologne Cathedral was the primary focus for German war damage propaganda in 1943. Thus far spared from damage, the cathedral was hit in an air raid of 29 June, affecting the vault and part of the facade. This damage was transformed in the commentary into total destruction and characterised as deliberate, 'the crowning glory of their destruction programme' and 'England's assassination of European culture', motivated by a cultural inferiority complex – a very similar argument to that used against the Germans in the First World War in connection with Reims Cathedral. Critical sentiments were collected from the 'European' or Nazi-controlled press, for instance 'A pearl of the world's culture destroyed' and 'satanic destructive mania' – a useful message to spread in countries under German control.[57] By selecting such examples of damage and presenting them in isolation, an impression of systematic historic monument targeting emerged, enabling the maximum propaganda value to be extracted from these events. A cartoon appeared in the *Völkischer Beobachter* of 2 July 1943 showing a British airman about to crush Cologne Cathedral, with burning ruins in the foreground and the caption 'Wer sprach von Hunnen?' ('Who mentioned Huns?'), suggesting that the Allies who had labelled Germans thus in 1914–18 could now be described in the same terms (Figure 3.2). The imagery and ideas used were the simple reversal of those employed against Germany in First World War visual propaganda on cultural damage – compare for example Figure 3.3, where Thor is depicted threatening a French cathedral, with a quotation from Heine beneath: 'The day will come, alas, when the old Germanic gods will awake from their fabulous tombs...Thor will rise up with his gigantic hammer and destroy the Gothic cathedrals'.

Further evidence of the incorrigible barbarity and lust for destruction of the British in particular was found outside Germany, for instance in the bombing of the Renault factory in Paris (Boulogne-Billancourt, to the south-west of the city) on 4 March 1942. Goebbels saw this episode as ripe for exploitation and

Zeichnung: Mjöln

Wer sprach von **Hunnen?**

FIGURE 3.2 'Wer sprach von Hunnen', cartoon from the front
page of the *Völkischer Beobachter* of 2 July 1943.
Photograph © Bibliothèque royale, Albert I, Brussels.

ordered that the industrial nature of the target be played down,
with the threat to culture emphasised instead:

It was always the English who said that an air raid on Paris would be cultural barbarism of the highest grade. Now the English have attacked their
old allies and don't seem much concerned about attacking the city they
nominated as the capital of culture.[58]

The assertion that the Germans themselves had never bombed the
French capital, at least not yet during this war, was used as a possible

method of turning French feeling against the British. The Vichy government joined the condemnation of the RAF decision to 'aim its heaviest blow against the capital', following their 'constant destruction of our beautiful towns on the Channel and Atlantic coasts'.[59] Besides this example of alleged Allied barbarism in France, the Germans routinely collected and publicised cases of British or Allied cultural aggression in Italy. The bombing of Rome on 14 July 1943 provoked especially energetic outrage in headlines such as 'Terror Bombers Attack Rome. Latest Crimes of British-American

FIGURE 3.3 'Le Dieu Thor, la plus barbare d'entre les barbares divinités de la Vieille Germanie', 1915, image d'Epinal by F. Clasquin.

Gangsters of the Air' and commentary along the lines of 'Such targeting can only be motivated by a profound hatred of Europe and its greatness'.[60]

This Britain-as-anti-European theme was developed in German propaganda and more general conclusions were drawn concerning the nature of the British and American motivations for area bombing: far from an attempt to destroy specific military and industrial targets, it was German and European culture and civilisation as a whole that the enemy wanted to destroy out of pure jealousy. As Goebbels put it in a speech given at the opening of the Great German Art Exhibition in Munich on 26 June 1943:

When British and American terror planes appear over German and Italian centres of art, transforming in less than an hour into rubble and ashes cultural monuments which it took centuries to build and to create . . . There is much more at stake than the terrorisation of the civil population. This is the fury of an historical inferiority complex that seeks to destroy on our side what the enemy himself is incapable of producing and has never been able to achieve in the past.[61]

In this line of propaganda, Britain was associated with America rather than with Europe, being geographically separate from the Continent and militarily allied to the US. European culture and history was defined as that which existed in Germany, 'Greater Germany', that is the countries occupied by Germany, and Italy, the Axis ally. While Britain at least had some culture of her own, albeit non-European and therefore inferior, America had no culture at all:

. . . a twenty-year old American terror-pilot can destroy a painting by Albrecht Dürer or Titian . . . when neither he nor millions of his compatriots have even heard of these venerable names . . . This is the cold-blooded cynical battle of Europe's descendants, upstarts from another continent who turn against their old ancestor because he is richer in soul and spirit and is profoundly artistic, inventive and creative, instead of the proud owner of sky-scrapers, cars and refrigerators.[62]

On this model, the Americans and their followers were materialistic, while the Germans were spiritual. The Americans could not buy the cultural and architectural treasures of Europe, so their intention was to destroy them, with the help of the British.

These then were the type of propaganda insults derived from the fact of cultural damage during the Second World War. Many of the arguments had already been used in 1914–18 and it was often just the direction of the criticism that was reversed in 1939–45, towards the Allies rather than towards Germany. The propagandists told essentially the same story of the wartime history of art and architecture in both wars, with chapters on barbarism and cultural atrocities, the systematic targeting of historic monuments and the artistic inadequacy of the jealous enemy. Beyond an examination of the ideas employed, the precise effect of propaganda and counter-propaganda is difficult to gauge, whether it be upon the public or governments. That at least some of the cultural propaganda had struck a nerve in the latter case can be determined less from what they published in revenge in the press and more from certain telling wartime activities provoked by embarrassment. These activities are the subject of the last section in this chapter, 'Guilt'.

PICTURING THE DAMAGE

In Britain, one way found to communicate the fact of war damage in bombed cities to the public, while at the same time controlling the manner of its presentation, was the commissioning of images of damaged buildings for inclusion in wartime exhibitions. The War Artists' Advisory Committee (WAAC), headed by Kenneth Clark under the aegis of the Ministry of Information, coordinated the recording of scenes of the effects of war, including the effects of bombing on buildings. The aims of the scheme were listed as follows:

First, that posterity should have some notion of what these extraordinary times looked like to the sensitive eye of the artist; secondly, to show contemporaries at home and overseas something of the war effort; and thirdly, to provide employment for a section of our best painters during what could inevitably be a difficult time for the arts.[63]

Although work could be submitted to the WAAC on a speculative basis, the recording of certain aspects of war was ensured by commissions, both at home and abroad. John Piper and Graham Sutherland produced images of architectural war damage in blitzed Britain, while Edward Ardizzone worked in locations such as Dunkirk and North Africa and Eric Ravilious in Norway, and Henry Moore sketched air raid shelters in the London Underground. The commissioning procedure was not a Goebbels-style exercise in total information control: the artists were free to work in whatever style they chose, as the intention was not that they should produce visual reportage, rather an artistic response to what they saw. It was, however, considered essential that these be 'eye-witness' accounts and that the artists should experience the scenes directly themselves. To this end, they were issued with the necessary 'sketching permits' – additional permission was needed to take photographs – and their journeys to war damage sites were expenses-paid. The subjects themselves were not entirely dictated by the Ministry of Information either – while some images were specifically commissioned, the artists were also free to propose additional subjects to the WAAC. An element of control did appear after the completed pictures were given to the Committee, when they were also submitted to the censor. The extent of destruction and the precise location of war damage sites were considered particularly sensitive subjects and artists were warned not to show their work to anyone else before submitting it.[64]

It was John Piper who took most interest in depicting the damage done to historic monuments. He recorded the damage to Coventry Cathedral the day after it happened, supplying the WAAC with a painting entitled 'Interior of Coventry Cathedral, November 15, 1940' on 24 November 1940. Other commissions included bombed churches in Bristol, after the raid of 24 November 1940 ('St. Mary le Port, Bristol'), and in the City of London, for instance 'Christ Church, Newgate Street, after its Destruction in 1940'(Figure 3.4), then the House of Commons, damaged on 1 May 1941 (Figure 3.5).[65] Several watercolours of buildings in Bath were commissioned immediately after the Baedeker raid of April 1942; watercolour was a suitably swift medium and images of damage to All Saint's Chapel and Lansdown Crescent commissioned on 30 April were purchased by the WAAC by 15 May (Figure 3.6).[66] Piper was especially attracted by the theme of damage to historic monuments, interested in the moment when 'the City churches crashed, when the classic and Perpendicular glory of England was burnt and stark' and depicting a vision of historic England threatened by modern bombs.[67]

Graham Sutherland was also commissioned to 'undertake for the Ministry of Information pictures of damage which may be caused by enemy action'.[68] His approach was rather different, focusing more on the forms taken by architectural destruction than on individual, identifiable damaged historic monuments. For his work on architectural damage in London he chose anonymous subjects such as the shape of a lift shaft in bombed offices and rarely named a specific building, a typical title being 'Devastation 1941. An East End Street', for an image showing a terraced street with only the facades still

FIGURE 3.4 John Piper, 'Christ Church, Newgate Street after its Destruction in 1940', 1941, oil on canvas over panel. Negative Number 4569. © Museum of London.

standing (Figure 3.7). Sutherland was interested in the aesthetic possibilities of bombed architecture, although wary of the inappropriate nature of such an interest in wartime:

The City was more exciting than anywhere else mainly because the buildings were bigger, and the variety of ways in which they fell more interesting. But very soon the raids began in the East End . . . and immediately became more tragic. In the City one didn't think of the destruction of life.[69]

Alluded to here is the tension between the imaginative and the

FIGURE 3.5 John Piper, 'The Ruined House of Commons', 1941, ink, watercolour and gouache.
Negative Number WAG430. Board of Trustees of the National Museums and Galleries on Merseyside (Walker Art Gallery, Liverpool).

reporting functions of war art – while the scenes and shapes of destruction could be formally interesting for an artist, the subject itself had further connotations, particularly for the residents of blitzed cities. Images of war damaged architecture also referred indirectly to human damage.

War damage to buildings in Germany and occupied France was naturally not an accessible subject for the WAAC artists, and the subject of cultural damage resulting from Allied bombing would in any case have been an unlikely commission. When the opportunity did arise to send an artist to France after the Allied invasion of Normandy, it was not the theme of war damaged cathedrals that was chosen. Sutherland was instead commissioned to produce images of V-2 rocket bases in northern France that had been destroyed by Allied bombing. He travelled to France in December 1944, visiting the 'Flying Bomb Depot, St Leu-d'Essèrent', and completed three paintings and a gouache for the WAAC of this subject – a subject depicting an unequivocally successful and positive result of bombing, as these rocket bases had recently been the cause of so much damage to south-east England. The cultural destruction caused in northern France was a more ambiguous result of the recent military operations and too sensitive a scene to paint.[70] The hope that more subjects might be available to artists during the Allied advance was expressed in the introduction to an illustrated book published in 1945, *War Through Artists' Eyes. Paintings and Drawings by British War Artists*:

With the invasion of the mainland of Europe the war's last phase has begun. As I write, our armies are gathering along the frontiers of Germany. New fields of experience and record are opening up. It is possible that the best war pictures are still to be painted.[71]

British artists were not, however, commissioned to paint the consequences of area bombing in Germany.

FIGURE 3.6 John Piper, 'All Saints Chapel, Bath', 1942, ink, chalk and watercolour.
© Tate Gallery.

FIGURE 3.7 Graham Sutherland, 'Devastation 1941. An East End street',
1941, ink and gouache on paper.
© Tate Gallery.

This wartime architectural damage imagery was put to a specifically wartime use. The pictures were not commissioned with the
simple intention of producing a record of the damage – they were
intended to be seen and to convey a certain message about the
architectural damage caused in Britain. They were made available
to the public in various ways. One of Piper's images of the damage
to Coventry Cathedral was made into a commemorative and
morale-boosting postcard, with a caption from a poem:

> 'That from the ruin of a church thrown down
> We see God clear and high above the town'.[72]

Another Piper Coventry scene was reproduced in the magazine
Horizon in January 1941 and was on show at the National Gallery
from October of the same year (Figure 3.8). This and other images
were exhibited throughout the war as part of an ongoing display at
the National Gallery in London, opening in July 1940 and continuing
until the end of the war.[73] This was just one of a number of wartime
exhibitions: besides the National Gallery exhibition, the Ministry of
Information organised a show of 'War Drawings by British Artists'
(1942), which travelled to schools around the country. The Royal
Academy in London held a postwar 'Exhibition of National War
Pictures' in October–November 1945.

The public was presented with war art that did not concern itself with battle scenes or the heroic last moments of soldiers. There were some traditional paintings, portraits of military leaders and 'portraits' of military equipment (ships, tanks and aeroplanes), but most images depicted scenes from the home front – as the 1942 catalogue to the 'War Pictures at the National Gallery' exhibition put it, 'The age of heroics is over. The artist's subject-matter is no longer confined to the battle-field: he must look for it in the blast furnace, the shipyard or the village street'.[74] War damage was a

FIGURE 3.8 John Piper, 'Coventry Cathedral, November 15th, 1940', 1940, oil on canvas over panel.
© Manchester City Art Galleries.

subject that many visitors to the exhibition in London would have had experience of and various images of architectural destruction reflecting that experience were included in the 1942 show, varying from a Sutherland 'East End Street' scene to Piper's 'All Saints Chapel, Bath' (this was exhibited shortly after the Baedeker raid there). There were no overt images of death or injury – scenes of damage to buildings alluded to this other experience of war on the home front, architectural ruins serving as visual equivalents for ruined lives. This visual propaganda was not of the 'hate the enemy' variety, but rather the kind which recorded and thus acknowledged the suffering of those on the home front in an indirect way. This would hopefully encourage fortitude and endurance at home, plus continued support for the war effort.

Other intended messages or meanings for these war damage scenes were suggested in the many publications containing reproductions of them which appeared throughout the war. Besides the National Gallery exhibition catalogues, two series of books of *War Pictures by British Artists* were produced, dividing the images by subject, including one on 'The Blitz' and one on 'Air Raids'. An introduction by J. B. Morton to the former book attributed an interesting function to images of ruined historic monuments and cities, that of resensitising people to the significance of the damage in a period when such destruction was so common as to be almost banal.[75] Stephen Spender's introduction to the book on 'Air Raids' suggested that war damage pictures could inform the public about churches and monuments they had scarcely noticed 'until they became, overnight, famous ruins', and perhaps interest them in the postwar rebuilding and town-planning process.[76] While Morton saw at least some 'lasting value' in the destruction in that new subjects and styles for art had been provided and great war art produced, Spender saw the bombed city as one of the essential, summarising images of the Second World War, as the trenches had been for the First World War.[77]

The efforts of the artists and the messages of these pictures were not always appreciated by the audience, however, and one 1941 review of the display singled out Sutherland's 'Devastation' series for particular criticism: 'His suggestion of mass effect, carried out chiefly in sombre reds, yellow, and black, has a certain dramatic quality, though the drawing . . . often appears a little flimsy. He is better [when he] represents a complete, easily recognizable scene, than in a picture like 'City, Twisted Girders' which, whatever one may think of its purely decorative quality, remains only a fantasy in shape and colour, conveying little of the whole of which it is a fragment'.[78] The norms of art criticism were not suspended for the duration of the war – what was demanded were 'realistic' scenes of identifiable ruins, a topographical approach rather than the stylistic experiments of modernist art.

A more topographical approach to recording the damage to historic monuments was taken by the National Buildings Record, which carried out a parallel operation to the WAAC's commissioning of images of architectural destruction. This organisation, first proposed in late 1940 after the bombing of Coventry, was inspired by the extensive bomb damage of the Blitz to record the appearance of Britain's architectural heritage – both damaged buildings and as yet undamaged buildings were included in the programme. Buildings were 'recorded' by means of photographs and drawings and the general aim described as follows:

The National Buildings Record has been formed because of the mutilation and destruction of English architecture by enemy attacks from the air. The protection of buildings is impossible, but it is within our power to make a record which will mitigate the loss by preserving the design for posterity.[79]

The visual records were also intended for use during restoration work. Priority was given to supposed architectural targets such as cathedrals and cathedral towns, particularly after the Baedeker raids.[80] The growing library of images had additional wartime functions: some were chosen for a series of travelling exhibitions, starting at the National Gallery in London in July 1943, then moving on to towns all over Britain (to twenty-six locations in all). It was also recognised at the first planning meeting for the National Buildings Record that one by-product of the programme would be 'good photographs for present propaganda'.[81] Some photographs were later used as illustrations for the post-war edition of NBR deputy director John Summerson's war damage survey, *The Bombed Buildings of Britain*.[82] The project attracted funding from American sources, with contributions from the Rockefeller Foundation and the Leverhulme Trust given extra connotations in the First Annual Report: 'The help from America, at time when the rich inheritance of British architecture was exposed to such tragic injury afforded a sure proof and recognition of the common culture which unites these two countries'.[83] Here Britain and America were seen as architectural, as well as military allies, the historic monuments of the former the concern of the latter.

THE WARTIME SYMBOLISM OF HISTORIC MONUMENTS

Despite the enormous extent of general architectural damage caused across western Europe during World War Two, some ruins had more symbolic value than others: destroyed historic monuments seemed to stand for or summarise the general devastation, if only because they were photographed and commented on more than residential or industrial areas of bombed cities. The symbolism of damaged architecture was also flexible, changing according to the needs of the interpreter. The attribution of 'meaning' to buildings is notoriously difficult but the wartime context lent itself well to the process, suggesting a variety of meanings for historic monuments – either ruined or intact – relating to possible significances of the war itself, ranging from the expression of national power to the idea of necessary sacrifice to rid the world of evil. What they had in common was a desire that such buildings should inspire patriotism and that damage to them should mean something, that it should not be simply a bland feature of the war, with no positive purpose or explanation, but a special aspect of the conflict to be acknowledged and rationalised.

Damaged churches naturally took on elements of religious symbolism, with the bombing of such buildings often conceptualised according to Christian beliefs about death and resurrection – after the endurance of such suffering, the rebuilding of the church would follow and good would thus triumph over evil. After the Baedeker raid on Canterbury, the Dean of the Cathedral described the result in the following terms:

The Cathedral has suffered damage, though not beyond repair; but with the sunlight streaming through its glassless windows it was more beautiful than ever. We feel that there is here a parable of what the war may mean.[84]

The more seriously damaged Coventry Cathedral was invested with similar meaning:

All night long the city burnt, and her Cathedral burnt with her – emblem of the eternal truth that when men suffer, God suffers with them. Yet the tower still stood, with its spire soaring to the sky – emblem of God's over-ruling majesty and love, which will help us to survive the suffering and build a city and a world founded on eternal love.[85]

The fact that the cathedral tower did not collapse along with the nave was interpreted as 'miraculous' and as 'a sign', mystery attaching itself easily to such events. The deliberate construction of a specific Coventry-symbolism followed the damage and inside the ruined structure reminders of the building's, and by extension the congregation's, suffering were erected in January 1941: the Charred Cross, made from two burnt wooden beams, stood on the Altar of Rubble, made of stone fragments.[86] Services were then held in the ruins on Good Friday and Easter Sunday 1941, thus further enhancing the connotations of continuity and renewal after suffering.

In contrast to Coventry, St Paul's Cathedral in the City of London was not seriously damaged during the Blitz, and acquired a rather different symbolic meaning in the wartime context. It was the great architectural survivor, symbol of British resistance, 'the unconquerable spirit that has sustained the fight'.[87] There was a tendency to imply that the 'good' British deserved to keep their cathedrals, while the 'bad' Germans did not. After a heavy air raid on the City, J. B. Priestley described the church in these terms in a radio broadcast: 'the Dome and Cross of St Paul's, silhouetted in sharpest black against the red flames and orange flames . . . like an enduring symbol of reason and Christian ethics'.[88] Such was the power of the sight, even Arthur Harris registered its significance, making a rare mention of an historic monument in his war memoirs.[89] The cathedral was hit on several occasions, causing relatively minor damage compared to that suffered by the burnt and gutted City churches close by, and consequently seemed permanently at risk, a situation with which many London residents could identify. The importance of the survival of St Paul's was even felt across the Atlantic, as described in an emotive report in the *New York Times* on the defusing of a bomb that landed close to the church:

These men were not burrowing their way towards death to rescue women and children. There was no military objective to defend . . . The only thing in danger was an old soot-covered building, just an inanimate pile of masonry that may yet crash down before the German fury. They risked their lives for a symbol. The dome that still stands, the dome that people watch so prayerfully, covers two and a half centuries of England. Over the city it is like a flag flying above the bloody deck of a beleaguered battleship. It may be shot away; but it must not fall while there are Britons who can save it.[90]

These inspiring sentiments encapsulate the summarising function of historic monuments in wartime, as what happened to these militarily inessential but curiously important buildings effectively expressed what was happening to civilians and cities in general.

They stood for a nation's history even more than usual and explained to the home front what the war was being fought to save.

If historic monuments acquired a heightened symbolic power during the war, this was particularly true for those which recalled previous conflicts. The self-consciously symbol-making Nazis found such buildings very useful, sometimes literally: after the capitulation of France in June 1940, the Germans decided that the armistice was to be signed at Compiègne, in the same railway carriage that had been used for the 1918 Armistice, thus crudely emphasising the reversal of power between the two nations. The railway carriage, Marshal Foch's private wagon, had been preserved as part of an Armistice museum. William Shirer, an American journalist brought to Compiègne to observe the scene reported that, for historical accuracy, Germany army engineers placed the carriage in its previous position, then Hitler himself sat in Foch's seat at the table for the signing of the new armistice on 22 June.[91] The carriage was then sent to Berlin, where it was later destroyed by an equally symbolic air raid. Meanwhile, Hitler was planning further historical humiliation for the French: a victory parade at Versailles was proposed for the twenty-first anniversary of the signing of the Treaty of Versailles in June 1919, with a speech by Hitler in the Salle des Glaces to recall the ceremony of German unification that had been held there in 1871. This spectacular employment of this very significant historic monument did not, however, take place.[92]

The victory parade was held in Paris instead, without Hitler but with a service of thanksgiving in Notre-Dame – this use of Paris was itself heavy with the symbolism of Franco-German hostilities, as the last such German parade had been held following the French defeat in 1871. Shirer reported the process of Nazi installation in the French capital, from the appropriation of the Hôtel Crillon on the Place de la Concorde for their headquarters, to the appearance of a swastika flag over the Assemblée Nationale. This particular invasion was not destructive – German soldiers seemed delighted to be there, taking photographs of historic monuments like tourists and visiting the Tomb of the Unknown Soldier at the Arc de Triomphe.[93] The possession of Paris and all her historic monuments meant more than the simple taking of an enemy capital.

While the Germans undoubtedly admired Paris, there was an attendant cultural rivalry in their regard for the 'cultural capital of Europe'. Hitler himself had for years formulated projects for the architectural improvement of Germany, appointing Albert Speer as his chief architect in 1934 to design buildings for the Reich that would make German cities as impressive as Paris. The Pergamon Altar in the Berlin Museum and the Olympic stadium in Athens were the ambitious influences for buildings such as the Tribune and the Stadium on the Nuremberg Zeppelinfeld (completed early 1934 and 1937 respectively and used for the Nuremberg rallies), intended as expressions of power, both political and cultural. This was building for posterity, so that the Reich might be classified by later historians in the same league as the Roman Empire, with similarly magnificent architectural remains. As Hitler himself said in his 1935 Nuremberg rally speech, 'No nation lives longer than the relics of its culture'.[94] The architecture of the new Reich was to mark a new period of strength in German history, cancelling out the defeats and weaknesses of the First World War and the Weimar Republic.

The inbuilt-posterity element of Nazi architecture was taken to an extreme by Speer, who developed a *Theorie von Ruinenwert*, literally 'theory of the value of ruins'. On seeing a building of modern concrete construction being demolished, Speer was disturbed by the unattractive appearance of the rusting iron reinforcements, and decided to use more traditional building techniques, employing stone rather than steel and concrete, so that his designs would be as aesthetically pleasing as the remains of a Roman temple when they in turn became ruins. He sketched an imaginary ruined Nuremberg Tribune for Hitler: 'Hitler . . . found the thought logical; he ordered that in future the most important buildings of his Reich should be erected according to this law of ruins'.[95] The ruin-value of the Zeppelinfeld buildings was tested rather sooner than planned (they were intended to last for a thousand years) during the Allied raids of January and February 1945, although they were not entirely destroyed, standing as they did on the outskirts of the town, and are today alternative tourist attractions.

This very deliberate construction of historic monuments appears vastly over-optimistic now, given the scale of architectural destruction in Germany during the Second World War. Hitler's interest in architecture has been studied in much detail, but should also be considered in the context of the later devastation of Germany's built heritage.[96] The rival 'Champ de Mars' of the Zeppelinfeld was just one of many architectural projects planned in great detail from 1933 onwards. From 1936, Hitler fostered plans for the improvement of Berlin:

Berlin is a great city but not a world-class city. Look at Paris, the most beautiful city in the world! Or even Vienna! These cities have been excellently planned. But Berlin is nothing but a disorderly accumulation of buildings. We must outdo Paris and Vienna.[97]

To this end, Speer was directed to design a broad, grand boulevard even wider than the Champs Elysées, lined with theatres, restaurants, a congress hall with a dome larger than that of St Peter's in Rome, a new opera house and a cinema for two thousand people, with a 'Berliner Triumphbogen' higher than the Parisian Arc de Triomphe at one end.[98] These plans were not realised, a common feature of Nazi architectural ambitions. Some buildings were completed, for example the 'Führerbauten' in Munich, including the Haus der Deutschen Kunst (opened July 1937), designed by Paul Ludwig Troost for exhibitions of Nazi-approved art, and Speer's Neue Reichskanzlei in Berlin. Otherwise, impermanent structures such as Speer's German pavilion for the 1937 Paris *Exposition Universelle* represented the policy of architectural improvement as often as 'real' historic monuments. Photographs of models and drawings of plans took the place of actual construction work in the many publications on the subject, for instance the magazine *Die Kunst im deutschen Reich – Die Baukunst* which first appeared in 1937.[99] It is interesting that two books on this theme, Gerdy Troost's *Das Bauen im neuen Reich*, and Speer's own *Neue deutsche Baukunst*, both appeared in 1943 – in the year in which the scale of architectural destruction in Germany increased, architectural plans for the future took on a new significance.

If the durability of the Third Reich was to be symbolised by its architecture, its fragility was symbolised in the most concrete manner by the general devastation of the war. Three of the worst damaged cities, Nuremberg, Munich and Hamburg, were all cities of significance for the Nazis and plans existed for their redevelopment. Each was given the title of honour *Führerstadt* and had been designated respectively city of party rallies, capital of the Nazi movement and city of commerce and exports, and as such had been singled out for architectural and town planning improvements.[100] In Munich, the redeveloped Königsplatz sported a series of grand buildings glorifying the Nazi Party, later to be damaged during Allied bombing. In Nuremberg, many monuments of significance to both German and Nazi history were destroyed, from the main market square which had been renamed 'Adolf-Hitler-Platz' in March 1933, to the opera house where the party rallies traditionally began with a production of Wagner's 'Die Meistersinger von Nürnberg'. Following a relatively light raid in March 1943, Goebbels reported Hitler as 'very much worried about the fate of this city'.[101]

Besides these cities favoured by the Nazi leadership, towns and historic monuments dating from all periods in German history were damaged or destroyed. From the late Roman basilica in Trier to the Romanesque churches of Cologne, to the Gothic cathedral of Münster, to the Römer in Frankfurt – the Town Hall of 1405 where Holy Roman Emperors had been elected – to Balthasar Neumann's Baroque *Residenz* in Würzburg, to the nineteenth-century museums of Berlin, to the modernist designs of the Weissenhof Estate in Stuttgart. It had been Hitler's intention that Germany become the premier European tourist destination – in Goebbels' Propaganda Ministry there was even a travel propaganda division – but the historic attractions, both old and new, were the victims of area bombing.[102]

Historic monuments with apparently secure peacetime meanings came to mean something rather different during the Second World War, whether it was an exaggerated or jingoistic version of their earlier significance or a new revised version, taking account of bomb damage. The interpretation of cathedrals and historic city centres in the light of national successes and failures in war lent them an air of vital importance to the life of the various countries even as they were being bombed and damaged, their very vulnerability adding to their symbolic power. These symbols were relatively easy to construct, even if the preservation of the physical historic monuments themselves was less of a priority for all concerned.

GUILT

The manipulation of cultural war damage by commentators and propagandists ensured that an air of wrong-doing hung over the ruined historic monuments of western Europe. One substantial indication of the perceived immorality of bombing historic city centres was the effort made by the Allies after the war to deny any wrong-doing – a case of protesting too much suggesting some feelings of guilt. This attitude may or may not have been influenced by the German propaganda on Allied cultural barbarism but, whatever the cause, the British and the Americans energetically advertised their wartime efforts to protect works of art and architecture, in contrast to their frequent failure to avoid it. That embarrassment was felt concerning the architectural, and of course other consequences of area bombing in Germany is demonstrated by the postwar treatment of Arthur Harris (discussed at the end of this section). But more evident embarrassment was experienced in connection with damage caused to historic monuments in France and Italy during the Allied operations there, particularly as the Germans in occupied France had carried out art protection activities there. Embarrassment about damage to enemy monuments was not felt to the same extent as that affecting the 'Allied' monuments of the occupied countries.

That cultural war damage could be bad for the Allied image was openly acknowledged by the American Commission for the Protection and Salvage of Artistic and Historic Monuments in War Areas – also known as the Roberts Commission – which specified in its postwar Report (1946) 'the incidental but important advantage to be immediately gained by proclaiming to the world, friends and enemies, our Government's practical concern in protecting these symbols of civilization from injury and spoliation'.[103] The Roberts Commission was established to promote this concern in August 1943, followed by the British Macmillan Committee in May 1944, and these organisations worked together with the armed forces, supplying 'Monuments, Fine Arts and Archives' (MFA & A) officers to inspect and advise on repairs to threatened or already damaged architecture.[104] Personnel for this additional army division were drawn from museums and universities, for instance James Rorimer of the Cloisters Museum in New York, Ronald Balfour of King's College Cambridge (killed in action in 1945) and Lord Methuen, a trustee of the National and Tate Galleries in London. MFA & A officers were sent to North Africa, Sicily and mainland Italy, then to Normandy during the Allied invasion there. They had a dual role: on the practical side, to arrange for repairs or temporary protection measures where necessary – or possible – and, on the propaganda side, to act as a visible Allied presence acting for the good of historic monuments, in order to counter Axis accusations of vandalism.

The role of the MFA & A officers in Normandy had been worked out well in advance of the invasion and both lists and maps of historic monuments in the war zones had been produced and distributed to the various armed forces involved to encourage avoidance of such buildings on the part of troops with less cultural priorities. During the invasion itself, however, it became clear that these optimistic provisions were rarely practicable on the ground. The lists and maps of monuments could not in themselves prevent cultural war damage and in place of this preventive role, MFA & A officers were relegated instead to organising repairs. Their original brief had been that '. . . if the Army was to be protected from scandal precautions must be taken in advance', but scandal limitation activities were mostly confined to the weeks and months following the destructive army actions.[105] Even then it was in reality extremely difficult for MFA & A officers to be effective, as there were only twenty of them for the whole of France and north-west Europe (including Belgium, Luxembourg, the Netherlands and eventually Germany) – their mission was understaffed, underfunded and underprioritised by military commanders to whom historic monuments would always be of secondary importance. The plans for cultural rescue drawn up in New York and London had also been over optimistic on the question of materials available for temporary repair work – monuments were often in a worse state than foreseen and there were rarely sufficient quantities of wood, tiles, tar and felt with which to reroof them. Historic monuments were also in competition with other types of building for labour and materials and were classified as 'non-priority' structures. Monument officers spent much time begging rides and materials from other army divisions, with low rates of success. James Rorimer recorded that '. . . I had to admit that up to the first week of October [1944] little had been done in giving assistance to historical monuments damaged by battle'.[106] In most cases, only a little rubble clearing had been done.

The Monument officers also took and collected photographs of war-damaged architecture, for propaganda use as much as for record keeping purposes. All photographs were subject to censorship, then captioned and designated as suitable for distribution in particular countries. One photograph of Cologne Cathedral relatively undamaged, for example, was passed by the SHAEF (Supreme Headquarters of the Allied Expeditionary Force) censor for general distribution and given the official caption: 'Prior to the capture of the city March 6, 1945, by troops of the First US Army, Allied planes carried out innumerable bombing attacks on nearby communications and industrial targets. Despite the blast damage, the cathedral remains structurally intact'. Thus the image was intended to send the positive message of only a little necessary damage caused to an important historic monument. By contrast, the more gloomy photograph of the devastation of Cologne around the cathedral shown in Figure 2.22 was judged unsuitable for use in Britain, France and North America, as it depicted the disturbing extent of the effects of Allied area bombing in Germany.

Besides the concerns of postwar reputation, it was also thought to be useful, at least at an official level, to demonstrate to the

French a concern for the safety of their historic monuments – the French being traditionally regarded as very culturally conscious, it was judged that this would help 'to promote our relations with the French'.[107] The benevolent activities of American and British monuments officers were publicised with the help of the French press.[108] French attitudes to their liberators were sometimes ambiguous, with humiliation and also anger at the death and destruction caused during the process of liberation colouring feelings towards the Allied armies. That some negative reactions to the cultural damage caused in France were expressed locally was hinted at but firmly played down in Allied accounts. French complaints about the extent of the destuction of their towns were described as 'a little, quite understandable, murmuring' which did not last long. More positive reaction was emphasised in reports: 'a French commission of experts reported that avoidable damage done by the Allies was negligible and that the extent to which the country's monuments had been preserved was almost miraculous'.[109] This was later supported by postwar French accounts, which attributed the cause of the cultural destruction to 'strategic necessities', 'the methods of total war', or, most neutrally of all, 'the fire', tactfully avoiding more specific mention of who inflicted the damage except when it was the Germans. The new *villes martyres* and their destroyed monuments were 'necessary sacrifices' or 'the price paid for liberation'.

One excuse given for mistakes made in the planned monument protection scheme was that such cultural/military operations had not been carried out before: as Woolley put it, 'Prior to this war, no army had thought of protecting the monuments of the country in which and with which it was at war, and there were no precedents to follow'.[110] The World War One German *Kunstschutz* operations (and the related propaganda campaign) did not feature in this Allied story of war and architecture. The existence of a Second World War German 'Commission for the Protection of Works of Art' was acknowledged in Allied publications, however – it even had the same name as the 1914–18 organisation, *Kunstschutz beim Oberkommando des Heeres*. This is an aspect of the German involvement with works of art perhaps less familiar than the art theft activities of the Nazis. Both Methuen and Rorimer commended the efforts of German monuments officers in safeguarding and preventing misuse of buildings of historic or cultural interest by troops in occupied France, although Rorimer commented less positively on a possible motivation for these activities: '. . . it must be remembered that the Germans envisaged complete subjugation of Western Europe. They wished to preserve everything which was to be part of the culture of Greater Germany'.[111] It was also acknowledged that German monuments officers had attempted to continue their operations during the Allied invasion, ironically protecting French monuments against British and American attack.[112] Besides desiring to limit damage, the Germans would have been as aware as the Allies of the propaganda virtue of being seen to be protecting, rather than destroying, historic monuments.

German officers chosen for *Kunstschutz* duties were art historians and museum curators, like their Allied equivalents, and were rarely Nazi party members, as a lack of direct contact with the Nazi hierarchy made them less suspect in the eyes of the French. Franz Graf Wolff Metternich, Professor of Art History at Bonn University before the war, was in charge of operations in occupied France from 1940 until 1942, and was particularly admired by Allied commentators.[113] He and other *Kunstschutz* officers worked with existing French authorities such as the *Beaux Arts* section of the Ministry of Culture and the *Monuments Historiques*, a body of architects and inspectors responsible for the maintenance of listed buildings. More actual repairs to damaged historic monuments were carried out in the earlier years of the occupation, between the initial invasion of 1940 and 1942, when supplies of materials and indeed permission for reconstruction of French buildings of all varieties ceased as the scale of British bombing of German cities increased and supplies were needed at home.[114] This work for occupied monuments-in-need has been much overshadowed by more notorious 'art protection' duties such as the removal of French- and Jewish-owned paintings to depots in Germany for 'safe-keeping'. It was this *Kunstschutz* procedure which took precedence over historic monument safeguarding from mid-1942 onwards, when a change in emphasis from protection to appropriation took place.

The duties of German monuments officers in occupied France also extended to the carrying out of research on the works of art and architecture under their control – a practice already established during the First World War, when German studies of monuments in north-eastern France and Belgium were published during the conflict.[115] As early as July 1940 plans had been made for a programme of research and publications, echoing the curious mixture of serious scholarly interest and cultural invasion of the earlier war. French historic monuments were appropriated by German art historians, who photographed and wrote about them, in addition to the occasional repair work. The research programme itself cannot be seen as entirely uninfluenced by the wartime circumstances, as a report by Wolff Metternich shows: the purpose of this research was to study 'the relations between German and French art and the work of German artists in France', with the results to be published in the series 'Researches into West European Art and Cultural History'. One project undertaken by the art historian in charge of the Paris *Kunstschutz* operation, Dr. Hermann Bunjes, was a study of 'the boundaries of French culture from the early Middle Ages to the beginning of the Thirty Years War'.[116] The themes chosen were comparative, competitive and concerned with marking out a new map of German artistic influence in Europe – the new map was naturally intended to show more German influence on France than vice versa, giving an art historical justification of current possession.

This was just one of the many varieties of ways in which historic monuments were used for cultural propaganda during the Second World War. Despite attempts at safeguarding these buildings, it was the propaganda produced in their honour which had the more lasting effects. Given the lack of actual preventive success, the alternative technique of presenting the situation in the most positive light became essential and propaganda instead of actual protective action was increasingly the method deployed by the Allies to deflect the charge of vandalism. British and American postwar publications attempted to minimise in their reports the amount of cultural damage caused, arguing that enemy forces had done the same, and the emphasis was very much on the protection given to buildings of cultural and historic interest, rather than to their destruction. As many of the MFA & A officers were art historians, such publications were not in short supply. Articles were given titles such as 'The Preservation of Historical Architecture in the War Zones', to emphasise the more positive aspect of Allied activities on the Continent, and a scenario was described in which damage was kept to a minimum and done only when absolutely necessary.[117] The motivation was to inform concerned art professionals and the curious public of the fate of historic monuments, without causing unnecessary alarm or creating the 'wrong' impression of Allied activities. To this end Leonard Woolley, an archaeologist and wartime 'Archaeological Advisor to the War Office', was ordered to 'arrange for the publication of more picturesque (and preferably illustrated) articles . . . supplemented by interviews with the Press, by broadcasts and by lectures'.[118] These 'picturesque' articles had titles such as 'Protection of Archives in Italy' (in *Antiquity*, June 1945), 'Our Troops saved Art Treasures' (*Sunday Times*, 27 August 1944) and even 'German Vandalism in Naples' (*The Times*, 26 November 1943). As Woolley admitted, it was all a question of emphasis:

The record of damage makes sorry reading – it is bound to do so. If we list the buildings that have been destroyed or damaged, it might well appear, as one familiar name follows another, that little had survived from the orgy of destruction. . . . It is necessary to look at things in a better perspective. . . . What we ought to do is take the total number of historic monuments in any one area and see what percentage of them has disappeared . . . At the beginning of the war the French authorities produced a list of 25 buildings essential to the history of French art. Of these only one suffered serious injury, the Cathedral of Rouen. . . . Three of the 25 buildings suffered minor damage; 21 are intact.[119]

Such statistical optimism would have been even less convincing in the more extreme case of damage in Germany but even there it was possible to find examples of relatively undamaged monuments to cite – the Dom in Aachen, for instance, and even Cologne Cathedral, which did look remarkably intact from a distance. Woolley wrote a postwar account of the effect of the war on historic monuments, carefully titled *A Record of the Work done by the Military Authorities for the Protection of the Treasures of Art and History in War Areas* (HMSO 1947). In the preface he stressed that the book was for the reader interested in architectural protection rather than architectural damage – an interesting choice of emphasis so soon after the war. The book was illustrated with two types of photograph: pictures of historic monuments damaged by the Germans, particularly in Italy, still standing in ruins, and pictures of buildings which had suffered Allied damage now covered in promising scaffolding, well on the way to repair.

Information on damage to historic monuments in both Italy and France was marshalled into the following formation: any cultural destruction inflicted by the Allies was an unavoidable military necessity, while most had in fact been carried out by the Germans, who had no such excuse themselves. Thus the Allied bombing of Pompeii was described as forced by the existence of a German command post in a hotel close to the site, while that of Montecassino was entirely the responsibility of the occupying German army. The 'worst' damage was attributed to the German habit of mining and exploding bridges on retreat, in Florence for example.[120] This version of events was maintained in the account of the Allied advance across Belgium:

In Belgium the stubborn resistance of the Germans had as a result that the damage or destruction assumed serious proportions and occurred on a . . . well-defined line. That line was punctuated by churches whose towers constituted the only useful observation posts in a flat country. The German use of these necessarily made them targets for the Allied artillery; on their retreat the Germans generally dynamited them so as to deny their use to us. . . .[121]

This description of events echoes that offered by the Germans during World War One to justify their targeting of church towers in France – an account that was rejected at that time. Occasionally, the emphasis shifts too far from Allied damage to German to be at all convincing: there seems to have been a particular reluctance to acknowledge and report the damage in Rouen. Here, unlike in Caen, major historic monuments, including the cathedral, were not avoided, but there was an opportunity to shift most of the blame onto the Germans, who had caused some damage in 1940 and again during the Allied invasion of Normandy. Woolley quotes from a 1944 report which judged that 'Comparatively little harm was done in recent operations and serious damage mostly dates from 1940'.[122] This assessment of relative responsibilities was repeated in Lord Methuen's *Normandy Diary*, published in 1952 and perpetuating the guilt-free story of Allied treatment of historic monuments there.[123]

This is not of course to suggest that the Allies were 'guilty' in the sense of having deliberately and needlessly bombed cultural targets in either France or Italy, rather that there was a press campaign to persuade a concerned public that they – and not the Germans – had done everything possible to avoid, safeguard and repair historic monuments in these war zones. A certain amount of guilt was felt that this was not in fact the case. For Allied-inflicted damage within Germany there was apparently little such guilt experienced and no such campaign to promote a caring and cultured image. Allied feelings of culpability concerning damage inflicted during the area bombing of Germany have been condensed and concentrated in the person of Arthur Harris and in the specific event of the bombing of Dresden at the end of the war. This is not to say that responsibility and misgivings do not attach to any other instances of damage or to anyone else involved in the Strategic Bombing Offensive, rather that Harris and Dresden have become the focus for expressed concern, over both the human and the architectural damage, both in the British and the German press. This anxiety manifested itself shortly after the bombing of Dresden on the night of 13–14 February 1945, extreme even by the standards of World War Two. Churchill distanced himself from the attack, despite his involvement in instigating it, suddenly concerned that 'we shall come into control of an utterly ruined land. . . . The destruction of Dresden remains a serious query against the conduct of Allied bombing. . . . The Foreign Secretary has spoken to me on this subject, and I feel the need for more precise concentration on military objectives . . . rather than on mere acts of terror and wanton destruction, however impressive'.[124] The combined targeting of civilians and architecture was particularly unambiguous in this case and it suited the leadership to portray this as a military, rather than a political error of judgement. Harris himself always insisted that the decision to carry out such attacks was taken at ministerial level, rejecting his nomination as scapegoat.

Blame naturally attached to him, however, as he had been Commander-in-Chief of Bomber Command since 22 February 1942, after which area bombing rapidly increased in frequency and scale, a strategic approach enthusiastically pursued and promoted by Harris. As a result of the political embarrassment felt after the war, he was not made Lord Harris, unlike his peers in the other sections of the armed forces, and was not allowed to issue the usual official 'Despatch' on the campaign, publishing the more personal record *Bomber Offensive* instead in 1947.[125] The extent to which this demonisation has persisted was demonstrated more recently by reaction to the placing of a statue of Harris outside the church of St Clement Danes in the Strand in London (the RAF church, itself damaged during the Blitz). The statue was erected in 1992 and unveiled by the Queen Mother, despite protests from the mayors of Dresden and Hamburg, and to the accompaniment of much adverse comment in the British press. The project of the Bomber Command Association, the statue was neither commissioned nor paid for by the government – although it has been argued that it might be read as expressing the attitude of the then ruling Conservative Party towards relations with Europe.[126] In any case, it continues to function as a symbol of British embarrassment about the effects of the Strategic Bombing Offensive. The effect of ruined historic monuments was rarely the focus of this embarrassment, however, and comment on and consciousness of the postwar condition of German cities has remained consistently minimal.

The fact of war damage to historic monuments was put to various uses by propagandists and commentators during the Second World War, from the branding of the enemy as uncivilised and barbaric with apparently concrete evidence, to attempting to either destroy enemy morale or boost home morale with the symbolism of the ruins. The stories told by both sides starred different monuments and alternative villains, although the message was often the same, and often consisted of a revival of First World War attitudes and insults. In the constructions of propagandists in particular, the wartime experience of monuments was given a shape not always recognisable on the ground or with the hindsight of historical analysis. If the use to which cultural war damage was put ran parallel to the occurrence of the damage itself on a rather separate agenda, the pronouncements of commentators also had little influence on events in practice. However elaborate and heartfelt the protestations at this 'war crime', the importance of historic monuments to propagandists was far greater than that attached to them by military commanders, who continued to bomb cathedrals and historic city centres regardless of contemporary attitudes towards this type of destruction. The military attitude to historic ruins is one of the subjects of the next chapter.

Notes

1. There are many studies of World War Two Propaganda. Of particular interest here are the study by Kris and Speier, *German Radio Propaganda*, and the comparative study by Balfour, *Propaganda in War 1939–1945. Organisations, Policies and Publics in Britain and Germany*.
2. The Casablanca directive is further discussed in Chapter 4.
3. In a memo from Portal to Churchill, dated 2 October 1941, quoted in Webster and Frankland, *The Strategic Air Offensive Against Germany 1939–1945*, Vol. I, p. 183.
4. 'In dem Inselreich wird kein Stein auf dem anderen bleiben' – from an article widely printed in the German press, for instance in the *Berlin Lokalanzeiger* of 11 September 1940.
5. Lochner, *The Goebbels Diaries 1942–1943*, entry for 6 March 1942.
6. Ibid., entry for 28 April 1942.
7. Churchill, *The End of the Beginning. War Speeches 1942*, 'Prime Minister for Two Years. A World Broadcast', 10 May 1942, pp. 100–7, this quote from p. 103.
8. Ibid.
9. For the Reichspropagandaministerium discussion on how to respond to Churchill's broadcast, see Boelcke, *'Wollt Ihr den totalen Krieg?' Die Geheimen Goebbels-Konferenzen 1939–1943*, pp. 238–9.
10. Harris himself, from then on associated with the less humane aspects of

area bombing, always maintained that an actor had been used to make
the broadcast and that he had made no contribution to the text, which
was also published in British newspapers. The reference to historic monuments makes Harris' involvement in the broadcast unlikely, given his
lack of concern for this type of damage (see Chapter 4). Harris, *Bomber
Offensive*, pp. 115–19.

11. Churchill, *Onwards to Victory*, 'A Speech at the Guildhall on receiving
the Freedom of the City of London', 30 June 1943, pp. 123–33, this quote
from p. 130.
12. See Williamson, *Though the Streets Burn*, p. 261, on worries about retaliation in Canterbury.
13. Churchill, *Into Battle*, speech broadcast on 14 July 1940, pp. 249–51.
14. *Daily Mail*, 30 April 1942.
15. Wimhurst, *The Bombardment of Bath*, unpaginated.
16. Speer, *Erinnerungen*, p. 291.
17. Reported in *The Times*, 3 May 1941.
18. See Gerald Kirwin, 'Allied Bombing and Nazi Domestic Propaganda', in
European History Quarterly, vol. 15, no. 3, July 1985, pp. 341–62.
19. Many such visits are recorded in Goebbels' diaries. See, for instance,
Lochner, *The Goebbels Diaries 1942–1943*, entries for 3 March 1943
(Berlin) and 10 April 1943 (Essen).
20. By January 1945, RM (Reichsmark) 114,459,590 in compensation claims
had been paid by the War Damage Office for damage caused by air raids
in Lübeck alone. This figure is quoted in the United States Strategic
Bombing Survey report *A Detailed Study of the Effects of Area Bombing
on Lübeck, Germany*, pp. 13–14. The War Damage Office only paid
claims made by private citizens – funding for damage to churches and
public buildings came from other government sources.
21. See the account in Harris, *Bomber Offensive*, p. 148, and Lochner, *The
Goebbels Diaries 1942–1943*, entry for 14 December 1942.
22. Lochner, *The Goebbels Diaries 1942–1943*, entry for 15 March 1943.
23. 'Wie lange dauert der Wiederaufbau?', by Ernst Wageman.
24. See Kris and Speier, *German Radio Propaganda*, pp. 457–9. On the plans
themselves, see Durth and Gutschow, *Träume in Trummern. Planungen
zum Wiederaufbau zerstörter Städte im Westen Deutschlands
1940–1950*.
25. Quoted in Bonn, Bundesminister für Vertriebene, Flüchtlinge und
Kriegsgeschädigte (ed.), *Dokumente deutscher Kriegsschäden*, p. 252.
26. On the plans for Orléans, see *Urbanisme*, January–May 1941. For other
projects, see the article 'Reconstruction' by Jean Royer in *Urbanisme*,
October–November 1941, and the 1943 book by Jean Vincent, *La Recon-
truction des Villes et des immeubles sinistrés après la guerre de 1940*.
27. *La Charte d'Athènes* listed the principles of town planning agreed at the
1933 Athens meeting of the Congrès Internationaux d'Architecture
Moderne.
28. The poem was published in *The Times* on 30 September 1940.
29. In a speech to the House of Commons of 28 October 1943, in Churchill,
Onwards to Victory, pp. 248–253, this quote, p. 252.
30. Lochner, *The Goebbels Diaries 1942–1943*, entry for 28 November 1943.
31. Two *Propagandaanweisungen*, of 12 October and 2 November 1940 limited the scope of the press on this subject. See Hagemann, *Publizistik im
Dritten Reich*, p. 445.

32. Lochner, *The Goebbels Diaries 1942–1943*, entry for 4 May 1942.

33. An episode recorded by Goebbels, ibid., entry for 10 May 1943.

34. Shirer, *Berlin Diary*, entries for 26 and 29 August 1940, pp. 380–4.

35. Boelcke, *Wollt Ihr den totalen Krieg?*, report of meeting on 30 March 1942, p. 225.

36. From a report of a meeting at the Propaganda Ministry on 11 August 1942, reprinted in Boelcke, *Wollt Ihr den totalen Krieg?*, pp. 269–70.

37. 'Konzentration der Kräfte', 16 August 1942, reprinted in Goebbels, *Das Eherne Herz*, pp. 428–35, this quote from p. 431. Goebbels favoured the 'royal we' in his speeches.

38. 'Ungebeugtes Berlin' was dated 29 August 1943. In Goebbels, *Der Steile Aufstieg*, pp. 438–9; the quotation is from *Das Reich*, Goebbels' official weekly, of 12 December 1943.

39. Reports on the 14 November 1940 Coventry raid appeared in *The Times* of 16 November 1940. The editorial judged that 'The Government have wisely concealed neither the name of this city nor the gravity . . . of the damage caused'.

40. Ministry of Information memorandum 174A, 31 March 1941, 'Preparation of Air Raid Commentaries' – this is quoted in McLaine, *Ministry of Moral*, pp, 129–31.

41. *The Times*, 12 May 1941.

42. The order was given on 31 March 1942. Boelcke, *Wollt Ihr den totalen Krieg?*, p. 225.

43. See Kris and Speier, *German Radio Propaganda*, p. 454.

44. See for instance the article 'Schamlose britische Gewalt terrorisiert Süditalien' in the *Völkischer Beobachter* of 14 October 1943.

45. Boelcke, *Wollt Ihr den totalen Krieg?*, p. 289.

46. Ibid., p. 348.

47. Ibid., entry for 8 May 1942, p. 238.

48. United States Strategic Bombing Survey, Morale Division, *The Effects of Strategic Bombing on German Morale.* The survey was carried out March–July 1945.

49. This collection was published by the Bundesminister für Vertriebene, Flüchtlinge und Kriegsgeschädigte in Bonn.

50. From an article in *The Listener*, quoted in Kent, *The Lost Treasures of London*, pp. 3–4.

51. See Rothnie, *The Baedeker Blitz*, p. 133, and Lochner, *The Goebbels Diaries 1942–1943*, entry for 8 March 1943.

52. This response of the British press to the Baedeker raids was even quoted in German newspapers, for instance the *Völkischer Beobachter* of 30 April 1942. The Goebbels directive is quoted in Kirwin, 'Allied Bombing and Nazi Domestic Propaganda', p. 343.

53. From an article on the bombing of Nuremberg at the beginning of 1945 in the *Nürnberger Tageszeitung* of 4 January 1945 – the paper was briefly revived as a two-page sheet after this, the most serious raid on Nuremberg, to revive morale.

54. *The Times*, 13 May 1941.

55. Reported in *The Times* of 30 April 1942.

56. From the *Völkischer Beobachter* of 26 April 1942.

57. The first quotation is from the *Frankfurter Zeitung* of 1 July 1943, the rest from the *Völkischer Beobachter* of 1 July 1943.

58. Boelcke, *Wollt Ihr den totalen Krieg?*, pp. 220–1; also Lochner, *The Goebbels Diaries 1942–1943*, entries for 5 and 6 March 1942.

59. From a statement to the press made by Paul Marion, Vichy Secretary of State for Information, quoted in *The Times* of 4 June 1942.
60. The headline appeared in the *Völkischer Beobachter* of 20 July 1943 and the quotation in the *Frankfurter Zeitung* of 21 July 1943.
61. From the speech entitled 'Unsterbliche deutsche Kultur. Rede zur Eröffnung der 7. Großen Deutschen Kunstausstellung', 26 June 1943, reprinted in Goebbels, *Der Steile Aufstieg*, pp. 339–46, this quote p. 341. The same message had been given in the opening speech of the same exhibition the year before, 'Bilde, Künstler, rede nicht!' (a quotation from Goethe inciting artists to action), on 4 July 1942, reprinted in Goebbels, *Das Eherne Herz*, pp. 374–82. The Exhibition was held in the Haus der Deutschen Kunst.
62. Goebbels, *Der Steile Aufstieg*, pp. 341–2.
63. From the introduction to the 1944 National Gallery catalogue of the exhibition 'War Pictures at the National Gallery' (London), unpaginated.
64. This advice is given to John Piper, for instance, in a letter from Leigh Ashton, dated 27 April 1940, in the Second World War Artists Archive at the Imperial War Museum, File GP/55/51.
65. Piper's painting of the House of Commons now hangs in the Palace of Westminster.
66. As confirmed in letters to Piper, dated 30 April and 15 May 1942, ibid.
67. The quotation is from John Betjeman's introduction to the book *John Piper*, in the Penguin Modern Painters series and published in 1944, p. 15.
68. From a letter to Sutherland, dated 3 August 1940, in the Second World War Artists Archive at the Imperial War Museum, File GP/55/57 on Graham Sutherland 1940–50.
69. Sutherland, in a letter to Edward Mullins, reprinted in *The Daily Telegraph Magazine*, no. 359, 10 September 1971.
70. Documentation and correspondence on this commission is contained in the Second World War Artists Archive at the Imperial War Museum, File GP/55/57 on Graham Sutherland 1940–50.
71. Newton, *War Through Artists' Eyes*, p. 10.
72. The poem, by one Anna Welcham, was the suggestion of the Director General of the Ministry of Information himself, according to a letter to Piper from Kenneth Clark, dated 22 November 1940, in the Second World War Artists Archive at the Imperial War Museum, File GP/55/51 on John Piper 1940–50. The postcard was produced with the help of the National Gallery.
73. These works of art, purchased by the state, formed a national collection of war pictures, most of which were dispersed after the war to regional galleries and museums in Commonwealth countries.
74. In the introduction to the 1942 National Gallery catalogue by Eric Newton, unpaginated.
75. Morton, *War Pictures by British Artists. No. 2 Blitz*, introduction, p. 7.
76. Spender, *War Pictures by British Artists. Second Series: Air Raids*, introduction, p. 5.
77. Morton, ibid., preface, and Spender, ibid., p. 6.
78. Review of 'War Pictures at the National Gallery' in *The Times*, 9 May 1941.
79. From the *First Annual Report of the National Buildings Record*, All Souls College, Oxford. For the Period ending April 12th, 1942, unpaginated. On the contemporary and very similar 'Recording Britain'

scheme, see Mellor et al, *Recording Britain. A Pictorial Domesday of Pre-War Britain*.

80. See the *Second Annual Report of the National Buildings Record*, For the period ending April 12th 1943.

81. The meeting was held at the RIBA on 18 November 1940 – this remark is quoted in Briggs, *Goths and Vandals*, p. 234.

82. Co-edited by Richards and Summerson, 2nd edition 1947. Summerson later suggested another function for the photographs: 'The records of bombed cities in their ruinous state are part of architectural and topographical history now completely blotted out by rebuilding, and it could be said that more destruction took place after 1945 than during the years of the Blitz' – from Summerson's introduction to the Royal Commission on the Historical Monuments of England publication *50 Years of the National Buildings Record 1941–1991*, p. 10.

83. Briggs, *Goths and Vandals*, p. 234.

84. From a letter to *The Times*, 4 July 1942, by Dr Hewlitt Johnson.

85. From a pamphlet by the cathedral Provost, published in 1941: Richard Thomas Howard, *The Story of the Destruction of Coventry Cathedral, November 14, 1940*, p. 9.

86. See Thomas, *Coventry Cathedral*, pp. 76–8. The Charred Cross and the Altar of Rubble were eventually incorporated into the new St Michael's.

87. According to *The Times*, quoted in Kent, *The Lost Treasures of London*, p. 33.

88. Priestley, *Postscripts*, p. 83.

89. 'I well remember the worst nights of the Blitz . . . with St Paul's standing out in the midst of an ocean of fire . . . '. Harris, *Bomber Offensive*, p. 51.

90. From the *New York Times* of 17 September 1940, also published in *The Times* of 18 September 1940.

91. Shirer, *Berlin Diary*, pp. 323–8.

92. Ibid., p. 346.

93. Ibid., pp. 316–23.

94. Quoted in Speer, *Neue deutsche Baukunst*, p. 7.

95. Speer, *Erinnerungen*, pp. 68–9.

96. On Nazi architecture see for instance Barbara Miller Lane, *Architecture and Politics in Germany 1918–1945* and Taylor and van der Will, *The Nazification of Art, Design, Music, Architecture and Film*.

97. Hitler, as quoted by Speer in *Erinnerungen*, pp. 88–9.

98. See ibid., pp. 87–94 for Speer's account, and Larsson, *Die Neugestaltung der Reichshauptstadt. Speers Generalbebauungsplan für Berlin* for more detail on the project.

99. On this discrepancy, see Barbara Miller Lane, *Architecture and Politics in Germany 1918–1945*, p. 212. Lane does not discuss the destruction of architecture during the war.

100. Speer discusses these plans in his introduction to *Neue deutsche Baukunst*.

101. Lochner, *The Goebbels Diaries 1942–1943*, entry for 9 March 1943.

102. One Hermann Esser was in charge of the travel propaganda unit. See Lochner, *The Goebbels Diaries 1942–1943*, entry for 20 March 1943.

103. From a letter from Chief Justice Stone to Roosevelt recommending the establishment of the Commission, dated 8 December 1942, quoted in *Report of the American Commission for the Protection and Salvage of Artistic and Historic Monuments in War Areas*, p. 1.

104. The Roberts Commission had the broadest brief, being concerned with the protection of both mobile works of art and architecture, while the Macmillan Committee was primarily interested in problems of restitution of and reparations for lost paintings.
105. The quotation is from Leonard Woolley's introduction to Methuen, *Normandy Diary*, p. xv.
106. Rorimer, *Survival*, p. 57. This book contains many details on the difficulties encountered by MFA & A officers.
107. Rorimer, *Survival*, p. 48.
108. Methuen, *Normandy Diary*, pp. 56–7.
109. Ibid., quotations from p. 73 and introduction (by Woolley), p. xvii respectively.
110. From Woolley's introduction to Methuen, p. xv.
111. Rorimer, *Survival*, p. x. See also Methuen, p. xxi.
112. Ross, 'The Kunstschutz in Occupied France', in *College Art Journal* May 1946, vol. 4, no. 4, pp. 336–52. The article includes an English translation of a Kunstschutz report covering the period 1 April to 5 June 1944. The author was a curator at Walters Art Gallery in Baltimore.
113. Judged rather too independent minded, he was replaced in 1942 by Bernhard von Tieschowitz. Other Kunstschutz officers included Josef Busley, Hans Hoermann and Felix Kuetgens.
114. For a French account of repairs to historic monuments carried out after the armistice in June 1940, see Verrier, 'Les Monuments historiques atteints par la guerre', in *Bulletin monumental*, 1940, tome XCIX, pp. 239–60. This and other professional journals in the field continued to be published throughout the war.
115. For instance, a book on Noyon's historic monuments was published from occupied Noyon itself by the temporary 'Verlag der Ortskommandatur' in 1917, entitled *Noyon. Seine Geschichte und seine Baudenkmäler*. See also a study by the architectural historians Paul Clemen and Cornelius Gurlitt of *Die Klosterbauten der Cisterzienser in Belgien*, based on extra research carried out during the occupation and published in 1916 (Berlin).
116. Wolff Metternich's report on research activities was published in English translation in Ross, 'The Kunstschutz in Occupied France', *College Art Journal*, vol. V, no. 4, pp. 336–52.
117. See the article with this title by Woolley, in *Journal of the Royal Institute of British Architects*, December 1945, pp. 35–42.
118. Woolley, *A Record of the Work done by the Military Authorities for the Protection of the Treasures of Art and History in War Areas*, p. 5.
119. Ibid., p. 40.
120. For Allied accounts of the events in Italy, see the *Report of the American Commission for the Protection and Salvage of Artistic and Historic Monuments in War Areas*, section on 'Mediterranean Theater of Operations', pp. 47ff., and that of the British Committee on the Preservation and Restitution of Works of Art, Archives, and Other Material in Enemy Hands, *Works of Art in Italy. Losses and Survivals in the War*.
121 Woolley, *A Record of the Work done by the Military Authorities for the Protection of the Treasures of Art and History in War Areas*, p. 51.
122. Ibid., p. 48–9.
123. Methuen, *Normandy Diary*, p. 24.

124.   From a note from Churchill to General Ismay and the Chief of the Air Staff, dated 28 March 1945 and quoted in Webster and Frankland, Vol. III, p. 112.

125.   The Despatch was eventually published in 1995 as *Despatch on war operations 23rd February 1942 to 8th May 1945*.

126.   The view of John Taylor in '"London's latest immortal" – the statue to Sir Arthur Harris of Bomber Command' in *Kritische Berichte*, XX 3, 1992, pp. 96–102.

4

Calculated Frightfulness

The expression 'calculated frightfulness', used in an article in *The Times* on damage to historic monuments in London, summed up the popular view that the bombing of city centre architecture was deliberate and controlled, rather than a random and unintended result of military activities with other targets.[1] As the bombing of cities and the consequences for civilians and buildings was a feature of 'total war', with its blurring of distinctions between military and non-military targets, historic monuments might be expected to feature regularly as specific targets in the bombing policy of both sides during the Second World War. As we have seen in Chapter 3, this expectation certainly featured regularly in the propaganda on cultural war damage, where the deliberate targeting of cathedrals was presented as concrete proof of the barbarity of the enemy, but official government and military statements of an intention to destroy buildings of cultural and historic significance were rare. Far from being regarded actively as 'fair game', at this level mention of historic monuments as military targets was little in evidence on either side.

On the contrary, official German statements of intent issued from Führer headquarters on the question of air warfare emphasise almost exclusively the targeting of industrial and war production centres. A directive of 6 February 1941 stated that the main focus of attacks should be the British aeroplane industry, bomb-making installations, ports and harbours. When this was impossible, due to weather conditions, 'towns of particular importance to the war economy' and transport centres were to be targeted. It was stressed that 'No decisive success can be expected from terror attacks . . .', by which was meant attacks on historic city centres and residential areas.[2] The policy was based on an assessment of past successes and failures of the Blitz and was not extended to include non-military targets until the issuing of the so-called 'Baedeker directive' of 14 April 1942, just before the Baedeker raids. This ordered that targets for air attacks would henceforth be selected 'to have the greatest possible effect on civilian life'.[3] Which aspects of civilian life was not specified and a direct threat to the safety of historic monuments cannot be concluded from this directive alone (of which more below).

Likewise, official British and Allied statements of intent concerning the aims of the bombing offensive in Germany contained no direct references to cultural or historic monuments as targets. Incitements to cultural attacks appeared occasionally in the press, for instance, in a letter to *The Times* of 13 September 1940, following Blitz damage in London: 'Europe might be the poorer for the disappearance of Nuremberg or Munich. But Europe even then would be less poor than she will be if no limit is put to the destruction of works of art ... The threat of such reprisals might also serve as a useful warning to the Italians'.[4] From the government, however, the most frequently stated intention was the destruction of German industrial targets in order to reduce war production capacity and this was the message of many Churchill war speeches, particularly those made during the 1943 series of raids known as 'the Battle of the Ruhr'.[5] An earlier debate in Parliament on the precise nature of the target in the March 1942 raid on Lübeck illustrates the government position, with the Minister resisting the urge to declare war openly on German historic monuments, but at the same time dismissing any objections to their incidental destruction as unpatriotic:

M. R. J. Davies asked the Secretary of State for Air whether the intensified bombing operations over Germany, including the attack on Lübeck, have involved a departure from the previously declared policy of his Majesty's Government that such operations would be confined to military objectives. Sir A. Sinclair – The policy of his Majesty's Government is unchanged. It is to destroy the enemy's capacity to make war. (Cheers) Mr. Davies – Has the right hon. gentleman seen the pictures in the Press, presumably permitted by the Ministry of Information, of the very terrible sights in Lübeck, apart from any military objectives? (Cries of 'What about Bath?') ... and cannot he do something to prevent all this destruction? Sir A. Sinclair – The best way of preventing this destruction is to win the war as quickly as possible. (Loud cheers)[6]

If this was the policy, it does not seem to have been a success: in Berlin, for example, it has been estimated that 70 per cent of industrial capacity was still functioning at the end of the war, despite the many air raids. As during the German raid on Coventry, the destructive effect was much greater in the historic and residential areas of the city, while the aircraft factories outside the town centre were not seriously damaged and were soon able to resume production.[7] Industrial structures were more easily repaired than older, more historically interesting varieties of building. One interesting source on the effectiveness of Allied air attacks on German war production is Albert Speer, who became Minister for Weapons and Munitions in February 1942. Speer recorded the success of attacks such as the 'Dambuster' raid of 17 May 1943, which destroyed the Möhne dam, causing flooding in the industrial Ruhr area, but reported a variable success rate for air raids on cities. In some cases, war production actually increased during the conflict, and most damaged factories were able to restore production levels in a matter of weeks after even the most major raid – even, for example, in Cologne.[8] He dated Germany's loss of what he called the 'technical' war, that is, the struggle to maintain production despite the raids, as late as 12 May 1944.[9] In comparison to this war on enemy industry, the unstated war on enemy historic monuments had longer lasting effects and was lost much earlier, despite its non-appearance in the official policy.

Despite the apparently clear-cut industrial objectives of the Strategic Bombing Offensive, the fact remains that most Allied raids were directed at the centre of German cities, not at the industrial outskirts. That the rationale for the attacks was not simply the destruction of industrial targets was stated by Arthur Harris himself: 'But it must be emphasised that in no instance . . . were we aiming specifically at any one factory during the Battle of the Ruhr; the destruction of factories . . . could be regarded as a bonus. The aiming points were usually right in the centre of the town . . .'.[10] The aim, according to Harris, was not to cause any specific type of destruction at all, but rather to do as much general damage as possible, causing as much disruption to civilian life as possible, rather like the German 'Baedeker directive'. This contradicts the most commonly stated justification for the activities of Bomber Command, but certainly corresponds more closely to the actual effect of the raids. If the aim was as claimed the deliberate targeting of industrial structures, the success rate was haphazard; if indiscriminate bombing was in reality the method used, the Strategic Air Offensive appears more efficient. This may, of course, have been a retrospective rationalisation of failure on the part of the Commander-in-Chief of Bomber

Command, but it seems on the whole to represent more accurately what happened than the usual model of a clinical programme to decimate centres of war production. On the question of the deliberate targeting of historic town centres, if we accept Harris's explanation this now seems to have equal status to the targeting of industrial zones and military installations, in that neither were systematically attempted, even if some incidental success was achieved in both areas.

If the officially stated priority of the purely military target can be doubted, enemy morale was the other main target mentioned in Allied directives and public statements, a rationale for area bombing used from 1942 onwards. More specifically, the destruction of residential areas where factory workers lived was proposed as an effective way to lower their morale and therefore their productivity.[11] Uninhabitable cities would, it was believed, cause such disruption and 'dislocation' of everyday life that the German war effort would be arrested on the home front. This Allied approach was formalised in the Combined Chiefs of Staff Directive for the Bomber Offensive of 21 January 1943, known as the Casablanca Directive, which outlined the morale-destroying function of air raids: 'Your primary object will be the progressive destruction and dislocation of the German military, industrial and economic system, and the undermining of the morale of the German people to a point where their capacity for armed resistance is fatally weakened'.[12] The role of the devastation of the historic areas of cities in the lowering of morale was not considered as a separate issue – it was the destruction of cities as a whole which was to be attempted, including all types of buildings, with post-offices, shops and railway stations of as much interest as museums and churches. As discussed in Chapter 3, the influence of such destruction on civilian morale was difficult to predict or assess. Observation of the earlier post-bombardment disruption in British towns such as Coventry served as a measure of the general effect, although it is interesting that even the German assessment of the effects of bombardment of British targets up until early 1941 found that 'The least effect of all . . . has been made upon the morale and will to resist of the English people'.[13]

Arthur Harris himself appears to have been wholly uninterested in the issue of cultural destruction. When asked whether he had been disturbed by the damage caused to large numbers of historic monuments during the 'thousand-bomber' raid on Cologne, his answer was simply: 'No'.[14] In *Bomber Offensive*, his 1947 account of air power during the war, he described the Luftwaffe attack on

Coventry without mentioning the damage to the cathedral, and judged the Baedeker raids 'an admission of defeat' by the Luftwaffe, as they were attacks on towns 'of only historical importance'.[15] The word 'only' here conveys the absolute lack of concern for the fate of historic monuments; for Harris, buildings of cultural importance did not signify in the sphere of war or the military mind, either as targets or as structures to be avoided. This does not exclude the possibility that the War Cabinet itself may have been more interested in cultural targeting; Harris always insisted that the choice of cities to be bombed was never his to make and that Bomber Command followed orders from the War Cabinet on which to target.[16] It would be difficult, however, to attribute a policy of deliberate cultural targeting to the Commander-in-Chief of Bomber Command himself.

It was the Luftwaffe who carried out the most unambiguous examples of bombardment where historic monuments appeared to be the primary target: for the Baedeker raids of 1942, the target towns were selected from those with the top two-star rating in the German tourist guide. Exeter, Bath, Norwich and York were attacked in that order in a concentrated programme starting on the night of 23–4 April. There were further attacks on Exeter and Norwich in early May, the series finishing in Canterbury between 31 May and 6 June (there were further attacks on Norwich later that year), with consequences for historic monuments already detailed in Chapter 2. Of these towns, only York represented anything approaching the status of a substantial military target, in the form of its railway junction, but in each case it was the historic town centres which suffered most damage. These raids appeared in Chapter 3 as a source of propaganda material and appear again in the present chapter as the provider of at least one solid example of cultural targeting.

The supporting evidence of the cultural damage done was to some extent confirmed by the stated intentions of the Germans. As mentioned above, there was an ambiguity in the order issued from Führer headquarters on 14 April 1942 to cause 'the greatest possible effect on civilian life', as this need not necessarily involve damage to buildings with specifically cultural or historical significance.[17] But after the April raids on Exeter, Bath, Norwich and York, this less ambiguous threat from 'a Wilhelmstraße spokesman' was published in *The Times*:

Our art connoisseurs know the English Baedeker thoroughly. They know where all the historic Tudor houses are, the exact position of Canterbury

Cathedral, where the spas are situated, and most of the famous castles and homes of the nobility. Our airmen will know how to find and hit them.[18]

The next day, Joseph Goebbels reinforced the impression of deliberate cultural punishment in a front page *Völkischer Beobachter* article on the 'second front' of aerial bombardment (in addition to the Eastern front), referring to the attacks on Bath, Norwich and York as the only way to bring Churchill to his senses and to prevent further attacks on German towns.[19] This had been preceded by a series of reports describing the raids as cultural *Vergeltungsangriffe* or 'revenge attacks', although the expression 'Baedeker raid' itself did not appear in the German propaganda and was more a feature of Allied commentary which sought to emphasise the cultural barbarism of the enemy.[20] Not all Luftwaffe raids in this period were upon primarily cultural targets, however: during May and June 1942, towns outside London without a two-star Baedeker rating were also on the receiving end of night air raids: Hull on 19 May, Ipswich on 1 June, Birmingham on 24 June and Weston-super-Mare on 27 June, for instance.[21] These raids were not highlighted in German propaganda as having been carried out for reasons of cultural revenge and the usual industrial and military targets were cited. It was only in the case of the Baedeker towns that the choice of air raid target and the explanations of post-raid propaganda seemed to coincide for once in a clear case of cultural targeting. For this reason the group of Baedeker raids has acquired a certain notoriety and an historical life of its own.

German propaganda presented the Baedeker raids as tit-for-tat reprisals for similar cultural damage inflicted by Bomber Command on historic German towns. The sequence of events was as follows: the British, the Germans claimed, invented the deliberate attack on the cultural target with the bombardment of Lübeck on the night of 28–9 March 1942, followed by attacks on Rostock between 23 and 26 April. Although cultural damage occurred, more so in Lübeck than Rostock, Britain did not advertise the raids as directed primarily at cultural targets, but it was precisely this aspect of the attacks that the German propagandists chose to focus on: the German threat published in *The Times* of 30 April specified that 'If England believes it necessary to destroy German cultural treasures, she must take the consequences'.[22] But the Baedeker raids themselves began on 23 April and it was only after the first crop of raids that this threat appeared. Goebbels' diary entry for 27 April includes the remark 'Like the English, we must attack centers (sic) of culture, especially such as have only little anti-aircraft'.[23] Confusingly, on 29 April, German radio was still broadcasting the industrial and military importance of the Baedeker towns, reported in the British press as perverse 'Nazi geography'.[24] The first raid on Canterbury on 31 May was immediately preceded by the 'thousand-bomber' raid on Cologne on the night of 30–1 May, the latter an attack so widespread that specifically cultural targeting seems unlikely. But once again, it was the cultural damage that the German press emphasised, with the bombardment of Canterbury appearing most convincingly as cultural revenge. By this time, the idea of cultural targeting had had time to establish itself, despite the fact that the British had been steadily attacking industrial Ruhr Valley targets in the same period.

The dovetailing of cultural targets and cultural propaganda represented by the Baedeker raids was an exception, however. In general, a model of cultural war damage restricted to the deliberate aiming of bombs at cathedrals and cathedral towns would generate a rather short list of provable cases. If the definition of cultural war damage is broadened a little, to include a wider range of buildings with cultural and historical connotations, the list becomes considerably longer. For instance, a series of German raids were made on British seaside resorts in 1943, causing damage to seafront facades, promenades and piers: from March to the first week of June, German fighter planes carried out daylight raids on Eastbourne, Hastings, Bournemouth, Brighton, Folkestone, Margate, Torquay and Yarmouth.[25] Goebbels himself placed these towns and targets in the same category as Canterbury or Bath, noting in his diary that Hitler 'shares my opinion absolutely that cultural centres, bathing resorts, and civilian cities must be attacked now; there the psychological effect is much stronger'.[26] Another variety of cultural targeting, this time one considered by the British Air Ministry, was the destruction of German forests, a plan conceived of in the summer of 1940 as a double strike at the heart of the German Romantic imagination and at supplies of wood. The Harz Mountains in the very centre of Germany were identified as a particularly significant target 'both from the material and psychological standpoints'.[27] Air raids on the Black Forest were carried out in early September 1940, to the accompaniment of newspaper headlines such as 'Black Forest set on fire by RAF'.[28] This demonstrates a certain amount of inventiveness on the part of the Air Ministry on the question of how Bomber Command was to be employed, beyond the narrow limits of the traditional military target.

The capital cities London and Berlin were also more-than-simply-military targets, with all their obvious political and historical significance, in addition to a high concentration of architecture symbolic of the power of the two nations. The Luftwaffe had shown their appreciation of the value of such a target during the prolonged Blitz on London and, as early as October 1940, the British had attempted direct hits on the War Office and Chancellery in Berlin.[29] Throughout the war, public buildings in both capitals were regularly targeted and regularly presented by the press as deliberately so – for instance, a heavy raid on London on 16 April 1941 was described as a cultural reprisal raid on the capital's historic centre, in return for an RAF attack on the centre of Berlin on 9 April.[30] An editorial in *The Times* on the London raid insisted 'There has never been a raid which has done less military damage. There has never been a raid which has done more damage to buildings and to objects which were part of the heritage of mankind'.[31] The Palace of Westminster, including the House of Commons Chamber, and Westminster Abbey were among the affected buildings this time.

The list of damaged or destroyed public buildings was particularly long in Berlin. After the raids of November 1943 (during the 'Battle of Berlin', involving numerous raids from the summer of 1943 to mid-March 1944), Goebbels recorded in his diary that 'The government quarter is nothing short of an inferno'.[32] Industrial buildings were also affected, but bombs dropped on the centre of the city had the most impact: Potsdamerplatz, the Reichstag, the Kaiserhof Hotel (Hitler's Berlin residence), the Chancellery, ironically including the Hall of Models on the top floor where Hitler kept plans for grandiose architectural projects, and Albert Speer's Ministry Headquarters, formerly the Academy of Arts building, were all hit, as were cultural monuments such as the Schloß Charlottenburg, which was partly burnt out, the Deutsches Theater, Schinkel's Staatstheater and churches such as the Kaiser-Wilhelm-Gedächtnis-Kirche.

The Germans feared a raid on the scale of those on Cologne and Hamburg and indeed such an attack on Berlin seems to have been favoured by Sir Arthur Harris.[33] He was encouraged to conduct regular raids on the German capital by a series of Air Ministry directives, which specified that Berlin was to be attacked whenever the weather or other factors prevented raids elsewhere – a default target. According to the Combined Chiefs of Staff directive of 21 January 1943, Berlin was in the category of 'objectives of great importance . . . from the political . . . point of view'.[34] Allied aggression towards Berlin's historic monuments was publicised in a

Newsweek article in September 1943 with the frank title 'Battle of Berlin. Opening Raids Show Capital Destined for Hamburg's Fate'. The article included a map of historic monuments in the centre of Berlin, with the caption 'Heart of the Reich: the buildings and monuments of Central Berlin formed a target for the RAF'.[35] If the official policy consistently omitted to mention the destruction of Berlin's historic monuments, the press were advertising another agenda, apparently supported with the evidence of the damage itself.

The deliberate devastation of Paris was also considered, if happily not carried out, indicating the extent to which cultural targeting was 'in the air' as a military possibility. Hitler regarded the French capital as admirable but expendable, an entire city of historic monuments and the cultural capital of Europe which could nevertheless be bombed if necessary. Hitler's attitude towards Paris was reported by Albert Speer who, along with the sculptor Arno Breker and the architect Hermann Giesler, was chosen to accompany Hitler on a cultural day trip to Paris after the capitulation of France in June 1940.[36] The Armistice between France and Germany was signed on 25 June 1940 and the artistic group flew to Paris three days later, landing at Le Bourget, then driving directly to the Opéra (designed by Charles Garnier, 1861–74), Hitler's favourite building. After a tour of monuments with Napoléonic connections such as the Arc de Triomphe, the tomb of Napoléon at the Hôtel des Invalides and the Panthéon, the final stop of the tour was the basilica of Sacré Coeur, built to atone for the defeat of France in 1870–1 (to Speer's stylistic disapproval: 'a surprising choice, even by the standards of Hitler's taste'). Then, after a visit of only three hours, the party left for the airport. The choice of grandiose commemorative monuments is interesting, given that this was Hitler's first and last visit to Paris. According to Speer, however, this appreciation of the architecture of Paris did not guarantee its safety, as Hitler remarked the same evening:

Wasn't Paris beautiful? But Berlin must become even more beautiful! I have often considered whether Paris should be destroyed . . . but when we are finished in Berlin, Paris will be a mere shadow. Why should we destroy it then?[37]

For Hitler, Paris and Berlin were in architectural competition and the fate of Paris was apparently dependent on the success of Speer's plans for the redesign of Berlin. The idea of the complete

destruction of Paris specifically because of its architectural significance or beauty was later replaced during the 1944 Allied invasion
of France by the order to destroy it while retreating – if Germany
could not have Paris, then neither would the enemy. As the Allies
approached the French capital, explosives had already been placed
in key parts of the city, under bridges and in electricity generators
but also in historic monuments such as Notre-Dame, the Opéra
Garnier and the Invalides. Hitlerian vandalism was avoided this time
when his orders were famously ignored by General von Choltitz,
the military governor of occupied Paris.[38] Hitler then decided to
apply this policy of *verbrannte Erde* (scorched earth) within
Germany itself in the increasingly likely event of enemy invasion,
and advertised this in a leading article in the *Völkischer Beobachter*
of 7 September 1944. A directive was issued on 19 March 1945 that
all buildings on Reich territory be destroyed, so that the enemy
should not profit by their victory.[39] According to Speer, who was
not in favour of this extremism, the directive was also intended to
apply to those historic monuments still standing after the Allied
bombardment, even those in Berlin.[40] In the event, the directive
was not acted upon, and the task of razing Berlin and its remaining
architecture fell to Allied bombers and Russian artillery. In the
competition for the most beautiful and impressive capital city, it
was Paris which survived the war virtually intact.

Returning from fantasies of architectural death and glory to the
level of actual damage to historic monuments, the more convincing
cases of deliberate cultural targeting, even according to the broader
definition of this phenomenon, represent a small amount of the total
cultural damage inflicted in western Europe. Far more substantial
is the list of cases of 'incidental' cultural damage, that is, when
historic monuments were damaged during the bombardment of
other targets for other reasons. The target books used by Bomber
Command pilots may have been known unofficially as the 'bomber's
Baedekers' but the towns and buildings marked on their maps were
not graded according to historical importance. Incidental cultural
damage occurred in both Allied and Axis territory; we must assume
for instance that all damage in France and the Netherlands inflicted
during the Allied invasion in 1944–5 falls into this category, along
with that occurring in Italy. One example in Britain is Coventry:
while it is the cathedral in Coventry that has become a symbol of
wartime destruction in Britain, it was the aircraft industry located
there rather than the church that was the main target during the air
raid of 14 November 1940. Coventry was also within range for the

German planes and large enough (approximately a quarter of a million people) to represent a significant target – the cathedral was not the only attraction for the Luftwaffe.[41] The many examples of German cities in the same situation included Stuttgart with its Bosch, Daimler-Benz and Zeiss-Ikon factories, and Essen, where the Krupps factory was in the centre of the town, rather than in the suburbs. One writer on air power, J. M. Spaight, claimed that this 'Jekyll and Hyde', dual cultural/industrial nature of some of Germany's most historically interesting cities made attacks on towns such as Munich inevitable.[42] In most cities there was very little that was not considered in some way a military target and on this point the official British history of the strategic air offensive makes an illuminating statement: 'Even the national churches pray for national victory'.[43] The 'thousand-bomber' raid on Cologne was also an extreme example of 'incidental' damage of another kind: official sources maintained that Cologne was only chosen as the target for the raid because weather conditions were not suitable for an attack on Hamburg that night.[44]

If the destruction of architecture was not a priority in the Allied strategic bombing of Germany, neither was the deliberate avoidance of historic monuments. This is an important point, as simple lack of concern is also effectively a policy – no decision was taken to spare, or to attempt to spare historic monuments, as is demonstrated by the high proportion of attacks which focused on the historic town centres of German cities, as opposed to the less architecturally significant industrial outskirts. The most detailed survey of architectural damage in Germany records consistently higher rates of damage in the *Altstädte*, or 'old towns', than in more recently built industrial or residential suburbs.[45] In Cologne, for example, 95 per cent of the *Altstadt* was damaged or destroyed, while only approximately 30 per cent of industrial or suburban areas were affected. In Münster, 63 per cent is the figure for damage overall, but more specifically 91 per cent of the *Altstadt* was damaged. For Mainz, the town centre was 80 per cent ruined, as opposed to 60 per cent for the city as a whole. The cathedral at Ulm may have been only slightly damaged, but the *Altstadt* surrounding it was 80 per cent ruined. Other cities large enough to offer a choice of zones for bombardment where significantly higher levels of *Altstadt* destruction occurred were Munich, Stuttgart, Freiburg im Bresgau and Frankfurt. From the start of the major area bombing raids on Lübeck, Rostock and Cologne onwards, the Air Ministry supplied pilots with 'zone maps' which divided cities into old town, residential and industrial areas, but their usage was not apparently aimed at avoiding damage to old towns or residential areas.[46]

The question remains as to whether it is possible to go further and suggest at least some positive interest on the part of the Allies in the destruction of cultural/historical zones of certain towns. It is true that some towns of primarily historic interest were not bombarded at all, for instance Bamburg, Göttingen and Heidelberg (the latter suffering only a blown-up bridge during the Allied invasion in 1945), but a rather longer list of equally impressive locations of particular importance in German history were bombarded. There was a cluster of such attacks towards the end of the war, although whether this implies a degree of deliberate cultural targeting is uncertain. Once again, selecting these examples from the many German cities bombarded may distort their significance but these towns did receive either their first or worst bombardment at this late stage of the war, suggesting a search for new targets. The centre of Trier, for instance, was subjected to twenty raids between 14 August and 24 December 1944, causing severe damage to the fourth-century AD basilica and the Liebfrauenkirche, one of the oldest Gothic churches in Germany. Nuremberg, a town of particular significance for the Nazis, was also particularly heavily bombarded at this late stage of the war. Location of the Nazi rallies of the 1930s and of the German National Museum, besides being Dürer's birthplace and a centre for the nineteenth-century pan-Germanism movement, Nuremberg received its worst raid on 2 January 1945. The town had been bombarded earlier in the war, but this raid focused on the *Altstadt*, leaving approximately 90 per cent destroyed. The report the next day in *The Times* referred rather unconvincingly to 'the chief aims being the industrial and railway centre of Nuremberg' – curiously, industrial and railway centres were the only types of target reported by the Allied press at this point in the war.[47]

The attack on Dresden on the night of 13–14 February 1945 was likewise concentrated on the historic town centre. This most notorious of Bomber Command's missions has always drawn criticism for the targeting of civilians with no apparent military justification, an extreme case even by the standards of World War Two, but it also caused the ruin of the Baroque city centre. Its status as a military target was doubtful: Dresden was a cultural centre, with relatively little industry or military significance, although it was these last two aspects which were emphasised in a BBC broadcast on the subject on 14 February 1945. Arthur Harris also maintained this justification in his account, describing Dresden as an important railway and communications centre and particularly significant for military activity on the eastern front.[48] It was also the largest German city still unbombarded in the Second World War. Although the effect of the attack was the ruin of historic monuments and the death of large numbers of civilians (including many refugees), neither target appears in the official rationale for the bombarding. With damage to non-military targets on such a massive scale, the official rationale becomes almost irrelevant.

Towns with even less specific military importance were also attacked in this late stage of the war, during the Allied progress across Germany: Würzburg, bombed once but heavily, on the night of 16–17 March 1945, lost many buildings of solely cultural interest, for instance Balthasar Neumann's Baroque Residenz. Similarly, the historic town of Hildesheim was devastated on 22 March 1945. During the last days of the Allied advance Potsdam received an attack on 14 April 1945 which concentrated on the historic old town. Finally, most probably accidental but with spectacular symbolism was the damage to Bismarck's former residence in Friedrichsruh, where on 29 April 1945 a bomb destroyed the Schloß and part of the Bismarck Museum, including the Anton von Werner painting of the 1871 ceremony marking the establishment of the German nation in Versailles. From an historical point of view this example of bombardment was so outstandingly appropriate that it is tempting to read into it the signs of deliberate targeting of an historic monument but, as with countless other examples of cultural damage, it is more likely to be evidence of the degree to which cultural damage was at the same time acceptable and uninteresting to the military strategists.

When considering the question of the possibly deliberate nature of cultural damage during the Allied area bombing raids on Germany it is important not to make too close a connection between intention and effect, deducing the former from the latter, or to base our assumptions on either the official stated motivation or on the perceived effect within Germany (or indeed on the perception publicised for propaganda purposes). A key source which bypasses some of this confusion is the United States Strategic Bombing Survey report on the British raids on Lübeck, a confidential military study produced in typescript form in October 1945, which gives a relatively disinterested account of the attacks, as the Americans were not involved in this particular episode.[49]

There are no direct statements as to the precise motivation for

the attack on Lübeck on the night of 28–9 March 1942, other than
that it was a good test case for the new technique of large-scale area
bombing. The official line on area bombing being that it was primarily directed at industrial and war production targets, it is
instructive to study the findings of the United States Survey as to
the actual effects of the raid on such buildings. It seems that very
little damage was caused to industrial structures, all of which were
situated outside the town centre: installations for iron and steel
production, ship-building, transportation and the fishing industry
were temporarily affected by an interruption in the electricity and
water supplies, but the report estimates that 80–90 per cent of
production capacity was resumed within a week of the attack.[50] A
small building close to the town centre used by the Deutsche
Waffen und Munitionsfabriken (German Weapon and Ammunitions
Works) for the manufacture of fuses was bombed and destroyed in
the March 1942 attack, but the main Lübeck branch of this more
military target was outside the centre and escaped damage. Some
temporary damage was done to the commercial life of the town as
a result of the damage to trading headquarters in the historic centre,
but importing and exporting activities soon resumed. For Arthur
Harris, at least, the raid was a success, if only as a test of his preferred strategy: 'It was not a vital target, but it seemed to me better
to destroy an industrial town of moderate importance than to fail to
destroy a large industrial city'.[51] As it was precisely the industrial
zones of the town which survived nearly intact, this seems a curious
criterion for success. After the March 1942 raid, Lübeck was free
of attacks until August 1944, when a precision raid was carried out,
causing some damage to the previously unaffected military and
industrial targets, but again production was rapidly resumed, for
example at the Dornier Werke, a factory manufacturing parts for
aircraft, which only suffered damage to non-essential areas of the
building.[52]

Whatever the Air Ministry rationale for the raid on Lübeck,
damage to buildings of cultural significance was its primary effect:
churches and timbered houses from the town's Hanseatic past were
the main material losses during an attack which focused on the
historic town centre. Ironically the very layout of the town, which
conformed to self-defence standards of previous centuries, contributed to the extent of the damage – a compact town with houses
built close together was easier to defend against more traditional
warfare methods, but made a perfect target for the incendiary
bombs of an area bombing raid.

As discussed in Chapter 3, that the only serious and lasting damage caused during the March 1942 raid was to buildings of cultural and historical interest was a fact not lost on German propagandists, who seized upon this effect, whether deliberately intended or otherwise, as evidence of British barbarism. We are left with the question, if cultural damage was the main effect, does it matter whether cultural damage was or was not the main target, particularly when there was no chance that historic monuments would escape damage in the course of such raid? It is an uncomfortable thought that historic monuments may simply have not entered into the Bomber Command equation, either as a target or as something to be avoided, but the evidence of the Lübeck raid and many others suggest this conclusion. This would make the wartime destruction of historic monuments a 'sin of omission' and negligence rather than a positive act, but does not necessarily legitimise it.

Given the ambiguities which emerge from an attempt to gain a clear picture of precise military intentions regarding the bombardment of historic monuments, another perhaps more fruitful approach to the question of whether historic monuments and ensembles were deliberately targeted might be to ask to what extent it was technically possible to either target or avoid specific buildings or areas of towns with the aircraft and bomb types available during the Second World War. Propaganda from both sides in the conflict on the subject of cultural targeting was hugely optimistic on this question, assuming an impressive degree of precision, particularly on the part of enemy aeroplanes, who were portrayed with a capacity to target specific historic buildings at will – any such damage caused by the home side was of course presented as accidental, lack of accuracy being a useful defence in case of embarrassing damage. Whether or not these propagandist assumptions were over-optimistic is the next issue, with the discussion focusing on the capacities of RAF aeroplanes and bombs.

Expectations of the ability of both the RAF and the Luftwaffe to target accurately and destroy comprehensively were varied at the beginning of the war, very high in some cases and very low in others. The concentrated German air raid on Guernica in 1937 had provided advance warning of the possible success of such bombardment techniques. William Shirer, an American journalist covering the German advance towards France in May 1940, confidently predicted that 'Hitler will bomb Paris and London to daylights within the next forty-eight hours' and was surprised during a journey through the Ruhr Valley where the factories appeared to be functioning as usual that RAF aeroplanes had not simply 'knocked out' the cities immediately.[53] In Germany, meanwhile, there was a contrasting underestimation of the capacity of RAF bombers: Shirer reported the stunned surprise of both Berliners and himself at the first big raid on the city on 25 August 1940.[54] As late as March 1942, on the occasion of the British raid on Lübeck, Goebbels himself expressed amazement as to the scale of the attack ('Stupendous numbers of works of art have fallen victim to the British craze for destruction'), and there was similar disbelief concerning the number of aircraft used during the 31 May 'thousand-bomber' raid on Cologne.[55] German expectations, or at least those presented by propagandists, changed thereafter to an attribution of super-efficiency to Allied bombers.

Accuracy of targeting and capacity to destroy are, however, different military skills. The former would enable the deliberate targeting of particular historic monuments, but the policy of the area bombing of German cities adopted by the RAF gave clear priority to the latter. Indeed, this policy was a direct response to the lack of accuracy demonstrated during earlier raids. The most precise plans for precision bombing of particular targets had been disrupted by adverse weather conditions and the need to fly high enough to avoid anti-aircraft fire. Reports of the accuracy of Bomber Command missions during 1940 and early 1941 were not optimistic and were themselves subject to inaccuracies, given the difficulty of even estimating the results of raids in the absence of reliable post-raid reconnaissance photography at this stage in the war.[56] To put this lack of accuracy into perspective, problems with weather and reconnaissance were still being reported nearly sixty years later during the 1999 Nato bombardment of Kosovo and Serbia: Nato aeroplanes were frequently unable to drop bombs due to heavy cloud cover obscuring targets, affecting even laser-guided bombs dropped from Harrier aeroplanes, and there was still uncertainty over the precise results on the ground.

Interest having shifted away from apparently unachievable precision bombing, from March 1941 onwards RAF raids were more often than not at night and took as their target whole German cities, rather than particular military or industrial installations. Plans were made for the destruction of forty-three German towns, chosen according to the criterion of population: only towns with 100,000 or more inhabitants were considered worth attacking at this stage. Shortly after Arthur Harris took over as Commander-in-Chief of Bomber Command on 22 February 1942, the attack on

Lübeck on the night of 28–9 March provided the first test case for the new policy. It was the first large-scale area bombing raid, involving seventy aircraft which discharged their bombs over the centre of the town in three waves.[57] From then on, while industrial areas of German cities were officially maintained to be the primary targets in such attacks, in reality historic town centres and residential areas suffered as much, if not more, damage. In Harris's view this was the most effective use of Bomber Command's air power, as attempts at precision targeting of military or industrial installations created extra risks for air crew without a corresponding success rate on the ground. The emphasis was firmly on the total destructive effect on the cities, rather than on precise attacks on any particular urban target, cultural or otherwise.

Area bombing raids on German cities were known collectively as the Strategic Bombing Offensive, to contrast the approach with tactical bombardment. Tactical bombing is the attacking of traditional military targets during battles, with air power playing essentially a back-up role to land and sea power – to destroy enemy supply and communications lines, for instance, thus weakening their ground forces. The concept of strategic bombing gave air power an independent role, with its own non-traditional targets to destroy, such as enemy industry. Arthur Harris was main architect of the Strategic Bombing Offensive and the attractions of an independent strategic role to a Commander-in-Chief of Bomber Command are obvious. The argument was that strategic bombing and large-scale destruction of German cities could shorten the war considerably, an effect observed after the Luftwaffe air attacks on Warsaw (September 1939) and Rotterdam (May 1940), both of which were followed by the surrender of local forces. With such a line of thinking dominating policy at the Air Ministry from February 1942, the development of techniques for accurate targeting of specific types of building of any type was of little concern to those conducting the bombardment of entire town centres.

Harris also maintained that this style of bombardment was not a purely British invention but rather the result of learning lessons from the Blitz and taking a German approach to its logical conclusion – something which the Luftwaffe themselves had failed to do.[58] This line of argument was common in British press commentary, which advertised the enemy origins of 'deliberately indiscriminate' air raids, a paradoxical but accurate term for the policy. That the Germans had planned for London what was later inflicted on Hamburg by the RAF was confirmed by Albert Speer and Joseph

Goebbels, both of whom complained of a lack of planning by Göring in the areas of quantity and quality of aircraft production.[59] A failure to produce adequate numbers of bombers meant that the intensity of Blitz-style bombardment of British cities could not be maintained. The Luftwaffe did have long-range aircraft capable of carrying large quantities of bombs, without which the Blitz would not have been possible, but they had half the range, less speed and less than a third of the bomb-carrying capacity of the British Lancaster, for instance. The Lancaster was the bomber aircraft most generally used by Bomber Command in its area raids and could carry up to 6,350kg of bombs at 290mph with a there-and-back range of 1,600 miles. It was aircraft such as the Lancaster, as well as relatively efficient levels of production, which made possible the area bombing of cities on the scale recommended by Harris.[60] Again, this was not military technology directed towards the targeting of particular historic monuments, as these heavy bomber aircraft facilitated large-scale rather than precision bombing.

Besides the aircraft used and the method of their deployment, another barrier to accuracy was the fact that most raids took place at night, as if you can see the target clearly in daylight there is a fair chance that the target can see and aim at you. This was a lesson learned partly from the Luftwaffe, who carried out most of their attacks at night – hence the Blitz period expression 'a bomber's moon'. Great feats of accurate targeting were popularly attributed to the German bombers, following the raid on Coventry on 14 November 1940, for example, when the survival of the cathedral tower among the general devastation around was perceived as a deliberate intention on the part of the Germans, the better to relocate the city centre in a repeat raid.[61] In reality, accuracy of targeting was reduced at night: by moonlight, individual buildings cannot be seen at over 3–4,000ft, and pilots flew much higher – at over 12,000ft – to avoid the blinding effects of night search lights on the ground.[62] Night area bombing was the favoured method of Bomber Command: if a whole town was to be the target of a raid, with attempts at precision bombing abandoned, night raids could not be any less 'on target' than the daylight variety, and at least the danger of anti-aircraft fire was diminished. The only restricting factor was the length of the night as in the summer long-distance missions, to Berlin for instance, were not possible due to the reduced amount of darkness. Night raids were largely the preserve of the RAF, as the Americans maintained (at least officially) a commitment to precision bombing during daylight hours as their contribution to the Strategic Bombing

Offensive.[63] From the point of view of the specific targeting of historic monuments, as with many other features of the Strategic Bombing Offensive, night bombing was not a method designed for this.

Despite the apparently essential inaccuracy of such bombing techniques, the accuracy of RAF bombing did improve significantly as the war progressed: according to Air Ministry figures, the percentage of bombs falling within three miles of the intended target was only 20 per cent in 1942 but increased dramatically to over 90 per cent by the end of 1944.[64] For targeting particular buildings or historic monuments, a margin of error of three miles is obviously not helpful, but it is a degree of accuracy sufficient for the accurate targeting of whole historic town centres. It became, then, at least increasingly possible with the available military technology to deliberately destroy this broader category of target that included historic monuments. Success rates were also high for smaller-scale raids on railway marshalling yards and rocket launching installations in occupied France between late 1943 and mid 1944.[65] Such improved precision bombing skills raises concerns as to why general area bombing was continued over Germany, with the number of such raids increasing later in the war, when less generally destructive methods were proving effective in France. It is in this period that questions concerning the ethics of area bombing become more pressing: quite apart from the further damage caused to already devastated city centres which is our central concern here, the loss of civilian life in Germany continued at a time when it could not be described as the unfortunate consequence of technical inadequacy, that is, inability to target accurately. On the narrower issue of ability to target particular historic monuments, it seems that although Bomber Command's methods effectively ruled out the targeting of particular cultural monuments, they did enable the deliberate targeting of historic town centres, which necessarily included particular monuments.

In addition to the issue of the accuracy of area bombing, we might also ask whether the use of certain types of bomb and bombing patterns had specific consequences for buildings of historical or cultural interest and whether this aspect of the available technology could have contributed to a deliberate attempt to destroy this category of architecture, as so often suggested in the propaganda. At the start of the war, there was no real knowledge of the precise effect that the various existing bomb types available could have on buildings, whether of architectural interest or not, and this was an aspect of air power which was learned through trial and error during the conflict, often through being on the receiving end. Bombs such as the 'bouncing' variety specially designed by Barnes Wallis to destroy the Ruhr dams in the raids of May 1943 are so famous as to have passed into the mythology of the Second World War, but the more mundane technology used to destroy city centres was similarly effective. One method was found to be particularly effective by both the RAF and the Luftwaffe: during the Blitz, the Germans had observed that high-explosive bombs in themselves did a disappointingly small amount of damage, whereas large quantities of incendiary bombs created the fires which caused long-term and widespread material destruction.[66] It was 4lb incendiary bombs which were found to be most useful since, despite being too small to aim, they could be dropped on a limited area in the largest concentration possible to achieve maximum effect. This had an especially dramatic effect on historic town centres: the older the town centre, the more likely the presence of wood in the buildings, the better they would burn – as Arthur Harris is quoted as saying, Lübeck was 'built more like a fire-lighter than a human habitation'.[67] The larger variety of high-explosive bombs – 4,000lb 'blast' bombs – were used to follow up the fire treatment. Towards the end of the war, when many German cities were already devastated, more high-explosive bombs were used, which completed the effect by knocking down those walls left standing by the earlier fires.[68] Such methods constituted a war-long programme of development of bombs and bombing techniques with which to destroy buildings in the concentrated areas of city centres. Even if quantity rather than quality of destruction of the built environment was the priority, a particularly destructive effect on fragile historic monuments must have been anticipated, even if not specifically intended. As seen in Chapter 2, some of the sturdier cathedrals stood up to such bombing techniques rather better than surrounding structures, but they were exceptions to the general destructive rule.

Descriptions of area bombing raids from witnesses in the targeted cities themselves give a sharp impression of the sheer defencelessness of urban architecture in the face of fire and bombs, for instance Albert Speer's account of one such raid on Berlin, during which his own Ministry building was badly damaged:

The raids on Berlin provided an unforgettable image . . . : the illumination of the falling flares, known to Berliners as 'Christmas trees', followed by the flashes of explosions, producing clouds of fire and smoke . . . ; the apocalypse offered a magnificent spectacle.[69]

The midnight view over Canterbury during its 'Baedeker' raid sounds very similar, even if the attack described here by a resident was on a far smaller scale:

I looked out of my window. By this time a few German raiders were circling over the city dropping flares. The city with every fine detail of architecture was picked out in the uncanny blue and yellow light. Chandelier flares hung in the sky . . . After about three minutes there was an ominous sound of bombs dropping on the north side of the city.[70]

The raids, however large-scale, did not simply consist of the random dropping of huge numbers of bombs in the general area of a town in the hope that some would hit the target. There were several stages to an RAF area bombing raid, starting with the activities of a 'Pathfinder Force' sqaudron, who dropped flares over the city to illuminate the target. This enabled the bomb-carrying aircraft to aim their successive loads of incendiaries and high-explosives with relative accuracy over the town centre. From the point of view of individual buildings, historic monuments or otherwise, the degree of exposure to damage was enormous and unpredictable. Arthur Harris made a distinction between the danger to buildings and that to their inhabitants, regarding the incendiary plus blast bomb combination as more 'humane' than the use of high-explosive bombs alone, as the former combination was particularly effective in the destruction of architecture and 'only caused a large number of casualties when they raised a fire-typhoon, as at Hamburg'.[71] This claim to have found a humane area bombing technique falls within the 'he would say that, wouldn't he' category of statements but the capacity for material destruction of Harris's preferred bombing method cannot be doubted.

Area bombing was of course not the only method of bombardment available during the Second World War and historic monuments were under threat from a range of military equipment and operations, exhibiting various degrees of destructive efficiency. During the German invasion of Belgium and northern France in May 1940, the 'Stuka' dive bomber was employed to bombard towns; the 'Stuka' literally dived to drop bombs of up to 1,800kg with some accuracy, given the proximity of the aeroplanes to their targets. German air and ground forces caused combined damage along the path of their invasion of France, although many important historic monuments, most notably a whole series of Gothic cathedrals – Beauvais, Amiens, Reims, Laon, Soissons and Noyon – largely escaped damage, a deliberate policy on the part of the Germans according to them and even to one French account.[72] Göring made a special point of mentioning this in his defence at the Nuremberg trials:

Now I wish to refer to art monuments, which I would call the buildings, churches, and other monuments – anything of a stationary character. Here I can say that perhaps sometimes I issued an order which stood in contradiction to my strictly military duties, because I strongly emphasized to my fliers that the magnificent Gothic cathedrals of the French cities were, under all circumstances, to be protected and not to be attacked . . . and that if attacks had to be made, precision bombing Stukas were to be used primarily. Every Frenchman who was present at the time will confirm this, that . . . those art monuments of such great importance or beauty . . . were saved and purposely so, in contrast to what later happened in Germany.[73]

If this cannot be confirmed, the lack of damage itself does at least imply that this type of military operation, with a more limited tactical use of air power, was less of a threat to historic monuments than area bombing.

Bomber aircraft themselves, belonging to both sides, hit historic monuments and city centres in their tactical role during the 1944 invasion of France and the progress of the Allied armies across Belgium and Luxembourg into Germany. A combination of aeroplanes, artillery and bombardment from ships caused the damage during this campaign, with the additional hazards of the general sweep of troops and equipment through the battle zones, sometimes creating new roads through bulldozed historic buildings, and the destruction of church towers which the enemy might exploit as observation posts.[74] The slower the progress, the greater the destruction, with towns defended and fought over sustaining greater general devastation.[75] This was also the case in Germany, as described in one soldier's account of the artillery bombardment of non-surrendering Münster on 2 April 1945: 'We gave Münster a chance to escape total annihilation when we sent forward an interpreter with a white flag to see the German commander . . . Then we turned on our big guns which were placed five miles from the city and they reduced the place to ruin'.[76] It might be argued, however, that this type of military operation involved incidental damage to particular historic buildings, in the course of battles with other aims. Area bombing, by contrast, had the destruction of cities and the buildings in them as its primary motivation and was, therefore, a strategy which explicitly and deliberately included the destruction of buildings of all types, including historic monuments.

In the later stages of the war architectural damage was also caused by German V-1 and V-2 rockets (the V was an abbreviation of *Vergeltungswaffen*, or 'revenge weapons'). Launched from bases in occupied northern France, it has been estimated that over 9,000 V-1 rockets were launched in direction of south-eastern England, from March 1944 onwards, followed by the faster V-2s. Antwerp also suffered rocket attacks, approximately 1,300 in total.[77] This type of threat to historic monuments represents another contrast with that of area bombing, in that the rockets took indiscriminacy of aim to its furthest extreme: once launched, the element of control over where exactly they fell was minimal, far less than for other forms of artillery or aerial bombardment.

This scenario was far from that of the mythical single aeroplane targeting a cathedral with pinpoint accuracy which appeared so frequently in the propaganda. The propagandist's optimism concerning the accuracy of bombing techniques was not supported by the military technology actually in use during the Second World War. But, if the ability to bombard particular historic monuments at will seems to be located firmly in the realm of wartime mythology, the deliberate and accurate targeting of the historic town centres which contained such buildings was indeed possible and practised by both the Luftwaffe and the RAF, and practised with increasing precision and regularity by the latter as the war progressed.

This ability raises the further question of whether it was technically possible to positively avoid hitting particular historic monuments in the course of military action. As is clear from the discussion above, this would be a most unlikely feature of the area bombing of city centres as practiced over Germany and it is no coincidence that Allied claims that historic monuments had been avoided during their attacks on enemy towns were largely limited to events in Italy, during the Allied progression northwards in 1943–4, and in France, during the 1944 Allied invasion. There was the occasional case of intact survival of a significant building during raids on German towns, in Ulm, for example, where the cathedral was only slightly damaged in the centre of a completely ruined *Altstadt*. Given the rarity of this occurrence in Germany, this should be regarded as accidental survival, the result perhaps of the relative robustness of a solid stone church structure. The Allies rarely made claims to having avoided bombarding German historic monuments; the following boast in *The Times* about Cologne Cathedral's survival of the 1942 Operation Millenium was an exception: 'Although it is situated near important industrial targets, the famous cathedral has clearly not been hit – a tribute to the

RAF's bombing accuracy'.[78] This unusual claimed concern for a historic monument was motivated by the recent Baedeker raids on British cathedral towns, sending the message that the Luftwaffe were targeting important architecture, while the RAF were avoiding it.

The Allied approach to avoiding historic monuments during their advance through Italy was in many ways a test case for later events in France, both in practical and face-saving propaganda terms. Many ancient Italian cities were either threatened or damaged by the military activity, beginning in July in 1943 in Sicily, then moving up through Naples in October. Montecassino, immediately north of Naples, was under siege by the Allies from mid-December, suffering the heaviest bombardment in February 1944. Concern for the historic monuments in their path had been expressed in a letter from General Eisenhower to the troops of 29 December 1943, and this was read out by President Roosevelt at a White House press conference on 15 February 1944, just after the Allied-inflicted damage at Montecassino: 'We are bound to respect these monuments so far as war allows . . .'.[79] That the best way to avoid destroying historic monuments was not to bomb the towns in which they were located is proved by the case of Venice, which was granted a special immunity by both sides in the conflict and thus suffered no damage at all, unlike nearby bombed Treviso, with its destroyed fourteenth-century townhall. The treatment of Venice also demonstrated that it was militarily and politically possible to take the decision not to bomb. This was an unusual decision, however, and further damage was caused throughout 1944 and 1945 to cities in the north of Italy, from famous industrial centres such as Turin and Milan, to famous cultural centres such as Pisa, Florence, Padua and Vicenza, this last suffering both Allied bombardment and German bridge-exploding tactics. While area bombing was not the method used during the campaign in Italy, enabling a far greater number of historic monuments to escape the levels of destruction achieved in Germany, it was by no means the case that all were successfully 'avoided', as was often claimed in later Allied accounts. The ruined Eremitani Church in Padua, with its shattered Mantegna frescoes, stands almost adjacent to the spared Scrovegni Chapel, with its still intact Giotto frescoes – if the one could be 'avoided' in the air raids of 11 March 1944, why not the other?

The treatment of Rome was a major test of both Allied and Axis policy with regard to historic monuments. An American air raid on Rome was carried out on 19 July 1943, causing some damage to the church San Lorenzo fuori le Mura situated close to the targeted railway lines. American sources claimed the existence of detailed plans to avoid any damage to monuments in the centre of Rome, for example target charts for air crew with important buildings circled in white and marked 'Must Not Under Any Circumstances Be Damaged'.[80] Rather contradicting this, a less sensitive attitude to the treasures of the past was revealed by Churchill in a speech to the House of Commons on 21 September 1943, shortly after the Italian capitulation: he revealed an Allied plan, happily not carried out, to bombard German forces surrounding the city, making the startling statement that the plan 'might have led to its complete destruction, but we were ready to try it'.[81] On the German side, a last-minute decision was taken not to defend Rome when the Americans eventually entered the city on 4 June 1944, thus not provoking further bombardment. The arriving American troops were reminded by General Mark Clark of the symbolic nature of the city, and of the importance of an Allied demonstration to the world of their respect for historic monuments, a tenuous respect that had fortunately not been seriously tested.[82]

In France there were accounts of deliberate low flying over Chartres by RAF crews, who reportedly risked being shot down by the enemy in order to avoid hitting the cathedral.[83] The most famously undamaged French historic monuments were those in Caen, where the two Romanesque abbey churches, St Etienne and Ste Trinité suffered only slightly amidst the general devastation of the town during Allied attempts to expel the occupying German forces (June–August 1944). There was even a suggestion that the two churches were deliberately spared because of their historical connections with England, having been established in the eleventh century by William the Conqueror and Queen Mathilde.[84] Other churches without these allegedly crucial English connections were not spared – the Gothic St Pierre, for instance. The survival of the Romanesque churches is indeed surprising, as approximately 85 per cent of the town as a whole was ruined, but it is doubtful whether we can accept this 'historical' explanation – their location at the edges of Caen is a more likely reason. It has been claimed that the Allied air forces were given detailed maps and briefings to help them identify and avoid historic monuments on the ground and that it was this preparation of the air crews which saved the Caen churches.[85] The question remains as to why other important build-ings were not spared, as the two Romanesque abbey churches were very much the exception in an overall map of severe damage across

Normandy. Rouen Cathedral is perhaps the most famous example of non-avoidance, and many less celebrated examples contradict this suggestion of deliberate monument-saving manoeuvres.[86]

The Allied forces, at least at the higher command levels, were apparently sensitive to the presence of buildings of cultural and historic interest in the chosen spot for the invasion. General Eisenhower, Supreme Commander of the Allied Expeditionary Forces for this campaign, issued a letter to the troops on 26 May 1944 similar to his 1943 caution on Italy, encouraging some care to be taken at least:

Shortly we will be fighting our way across the Continent of Europe in battles designed to preserve our civilization. Inevitably, in the path of our advance will be found historical monuments and cultural centres which symbolize to the world all that we are fighting to preserve. It is the responsibility of every commander to protect and respect these symbols wherever possible.

The 'wherever possible' reflected the Hague Convention position on avoidance of damage to historic monuments, and the letter continues in this less than wholehearted vein:

In some circumstances the success of the military operation may be prejudiced in our reluctance to destroy these revered objects. Then, as at Cassino, where the enemy relied on our emotional attachments to shield his defense, the lives of our men are paramount. So, where military necessity dictates, commanders may order the required action even though it involves destruction to some honoured site.[87]

Whether even such limited sentiments were echoed in action on the ground is unclear. One American officer charged with the care of historic monuments in France reported that the preservation of historic monuments was not generally a military preoccupation and that the dictates of 'military necessity' were more compelling than the recommended respect for history.[88] Whether the few examples of significant buildings left standing intact among the ruins – the Gothic cathedral of St Pierre in Coutances, for instance – are evidence of Eisenhower's policy in action was information not even available to Monuments Officers such as Rorimer, who wrote 'I wanted desperately to believe that Coutances was evidence of the Allied consideration for great monuments'.[89] This uncertainty is reiterated in the 1946 *Report of The American Commission for the Protection and Salvage of Artistic and Historic Monuments in*

War Areas, which also might be expected to present more concrete data on the deliberate avoidance of historic monuments if such a policy had in fact been carried out.[90] The importance of such monuments to the military commanders should not, it seems, be overestimated.

If definite instances of the intentional targeting of historic monuments are rare, indisputable cases of intentional avoidance of these buildings are equally elusive, even if claims to the latter military achievement were more common, particularly on the part of the Allies. Indeed, bombing techniques developed during the Second World War made the destruction of monuments in targeted historic town centres inevitable. In the absence of a positive stated Allied policy of bombarding buildings of historic and cultural importance in Germany, the strongest impression given is more that of a lack of interest in avoiding them on the part of air forces and governments, except towards the end of the war, when a succession of historic cities were devastated. In general, the physical effects of war on historic monuments were of far more interest to propagandists exploiting the symbolism of this aspect of the Second World War than to those with the power to damage such buildings. It was only after the war that governments, notably those of the Allied countries, became considerably more interested in the wartime fate of historic monuments, exhibiting a concern that was little in evidence in practice during the fighting. This post-war cultural concern is the subject of the next chapter.

Notes

1. *The Times*, 1 November 1940.
2. The translated directive is printed in H. R. Trevor-Roper, *Hitler's War Directives 1939–1945*, pp. 102–3. For the original German text, see Walther Hubatsch, *Hitlers Weisungen für die Kriegsführung 1939–1945. Dokumente des Oberkommandos der Wehrmacht*, Frankfurt am Main 1962.
3. The order appears in the original German and in translation in Collier, *The Defence of the United Kingdom*, p. 512.
4. From a letter to the Editor from Robert Byron, the traveller, art historian and critic, 'Works of Art – their Position in War'.
5. In a speech at the Guildhall on 30 June 1943, for instance, and in a 'Message of Congratulations on the great air offensive against Germany' of 11 October 1943 (where he says of British and US Air Forces that 'we shall together inexorably beat the life out of industrial Germany, and thus hasten the day of final victory'). Both are published in Winston

S. Churchill, *Onwards to Victory*, pp. 123–33 and 232–3. This is also the message of Spaight's *Bombing Vindicated*.

6. The exchange was published in *The Times*, 30 April 1942.
7. Beseler and Gutschow, *Kriegsschicksale Deutscher Architektur*, vol. 1, entry on Berlin; on Coventry, see Thomas, *Coventry Cathedral*.
8. Speer, *Erinnerungen*, Chapter 20, chapter on 'Bomben', pp. 291ff. See also Webster and Frankland, *The Strategic Air Offensive Against Germany 1939–1945*, vol. I, p. 478.
9. Speer, ibid., p. 357.
10. Harris, *Bomber Offensive*, pp. 146–7.
11. Ibid., p. 76.
12. Webster and Frankland, *The Strategic Air Offensive Against Germany, 1939–1945*, vol. IV, Appendix 8, pp. 153–4.
13. H. R. Trevor-Roper, *Hitler's War Directives 1939–1945*, pp. 102–3.
14. In an interview with David Irving, recorded in Irving, *Und Deutschlands Städte starben nicht*, p. 49.
15. Harris, *Bomber Offensive*, pp. 87 and 122.
16. Ibid.
17. For the text of the directive, see Collier, *The Defence of the United Kingdom*, p. 512.
18. *The Times*, 30 April 1942. Wilhelmstraße in Berlin was then the German equivalent of Downing Street, the street of government.
19. *Völkischer Beobachter*, 1 May 1942. The article 'So etwas wie eine zweite Front' (1 May 1942) is reprinted in Goebbels, *Das Eherne Herz. Reden und Aufsätze aus den Jahren 1941–2*, pp. 302–8.
20. The origin of the expression 'Baedeker raid' is uncertain, but was attributed by Goebbels to a press officer in the German Foreign Ministry. Goebbels did not approve of the expression, seeing it as a gift to Allied propaganda. See Lochner, *The Goebbels Diaries 1942–1943*, entry for 2 May 1942.
21. For the complete list see Collier, *The Defence of the United Kingdom*, Appendix XXXVII, pp. 513–14, 'Principal German Night Attacks, 1942 (compiled from British and German sources)'.
22. *The Times*, 30 April 1942.
23. From the translation by Lochner, *The Goebbels Diaries 1942–1943*, entry for 27 April 1942, pp. 189–90.
24. See *The Times* of 5 May 1942, 'Nazi Geography. Exeter described as a "Harbour Town"': 'Apparently Goebbels has decided that it is not a good idea to emphasize the fact that cathedral cities are the avowed targets, so that Exeter was yesterday variously described as a "port", "harbour town", and "important traffic junction"'. See also Niall Rothnie, *The Baedeker Blitz. Hitler's Attack on Britain's Historic Cities*, pp. 131–3.
25. Collier, *The Defence of the United Kingdom*, Appendix XXXIX, p. 517.
26. Lochner, *The Goebbels Diaries 1942–1943*, entry for 27 April 1942, pp. 189–90.
27. According to directives to Bomber Command of 24 and 26 June, and 24 July 1940. The quote is from the latter (directive from Air Vice-Marshal W. S. Douglas to Air Marshal Sir Charles Portal), which is reprinted in Webster and Frankland, *The Strategic Air Offensive Against Germany 1939–45*, vol. IV, Appendix 8, pp. 121–3. The highest mountain in the Harz Mountains, the Brocken, features in German legend as the location for the witches' conference on Walpurgis Night (1 May).

28. *The Times*, 5 September 1940.
29. Webster and Frankland, *The Strategic Air Offensive Against Germany 1939–45*, vol. IV, pp. 218–19. According to the Bomber Command report of 7 October 1940, the result of the attack was uncertain.
30. *The Times*, 18 April 1941.
31. *The Times*, 13 May 1941.
32. Lochner, *The Goebbels Diaries 1942–1943*, p. 523, entry for 24 November 1943.
33. Harris, *Bomber Offensive*, p. 180.
34. The Combined Chiefs of Staff Directive of 21 January 1943 and the Air Ministry Directives of 28 January, 17 February and 17 April 1944 are reprinted in Webster and Frankland, *The Strategic Air Offensive Against Germany, 1939–1945*, vol. IV, Appendix 8, pp. 153–4 and 162–5.
35. *Newsweek*, 6 September 1943.
36. The incident is recorded in Speer's memoirs, *Erinnerungen*, pp. 185–8. Hermann Giesler had been appointed by Hitler to redesign Munich, just as a redesign of Berlin had been commissioned from Speer.
37. Ibid p. 187. On Speer's designs for a new Berlin, see L. O. Larsson, *Die Neugestaltung der Reichshauptstadt.*
38. For a lively if anecdotal French account, see Pierre Taittinger, . . . *Et Paris ne fut pas détruit*, particularly pp. 17–21 and 151–69.
39. For a translation of the directive, see Trevor-Roper, *Hitler's War Directives 1939–1945*, pp. 293–4.
40. Speer, *Erinnerungen*, pp. 411–12.
41. On the bombardment of Coventry, see Thomas, *Coventry Cathedral*, and Campbell, *Coventry Cathedral.*
42. Spaight, *Bombing Vindicated*, p. 92.
43. Webster and Frankland, *The Strategic Air Offensive Against Germany 1939–1945*, vol. I, p. 15.
44. Ibid., vol. I, pp. 405–6.
45. All statistics are taken from Beseler and Gutschow, *Kriegsschicksale Deutscher Architektur*, vols. 1 & 2. Entries on individual towns are organised by region (or Land), then alphabetically.
46. Webster and Frankland, *The Strategic Air Offensive Against Germany 1939–1945*, vol. I, p. 475.
47. *The Times*, 3 January 1945.
48. Harris, *Bomber Offensive*, p. 242. This was also the justification given in the report in *The Times* of 15 February 1945: 'At this moment Dresden is a place of vital importance to the enemy. As the centre of a railway network and a great industrial town, it has become of the greatest value for controlling the German defence against Marshal Konev'.
49. The full title of the report is United States Strategic Bombing Survey. Area Studies Division Report No. 7, *A Detailed Study of the Effects of Area Bombing in Lübeck, Germany*, 27 October 1945.
50. Ibid., p. 12.
51. Harris, *Bomber Offensive*, pp. 105–6.
52. United States Strategic Bombing Survey. Area Studies Division Report No. 7, *A Detailed Study of the Effects of Area Bombing in Lübeck, Germany*, pp. 48–52.
53. Shirer, *Berlin Diary 1934–1941*, entries for 16 and 19 May 1940, pp. 267–71.
54. Ibid., entry for 26 August 1940, p. 380. Shirer made a broadcast for CBS

during the night raid, the sound of anti-aircraft flak as background to his commentary.

55. Lochner, *The Goebbels Diaries 1942–1943*, entry for 31 March 1942 and Boelcke, *Wollt Ihr den totalen Krieg?*, entry for 1 June 1942.

56. See Webster and Frankland, *The Strategic Air Offensive Against Germany 1939–1945*, vol. I, section on 'The Coming of Area Bombing', pp.167–87.

57. The attack is described ibid., vol. I, pp. 391ff. in an account based on Bomber Command Executive Orders and Raid Reports.

58. Harris, *Bomber Offensive*, pp. 85–6.

59. Speer, *Erinnerungen*, pp. 296–7 and Goebbels in Lochner, *The Goebbels Diaries 1942–1943*, entries for 21–2 May 1943. On Luftwaffe capacity in general, see Cooper, *The German Air Force 1933–1945. An Anatomy of Failure*.

60. For comparison, one Luftwaffe plane in use at the start of the war, the Dornier Do 215, could carry up to 2,000kg of bombs at 250mph, with a range of c. 940 miles. For more detail on types of aircraft used during World War Two, and on anti-aircraft guns, see Hogg, *The Encyclopedia of Weaponry*, pp. 146–50.

61. An anecdote reported in Thomas, *Coventry Cathedral*, pp. 73–4.

62. Webster and Frankland, *The Strategic Air Offensive Against Germany 1939–1945*, Vol. I, p. 206.

63. As stated in the June 1943 Pointblank plan which set out the terms of the combined Allied air offensive in Germany; see Webster and Frankland, *The Strategic Air Offensive Against Germany 1939–1945*, Vol. II, pp. 22–3.

64. Quoted in the United States Strategic Bombing Survey, Military Analysis Division, Report No. 4 – Description of Royal Air Force Bombing, pp. 8–9 and Graph H.

65. A source of pride to Harris himself: see Harris, *Bomber Offensive*, p. 208.

66. Speer, *Erinnerungen*, p. 297.

67. From a letter dated 29 April 1942, quoted in Webster and Frankland, *The Strategic Air Offensive Against Germany 1939–1945*, Vol. I, p. 391.

68. On bomb types and usage generally see the United States Strategic Bombing Survey, Military Analysis Division, Report No. 4 – Description of Royal Air Force Bombing, section on 'Area Bombing Methods', pp. 2ff; Hampe, *Der Zivile Luftschutz im Zweiten Weltkrieg*, pp. 537ff, and Webster and Frankland, *The Strategic Air Offensive Against Germany 1939–1945*, Vol. IV, Annex IV, 'Bombs and Bombsights', pp. 31–9.

69. Speer, *Erinnerungen*, p. 301.

70. An account from Williamson, *Though the Streets Burn*, pp. 249–50.

71. Harris, *Bomber Offensive*, p. 238.

72. See Verrier, 'Les Monuments historiques atteints par la guerre', in *Bulletin Monumental*, 1940, pp. 239–260.

73. Trial of the Major War Criminals before the International Military Tribunal, Vol. IX – Proceedings 8 March 1946–23 March 1946, p. 330.

74. This practice, common during the First World War, is referred to in Methuen, *Normandy Diary*, p. 27. On the fate of a French church demolished to make a new road, see Rorimer, *Survival*, p. 13.

75. For a general overview of damage caused in this campaign, see the *Report of the American Commission for the Protection and Salvage of Artistic and Historic Monuments in War Areas*, section on 'European Theater of Operations. 1. France, Belgium, Holland, Luxembourg', pp. 94ff.

76. Quoted in *The Times*, 3 April 1945.

77. For more detail on V-1 and V-2 rockets, see Longmate, *Hitler's Rockets*.
78. *The Times*, 8 June 1942. The headline was 'Havoc in Cologne. 5,000 acres heavily damaged'.
79. The letter is reproduced in the *Report of The American Commission for the Protection and Salvage of Artistic and Historic Monuments in War Areas*, pp. 48–9. The American Commission was also known as the Roberts Commission, after its chairman.
80. Ibid pp. 68–9.
81. The speech is reprinted in Churchill, *Onwards to Victory*, pp. 189–216, this quote p. 199.
82. *Report of the American Commission for the Protection and Salvage of Artistic and Historic Monuments in War Areas*, p. 71.
83. An incident recorded in Woolley, 'The Preservation of Historical Architecture in the War Zones', *Journal of the Royal Institute of British Architects*, vol. 53, December 1945, pp. 35–42.
84. For this suggestion, see the account of the wartime fate of Caen by Roubier and Réau, *Caen*, Introduction (unpaginated). A less monument-oriented account is that of Gosset and Lecomte, *Caen pendant la bataille*.
85. Woolley, 'The Preservation of Historical Architecture in the War Zones', *Journal of the Royal Institute of British Architects*, vol. 53, December 1945, pp. 35–42.
86. For an impression of the full range of damage, see Verrier, 'Les Monuments historiques atteints par la guerre' in *Bulletin Monumental*, vol. XCIX, 1940, pp. 239–60 and Methuen, *Normandy Diary*.
87. Quoted in Rorimer, *Survival*, pp. x–xi.
88. Ibid., Chapter 1, 'Normandy'.
89. Ibid. p. 17.
90. On this point, see pp. 98–9 of the Report.

5

European Ruins and Reconstruction

As the war ended, desolate cityscapes stood across western Europe and the former enemies were confronted with the shared problem of how to rebuild. Besides the huge challenges of economic and political reconstruction, the less urgent but equally sensitive issue of how to deal with large quantities of ruined historic monuments in largely destroyed town centres confronted all of the affected countries. This chapter deals with the nature of the postwar response to the recent cultural destruction, from practical considerations to the rationalisations of embarrassed governments.

One postwar response to the widespread damage to western European historic monuments and cities that emerged immediately after the Second World War was the possibility of this feature of the conflict being judged criminal. The war crime of the deliberate bombardment of cultural targets was mentioned, if only briefly, during the Nuremberg trials, as part of the interrogation of Göring. The International Military Tribunal at Nuremberg tried the defendants according to the existing international laws of war, the Hague Conventions, which did, as we have seen in Chapter 1, forbid the destruction of buildings of cultural and historic importance in the absence of military necessity, but did not specifically cover their destruction as a consequence of air warfare. This point was made by Albert Kesselring, the Luftwaffe equivalent of Arthur Harris in the early years of the war and a witness in the defence of Göring, who insisted that any cultural damage done was justified by military necessity – during the bombardment of Rotterdam and Coventry, for example, where he claimed that every possible precaution was taken to ensure that 'the highest degree of accuracy could be obtained and regrettable deviations into the perimeter of the objectives could be avoided'.[1] When asked directly 'Did you . . . spare art treasures and churches as much as possible?', Kesselring predictably responded 'I regarded it as a matter of course as my duty to spare centers (sic) of art and learning and churches, and I gave orders accordingly, and acted accordingly myself in all my operations and tactical measures'.[2] Göring himself testified to his own careful concern for historic monuments during the 1940 invasion of France.[3] The interrogators did not pursue this line of questioning beyond these rather leading questions and no thorough attempt was made to indict Göring for the destruction of historic city centres by air bombardment or by other means. The absence of dogged legal determination on this issue must be at least partly attributed to the fact that, if Göring and the Luftwaffe could be described as guilty of this cultural crime, so could Allied forces. Equally awkward questions could be asked about the Strategic Bombing Offensive and the Allies were unlikely to attempt a prosecution of a former enemy for a crime they had committed themselves – a safer path was simply not to characterise it as a crime at all, on either side. The 'war crime' of indiscriminate bombing of historic cities with the consequent destruction of historic monuments was in effect not pursued at the Nuremberg trials, for the pragmatic reason of Allied face-saving.

EVENTUAL PHOENIXES

Whatever the legal or moral status of the cause of the destruction, the architectural aftermath of the Second World War remained to be dealt with, a very practical problem common to all western European countries. This is not the place for a detailed discussion of the postwar political situation in Germany, Britain and France, but certain aspects of postwar western Europe had particular influence on the postwar treatment of and attitudes towards the repair and reconstruction of war damaged historic monuments. While most western European nations either retained or regained their sovereignty, including that over their own ruins, Germany did not. Between the German surrender on 8 May 1945 and the establishment of the Federal Republic of Germany in the west in May 1949 and the German Democratic Republic in the east in October 1949, Germany was under the control of four occupying powers: Britain, America, France and the Soviet Union each set up a military government in their allotted zones, carrying out their own independent policies for the reconstruction of the country. The British controlled the top left hand quarter of Germany, from Cologne in the south-west to Hamburg and Lübeck in the north east; the Americans controlled Hessen and Bavaria; the east was under Soviet government and the French had the far south-west of the country, plus the regions bordering on its own territory, including the Alsace-Lorraine area, much exchanged between France and Germany since 1871. This division was partly accidental, depending on whose armies were where when Germany surrendered, and partly deliberate, as France was allocated its own Occupation Zone on de Gaulle's insistence.

There was some consensus on how the zones should be governed and the Potsdam Agreement of 2 August 1945 formalised the policy, consisting of a combination of chastisement and exploitation for reparations purposes on the one hand and reorganisation and reconstruction on the other. The emphasis, positive or negative, was left up to the individual military governments – historians have suggested that the Soviet-controlled zone took the most exploitative approach in terms of stripping the country of what resources and industrial installations remained, but the western powers were not entirely innocent of this, especially France. The experience of a particularly vicious style of warfare or of occupation informed postwar attitudes towards the defeated Germany. British and American histories of their conduct in what eventually became a single 'bi-zone' naturally emphasise the more positive policies of rebuilding, re-education, disarmament and denazification, but asset-stripping took place here too. The emphasis was very much on economic, rather than on cultural reconstruction and little progress was made on the latter between 1945 and 1947. It was the Marshall Plan, first proposed by the American Secretary of State George C. Marshall on 5 June 1947 and funded by the Americans, which encouraged movement, with measures such as the currency reform and birth of the Deutschmark in 1948.

Part of the problem in the early postwar period in Germany had been that countries such as Britain and France, themselves economically stretched by the war, were responsible for solving the massive food, housing and healthcare problems in their respective zones. There was a constant tension caused by the need to provide absolute necessities for survival in Germany, while rationing and the need for postwar reconstruction existed at home. Despite receiving more Marshall aid than Germany, Britain and France were not in a position to fund the luxury of historic monument repairs at home, let alone on the former enemy territory of Germany.[4]

From this brief survey it is not difficult to deduce that in the immediate postwar period the restoration of historic monuments was not always a priority. In worst-damaged Germany in particular buildings of cultural and historic interest were in competition with housing for scarce materials and labour. According to former West German government statistics, 20 per cent of living accommodation had been completely destroyed during the war, and a far greater percentage had been damaged to varying degrees.[5] The first priority for local authorities, survivors and returning refugees was the repair of apartments and the construction of temporary shelter and hospitals. This was an intimidating task – in the city of Mainz alone, only 1,300 apartments had been repaired or built by mid-1947 and 20,000 inhabitants had still not been rehoused.[6] This was the subject of the postwar *Trümmerliteratur* ('rubble literature') of authors such as Heinrich Böll, who described the citizens of Cologne collecting rubble from the ruins to repair their damaged houses, with no mention of their damaged historic monuments.[7] In France too the new *Ministère de la Reconstruction* presided over an inadequate budget and much rubble.[8] Meanwhile, in Britain, there was also a postwar housing shortage, albeit much less serious, exacerbated by the Blitz and the fact that few new homes were built during the war years.[9] In 1952, Coventry City Council opposed the plan for a new cathedral on the grounds that the money and materials could be better spent on essential housing than on non-essential churches.[10]

In Germany, the British, American and French authorities controlling the supply of what little building materials there were did release some for urgent work on historic monuments. This they were in theory obliged to do under the terms of the Hague Convention, which specified that the military government of an occupied nation was responsible for the maintenance of buildings of cultural and historic importance. Thus the Allies were in the curious position of being legally required to care for buildings they had only recently been bombing. One notable case was that of the Residenz in Würzburg, where Allied MFA & A officers worked together with civilian German staff to find the quantities of wood necessary for a roof to protect a surviving Tiepolo ceiling from the winter weather.[11] On the question of why so much effort was made in the case of this particular historic monument, it should be remembered that Würzburg was badly damaged by Allied bombardment in March 1945 during the invasion of Germany,

despite being of no military significance. An extra tension in the
relationship of the occupying authorities to the buildings of the
former enemy was provided by the reparations issue: as an economically ruined Germany could only pay 'in kind', reparations
were claimed by the victors in the form of building and industrial
materials; the dismantling of German factories was authorised by
the Reparations Plan formally approved in March 1946.[12] Victor
Gollancz gave a critical account of this activity after a visit to the
British Zone in October–November 1946: 'But as I drove through
ruined Cologne at late dusk . . . for a moment I just couldn't believe
that we were deliberately, eighteen months after the end of the war,
adding further ruin to this unspeakable desolation'.[13] Although
little attention was paid to them at all, churches and other historic
monuments were at least not used as sources of reparations in kind.
Their loose stones and bricks did sometimes find their way into the
makeshift home repairs of local residents.

The Allies were considerably more interested in the wartime
fate of mobile works of art, on the evidence of their postwar cul-
ture-related activities in Germany. The British and American
organisations established to oversee the treatment of art and architecture during the Allied invasion of France, Italy and Germany
(the Macmillan Committee and the Roberts Commission) demonstrated an equal interest in both types of cultural heritage in France
and Italy but, on entering Germany, were more concerned with
retrieving paintings than with protecting bombed buildings. Such
resources as were available were invested in the search for the
many art depots in the occupied areas – the notorious depots at
Neuschwanstein in Bavaria and the Alt Aussee mines, where Van
Eyck's 'Ghent Altarpiece' was rediscovered, were just two of the
396 depots found by May 1945 alone.[14] But this change of emphasis
in the Allied art mission was not simply the result of the sheer
quantity of paintings to recover and return to their original locations
and owners. As the American MFA & A officer J. J. Rorimer put it,
'Finding stolen objects was, of course, more spectacular'.[15] Bombed
historic monuments, ruined and ugly, in such quantities as to make
the task of restoration seem impossible, were a less attractive focus
for the occupying armies than the dramatic rescue of intact paintings
– a more positive, image-enhancing task for the victorious Allies,
where results could be achieved quickly, perhaps even obscuring
for a world audience the issue of the amounts of architectural
damage done. The retrieval operations certainly received the most
publicity. The recovery and restitution of mobile works of art was a

popular postwar activity and commissions charged with this duty were established in France, Belgium and the Netherlands, as well as in Germany. In addition to the operations carried out by the Allied armies under the auspices of the Roberts Commission and the Macmillan Committee, private organisations were set up to help co-ordinate the return of stolen paintings, many of them based in London.[16]

There was an additional motivation for this hunt for mobile works of art: as the German border was crossed, the issue of 'compensation for works of art stolen or wantonly destroyed by the enemy' became paramount.[17] Many of the paintings stored in the depots and salt mines were from German art collections, but there were also famous works belonging to Germany's former enemies. In the case of the latter, the policy was to repatriate the works with the maximum publicity. A notable example was the retrieval of medieval stained glass windows from Strasbourg Cathedral from a salt mine outside Heilbronn and their ceremonial return in September 1945. Removed to Germany from their storage place in the Dordogne in May 1944, the windows were the first works of art to be returned to France – symbolic of the now definitively French nature of the disputed region of Alsace, and of the Allied role in the cultural revival of Europe. This point was reinforced in French publicity and in an American documentary.[18] The other category of German-owned paintings received a different kind of attention, being suggested as a possible source of cultural reparations. This idea of cultural 'reparations in kind' the Germans found difficult to accept: Konrad Adenauer (the pre-war mayor of Cologne and later first chancellor of West Germany), for instance, was concerned that 'School of Cologne' paintings from the Wallraf-Richartz collection might be confiscated from their hiding places and taken to America to be added to museum collections there.[19] In the case of the Cologne paintings, this did not happen, possibly due to Adenauer's good relations with the Americans, but works of art from the collection of the Kaiser Friedrich Museum in Berlin, discovered by the US army in April 1945, were indeed taken to Washington DC and stored in the National Gallery of Art. This provoked protest in Germany and in America: in January 1946 the *College Art Journal* printed both an official statement justifying the move, listing the paintings taken and insisting that they were there for safe-keeping, not for eventual display, and letters arguing that the practice 'established a precedent which is neither morally tenable or trustworthy' and disapproving of the proposal that the paintings would only be given to the Germans if 'the nation had earned the right to their return'.[20] The idea of a cultural ransom to encourage good political conduct was a curious one, and has the air of a rationalisation produced after the event, although it might also demonstrate a continuing belief in the symbolic power of art on the part of some politicians.

While attention was diverted by the wartime experience of paintings and sculpture, for many damaged historic monuments the years immediately following the end of the war were a period spent in architectural limbo. Rubble and debris were cleared, temporary measures taken to prevent further deterioration – the construction of a temporary roof here, the shoring up of a dangerous vault there – but positive rebuilding was not undertaken for years in most cases. In Germany in particular, there was a sharp contrast between the reality of the restoration situation and promises made by the propagandists during the war. The architectural historian Paul Clemen wrote:

Then we dreamed of an immediate start to the rebuilding of destroyed cities, with all their monuments, even if we didn't believe the words of the cheerful windbags from the Propaganda Ministry, who assured the world that all the destroyed cities would be reconstructed in two or three years, more beautifully than before.[21]

Any early optimism soon evaporated. Apart from the material and manpower difficulties, postwar restoration work was further hampered by the destruction or unavailability of the architectural records and photographic archives, without which restoration work could not begin. For example, the postwar task of Franz Graf Wolff Metternich, then in charge of monument conservation in the north Rhineland area, was made even more difficult by the wartime destruction of his regional headquarters and the dispersal of building plans and documents elsewhere.[22] Wolff Metternich described the progress of work in his region: firstly, restoration priorities were decided and a list of around seventy of the most important historic monuments drawn up. An application for building materials to carry out emergency repairs and the stabilisation of threatened structures was made each month to the *Kunstschutz* department of the occupying military government.

Buildings that were not state-owned were more reliant on private funding, such as it was, and local organisations were formed to attract support, such as the *Gesellschaft der Freunde des Wiederaufbaus der*

Stadt Köln ('Society of the Friends of the Reconstruction of the City of Cologne'), which had taken the prudent step of electing the influential Konrad Adenauer as its president. Many 'lesser' monuments, such as private houses, were left unprotected and deteriorated further. Even 'major' monuments suffered postwar damage due to protracted neglect, for instance the Romanesque church St Maria-im-Kapitol, the apse of which collapsed in June 1948. As for the time scale of historic monument restoration work, by early 1946 most damaged buildings were largely untouched, and just a little rubble clearing had been done. Wolff Metternich estimated that by the end of 1946 over one hundred monuments were receiving attention, but that by the spring of 1948 only this essential stabilisation work had been carried out in the majority of cases. Progress in Cologne in 1950 was described as most unspectacular: 'Although much has been achieved, the greater part of the reconstruction of Cologne monuments remains a task for the future'.[23] Costs were high: even the relatively undamaged Dom in Aachen would, it was estimated in 1948, cost as much as one and a half million Marks.[24] Cologne's Romanesque churches only very gradually acquired their pre-war form. While waiting for funds and materials, a competition was held to decide how to restore St Maria-im-Kapitol – the debate was whether to restore its original eleventh-century appearance or not, and if so, what that original appearance might have been, disguised as it had been behind the additions and decorations of later centuries – and most basic structural work was completed by 1957. More decorative restoration work was not finished until 1984, when the church was definitively reopened on Christmas Eve. St Gereon, with its ruined Dekagon, had a similar postwar experience: although work was begun in 1949, the reconstruction of the Dekagon itself only started in 1957 and work on the north tower was just beginning in 1984. The finishing touches to these restorations were carried out as the fortieth anniversary of VE day approached.

Progress was no faster in Britain, with most work also beginning after the Marshall Aid year of 1949. No major reconstruction work had been carried out in Canterbury by 1949, for example, and in Plymouth work started on St Andrew's church in January 1949, nearly eight years after the bombing of the town. It was completed in 1957, with stained glass windows designed by John Piper installed in the 1960s.[25] That this was a matter of priorities rather than pure lack of materials is indicated by the swifter rebuilding of the House of Commons Chamber between 1947 and 1950 – this particular monument was formally reopened on 26 October 1950.

Other London damage was less of a priority. In the major London museums, for example, only minor repairs had been carried out by March 1948, enough to allow them to remain open to the public but substantial reconstruction work on out-of-access rooms and buildings was incomplete.[26] City of London churches received attention little by little throughout the 1950s and 1960s. The most publicised single rebuilding of a historic monument was that of Coventry Cathedral, the new church being completed in 1962, also with stained glass by John Piper in the baptistery, an appropriate commission since it was Piper who had produced the first images of the ruined church in 1940. This was a more glamorous project than the extensive repairs needed by most damaged architecture.[27]

A similar pace of monument reconstruction was achieved in France. One frustrated commentator suggested that the interminable eyesore ruins should at least be concealed behind giant reproductions of the monuments in their pre-war state, a measure which would encourage tourism and create jobs.[28] In France, however, there was an extra complication: the cost of the damage caused by the Allied invasion was a source of some anger on the part of the French, and of corresponding embarrassment on the part of the British and the Americans. Happy that Paris had been spared – as Jean-Paul Sartre rather ambiguously put it, 'The English, for their part, having flattened Lorient, Rouen and Nantes with their bombs, had decided to respect Paris' – there was nevertheless resentment of material and cultural losses caused by their wartime allies.[29] Post-liberation Allied propaganda attempted to convey a more harmonious message, for instance with this photograph of an American soldier and a Frenchman working together to repair a damaged church (Figure 5.1), to which the official caption was 'The church was one of the few edifices . . . wrecked by American artillery and planes, which avoided hitting the structures wherever possible'. Lord Methuen's view in his *Normandy Diary* entry for 9 September 1944 was 'I cannot help wondering who is going to foot the bill, and yet it is inconceivable that the more important of the damaged monuments will not be restored'.[30] One possible solution was Allied funding for restoration of particular historic monuments and of whole towns, such as Caen, Lisieux and Saint-Lo – it was proposed that towns in Britain and America should 'adopt' a damaged town or building in France and make some contribution, however symbolic, to the reconstruction process.[31] The spire of the Gothic church of St Pierre in Caen was restored with the help of American funds but this and other particular instances of generosity could

FIGURE 5.1 Post-liberation Allied Forces photograph of the bombed
church of St Malo in Valognes: 'Church salvage work begins in Normandy'
(Macmillan Committee photograph).
The Conway Library, Courtauld Institute of Art.

not cover the total cost of France's damaged monuments. Church
spires were often rebuilt last of all, being unnecessary for religious
ceremonies – it was temporary roofing that took priority, besides
the return of stained glass taken down before the war.[32]

RUINS, RECONSTRUCTION OR NEW CONSTRUCTION

The material and financial barriers to the rehabilitation of historic
monuments were problems shared by all countries in western
Europe and another shared problem was that of precisely how to
rehabilitate these buildings when the opportunity arose. The two
principal approaches to damaged historic monuments were neatly
summed up in the foreword to the first postwar edition of *Die
Kunstpflege*, the German journal dealing with restoration issues:
'The problem: reconstruction or new construction, to preserve or to
relinquish, pious revival or bold redesign'.[33] The scale of the ruins

encouraged the view that the bombed city centres should be demolished, clearing a space for new towns, while respect for historic monuments seemed to make rebuilding rather than new building the only option. This issue is specifically western – in some non-western cultures, Japan for instance, it is the building technique which it is considered essential to preserve, rather than the original fabric of a monument. If the technique has been safeguarded by careful teaching, the replacement of an 'old' structure with a new one in exactly the same style is unproblematic.[34] The western tradition of architectural conservation has by contrast placed the emphasis on the physical survival of historic monuments.

In practice, there was an extreme option open to those charged with the ruins: in the case of the most seriously damaged buildings, those which appeared unreconstructable, demolition was the obvious course of action. This was not always carried out on the recommendation of experts after careful consideration: demolition was a common means of solving the problem of unstable structures in the aftermath of a raid and the decision was sometimes taken by soldiers detailed to clear a bombed area. This resulted in some historic monuments being knocked down unnecessarily and was nearly the fate of the tower of Coventry Cathedral, according to one alarming anecdote: a soldier, assuming that the slightly leaning tower had received structural damage in the raid and subsequent fire which destroyed much of the rest of the building, decided to demolish it for safety reasons, but was persuaded not to by a chance passer-by who informed him that the tower had always stood at an incline.[35] Such lucky reprieves were not always available and this danger was yet another factor threatening the survival of historic monuments in this period. It was a particularly serious problem in Germany, where a combination of necessity, urgency and absence of expert opinion led to the razing to the ground of entire neighbourhoods of historic buildings and ensembles. Cost was an unavoidable factor here, as demolition and rebuilding from scratch using concrete could be less expensive than attempting to gather sufficient quantities of stone for an authentic reconstruction.

The more architecturally significant structures were generally safe from postwar destruction and the older and rarer the building, the more likely it was to be restored. Of the many City of London churches damaged during the Blitz, only St Alban, Wood Street was substantially knocked down, leaving only the Wren Gothic-style tower. The buildings immediately surrounding historic monuments were not always so fortunate – the structures around St Paul's

Cathedral were not subject to this urge towards preservation, for instance. This in itself was regarded as a benefit by some, as it disengaged important buildings from structures which obscured a clear view of them; Figure 5.2 shows a view of the slightly damaged east end of St Paul's with the remains of demolished buildings in the foreground.

One alternative to demolition in the case of historic monuments unsuitable for reconstruction was the preservation of the ruins. In

FIGURE 5.2 St Paul's Cathedral, London, after the war.
© Warburg Institute, National Monuments Record.

practice, many buildings of this type stood as ruins for some years during and after the war, due to the slow progress of repair and reconstruction, but it was one step further to decide to keep them in this state permanently. The ruined church of St Andrew's in Plymouth was transformed into an open-air church as early as 1943, intended as 'a fitting memorial to symbolize the city's grief and honour . . . [and] to the forty churches of all denominations which the enemy has destroyed' (Figure 5.3).[36] Although St Andrew's was later reconstructed, the equally ruined Charles Church was chosen to perform this memorial function.[37] This practice was later adopted as part of the solution for the largely-destroyed Coventry Cathedral, where the ruins of the old church were preserved alongside the new building. The remaining walls and arcade were stabilised, the floor grassed over and the windows of the relatively intact tower glazed. The same approach was taken in the case of the Kaiser-Wilhelm-Gedächtnis-Kirche in Berlin, where the original tower of the destroyed church was kept as a commemorative foil to a new structure (Figure 5.4). In both Britain and Germany, the

FIGURE 5.3 St Andrew's Church, Plymouth as 'garden ruin'.
© Crown Copyright. National Monuments Record.

FIGURE 5.4 Berlin, the war-damaged
Kaiser-Wilhelm-Gedächtnis-Kirche partly preserved beside
the new church (designed by Egon Eiermann 1959–61).
Bildarchiv Foto Marburg, neg. no. LA 1625/84.

preserved ruins of churches served as memorials to the dead and
to other destroyed buildings – St Alban in Cologne, for instance,
and in London Christ Church, Newgate Street and St Anne, Soho.
Churches in city centres were most suitable for this new postwar
function, due to their sacred status and spiritual connotations, even

for non-believers, and to the striking appearance of these architectural fragments in the midst of urban reconstruction. Towers still standing suggested defiant survival and optimism, positive connotations to counter the negative forces of war and destruction. There was also the more prosaic reason of their redundancy in cities with too many churches for less devout populations.

A campaign in favour of this use of damaged churches was conducted in Britain. An article suggesting the preservation of at least some ruins on the Plymouth model was published in the *Architectural Review* of January 1944, then the proposal was repeated in a letter to *The Times* of 15 August 1944, signed by Kenneth Clark, John Maynard Keynes and T. S. Eliot among others. The argument was that traditional war memorials would be inappropriate: 'In this war conditions have been different. England has itself been in the battle and London is still in it. Could there be a more appropriate memorial of the nation's crisis that the preservation of fragments of its battleground?'[38] The campaign was further reinforced with the publication of a book of essays on the subject in 1945, entitled *Bombed Churches as War Memorials* (edited by W. R. Matthews, the Dean of St Paul's), including articles such as 'Ruins for Remembrance' by Hugh Casson. In general, it was seen as particularly important not to remove all traces of the Blitz in which so many people lost their lives. The wounded churches could stand metaphorically for the wounded populations of bombed cities, just as they had done during the war, when civilian deaths were alluded to indirectly in reports of architectural damage.

On the practical level of establishing the ruins as monuments, a common format chosen was the 'garden ruin', with the architectural remains surrounded with flower beds and lawns. In London, continuing the garden theme, Christ Church, Newgate Street was given 'replacement' aisle pillars in the form of trees. This was a typical Romantic vision of the aesthetic possibilities of a ruin, inviting parallels with other popular ruins such as Tintern Abbey or Fountains. The eighteenth-century fondness for decaying architecture had extended to the construction of fake ruins as architectural features for gardens – now the bombarded city centres could have the real thing, hopefully with all the charm of the classical ruins of Rome. Some went so far as to advocate the preservation of some ruins on purely aesthetic grounds:

The architecture of destruction not only possesses an aesthetic peculiar to itself, it contrives its effect out of its own range of raw materials. Among

the most familiar are the scarified surfaces of blasted walls, the chalky sub-
stance of calcined masonry, the surprising sagging contours of once rigid
girders and the clear siena colouring of burnt-out brick buildings, their
rugged cross-walls receding plane by plane, on sunny mornings in the City
[of London].[39]

Making a virtue out of a necessity, this view that the primary interest
of a damaged building was visual rather than moral or commemorative was that of a 'connoisseur of ruins'.[40] These were ideas
approaching those of Albert Speer's theory of the value of ruins,
which posed the perverse question 'what makes a good ruin?'
    Such sentiments were unlikely to appeal to the non-specialist,
for whom an historic monument ruined by the recent war may
have had considerably less romantic connotations than an older,
elegantly moss-covered structure, ruined in some more obscure
historical conflict and never seen intact by the viewer. The response
to the proposal published in *The Times* was not entirely positive,
the suggestions provoking the following protests: 'Such ruins would
be a morbid commemoration of a successful assault by the forces of
evil . . . And, surmounting the wreckage, the only appropriate finial
would be the swastika . . .'; 'such ruins of disintegrated and calcined
stones are usually associated with a civilization which has passed
away . . . ; the symbol should be that of the phoenix rather than the
collector of antiquities'.[41] There was similar resistance to the idea
in Germany: not all ruins were aesthetically pleasing and there
was a reluctance in some quarters 'that recent ruins should stay
standing in a developing city like rotten teeth', as Paul Clemen put
it in a postwar plea for the swift reconstruction of historic monuments.[42] Not all damaged historic monuments had the potential
to be a future Colosseum and too many left in this condition might
evoke more negative sentiments of hatred for the former enemy,
standing as reminders of the conflict rather than sad symbols of
mutual suffering and reconciliation. This had been the conclusion
of a similar debate after World War One – a debate which Clemen
had himself taken part in – when the damaged cathedrals of
north-eastern France were all restored eventually, leaving only a
few overt scars to commemorate the wartime shelling, most notably
at Reims where the stonework calcined in the 1914 fire is preserved inside the west front.[43] For Clemen the conclusion was the
same in 1946: 'The word that shines before us is 'construction,
construction' – also a symbol for our resurrection as a nation'.[44]
    The decision having been taken to restore a particular building or

architectural ensemble rather than to demolish or retain it as a ruin, the question was then whether to rebuild in the original style or to construct something partly or entirely new. A 1949 edition of the German journal *Kunstchronik* stated the problem clearly with reference to the Alte Pinakothek in Munich, a nineteenth-century neo-classical museum designed by Klenze: 'Neither a total ruin nor a lightly damaged building whose restoration can be taken for granted' – the half-ruined half-intact structure dictated neither a redesign nor a stone-by-stone rebuilding.[45] In practice, most restoration work involved a pragmatic combination of both approaches, but each represented a distinct attitude towards the preservation of historic monuments, enthusiastically maintained by their respective supporters in the postwar debate on reconstruction. If for many buildings of cultural and historic interest reconstruction rather than redesign was an automatic choice, the same was not true for historic town centres as a whole, which were more likely to be replanned in a more contemporary style, and the results are visible today in the common sight in many western European cities of restored stone churches and monuments surrounded by structures of postwar design and materials.

Individual historic monuments were almost always restored to their original appearance, or something very closely approximating it. This was common practice in Britain, Germany and France. New elements or materials were sometimes introduced during reconstruction, out of material necessity or for symbolic reasons, but gradually throughout the fifties, sixties and sometimes even the seventies, these buildings reappeared.[46] The decision to build an entirely new cathedral in Coventry was unusual and resulted from the extreme nature of the structural damage to this church. Many historic monuments had retained more of the essential elements on which to base a reconstruction, such as intact and stable outer walls. That a faithful restoration should be carried out seems in retrospect 'natural', an obvious decision to take, but was subject to debate at the time. In Cologne, for instance, the question of how, or indeed whether, to restore the many damaged churches was considered by different interest groups in the immediate postwar period, not all of whom shared the view that 'naturally' a Romanesque church should be restored in the original style. As discussed above, local government officials had other building priorities, but even the Church was capable of a pragmatic approach to their own monuments, arguing that what needed was a building in which to worship, whether original, restored or brand new. It was primarily architectural historians, particularly those employed by the local *Denkmalamt* ('monuments department'), who championed restoration for aesthetic and historical reasons.[47]

This was a problem for secular as well as for ecclesiastical historic monuments: an especially heated debate was provoked by the question of what to do with the destroyed Goethehaus in Frankfurt. Hardly a stone remained of this building after an initial light bombardment in November 1943, followed by total destruction in March 1944, making the choice in this case that between constructing a copy of the original building from the foundations upwards or building a house in a different style. The director of the Goethehaus, Ernst Beutler, favoured the former option and canvassed support for an historical reconstruction from members of the German intellectual establishment, including Max Planck, Karl Jaspers and Hermann Hesse. The argument went that this was, after all, the childhood home of the German national poet (Goethe was born there in 1749) and had contained the attic room in which he wrote *Die Leiden des jungen Werthers*. Others were in favour of a less pious, more modern monument to Goethe, arguing that it was more important to preserve the memory of the great man himself than the style of his former house. Beutler's faction won the debate, gaining additional momentum from the approaching two-hundredth anniversary of Goethe's birth, and the house was re- rather than newly-built, with the first stone ceremonially laid in July 1947 (it was completed in 1951).[48]

Attitudes towards faithful or unfaithful restoration changed over the decades following the war and those historic monuments which did not receive attention in the first wave of restoration work in the late 1940s and 1950s were less likely to re-emerge with their original appearance. The Leibnitzhaus in Hannover, for example, was not rebuilt until 1981–3 and received a more modern treatment, whereby some skeletal remains of the 1648–52 Renaissance wooden facade were incorporated into a new design on a new site. The immediate postwar anxiety to recover the lost appearance of treasured buildings had faded by this stage of Germany's postwar reconstruction.

Recovering the lost appearance of entire historic city centres was an even more ambitious project than the reconstruction of individual monuments, and it was not feasible in the materially-stretched postwar years to rebuild entire streets in the decorative styles of past centuries. Nuremberg is a rare example of a badly damaged city requiring substantial reconstruction where the decision was taken to restore the original appearance of the historic town centre as far as possible. Besides the restoration of churches, town hall and other public buildings, old streets in the former *Altstadt* were reconstructed, not with copies of former houses, but using designs and materials in keeping with what had stood there before, on roughly the same street plan. Straight lines and overt use of concrete were deliberately avoided and loyalty to the local pink stone, even in new buildings, gave the 'new' *Altstadt* a certain visual unity.[49] This was an option available in the case of a small or medium sized *Altstadt*, such as Nuremberg or Lübeck, but not for a devastated city on the scale of Hamburg. It was not a popular option in Britain, where the new town plans imposed on bombed cities such as Plymouth and Coventry were resolutely modern in emphasis.

In France those favouring a modern reshaping of damaged towns conceived their task on a grand scale – a 1945 edition of the modernist architectural journal *Urbanisme* recalled Pericles' 'modern' redesign of Athens, calling for the same spirit of innovation and forward thinking in the reconstruction of postwar France.[50] This was also the message of the 1945–6 *Exposition de la Reconstruction* in Paris, where a quote from de Gaulle greeted the visitor: 'The great task, the national task, the sacred task, is Reconstruction'.[51] The modernist option had been advertised earlier during the war in local exhibitions in damaged towns such as Orléans (in October 1940), with the war damage to historic city centres presented as an opportunity to sweep away the old to make way for the inevitable new.[52] In 1941 Le Corbusier had even published a proposal for the replanning of Paris, entitled *Destin de Paris*, a faintly sinister title given the wartime publication date. As a coda to his modernist redevelopment, the author suggested that a Corbusian Paris would be far more likely to survive an air raid, with its reinforced concrete structures and wide open spaces replacing the fragile houses and narrow streets of the traditional town plan – traditional towns were, as he put it, 'destined for destruction'.[53] Historic monuments were accorded only a conditional survival in his text for 'The Charter of Athens', a modernist architectural manifesto, published the same year: 'Not everything from the past has, by definition, a right to survive; it is better to choose wisely what should be respected'. Here the value of historic architecture has been relativised and an unquestioning preservation of the past branded sentimental. Le Corbusier also disapproved of the building of imitation 'old' structures to harmonise with historic monuments, a practice which he believed transgressed 'the great lesson of history. Never go backwards . . .'.[54] These were uncompromising views, not adhered to to the letter by less architecturally radical town planners, but the reconstruction of damaged historic town centres in France was not conducted *à l'identique*, or in close imitation, as it had been after the First World War, in Arras for example.

Most bombed German cities also gradually acquired a compromise appearance of old where possible and new where necessary. The most extreme example of a total modern replanning of a town there was that of Mainz, where the practical necessity of concrete and straight lines was transformed into a progressive symbol of the redevelopment of German society. Mainz lay within the French-controlled sector of Germany and it was a French architect and town-planner, Marcel Lods, who produced a Le Corbusier-style design to make Mainz 'the world's most modern city'.[55] Few such complete modernist plans had been proposed by German architects and the design was met with suspicion by the Mainz town administration. Senior Councillor Petzold expressed the following concerns:

Intellectual and cultural issues are not peripheral to the replanning process in our cities – they constitute the central problem. The question today is whether we approve wholeheartedly the organisation . . . of our lives according to the principles of the machine and of technology, and in doing so celebrate the triumph of that technology, or whether we perceive a certain danger to humanity, however necessary technology might be in providing for the masses.[56]

An understandable concern, given that it was new 'technology' that had made reconstruction necessary. In addition to this resistance to a futuristic model for the new Mainz, there was also anxiety over the French origin of the plan – it was thought inappropriate, even sinister, that a German city should lose all its former characteristics at the hands of a French architect. This was an interesting reversal of World War One French paranoia about German modernist plans for the rebuilding of bombarded towns in north-eastern France. The modernist 'international style' of architecture was apparently not considered as entirely nation-neutral. Marcel Lods was not approved as architect-in-chief for Mainz in a vote at the town council in April 1948, and his plan was not carried out.[57]

In Germany, there was extra weight and significance to this conflict between those who wanted complete renewal, looking exclusively to the future, and those with more literally conservative opinions on the postwar fate of bombed cities. Architectural tastes had additional connotations of attitudes towards Germany's recent past. A desire to erase the past was countered by the view that it was not necessary to demolish all remnants of the country's architectural heritage, particularly that which had existed long before the advent of the Nazis, even if some architectural styles and some cities had been adopted by them and associated with their cause. In Britain and France, the debate was not as complicated with extra-architectural factors, and the choice of a predominantly contemporary style for the reconstruction of towns was not interpreted as a flight from the past, more as a positive opportunity to improve upon it.

All references to reconstruction in Germany so far have been to that which took place in the former West Germany but a parallel, if differently conceived, rebuilding of historic monuments was carried out in the former East German state. The division of the country into East and West was accompanied by a corresponding split in restoration and reconstruction policy. One consequence of this is that no single publication catalogues the fate of German historic monuments during and after the war – there are instead separate lists for East Germany (Götz, *Schicksale deutscher Baudenkmale im zweiten Weltkrieg*, 1978) and for West Germany (Beseler and Gutschow, *Kriegsschicksale deutscher Architektur*, 1988). Such was the separation administratively and intellectually that even the two sectors of the previously divided Berlin are dealt with separately, one in each book, with the West German story of cultural war damage stopping at the Brandenburg Gate, where the East German story begins.

Both restoration programmes had their own political connotations: while the rebuilding of West Germany was presented as the construction of a 'new' Germany, free of an uncomfortable historical past, the rebuilding of East Germany was presented as symbolic of the 'anti-fascist, democratic and socialist' ideals of this state.[58] The *Kulturpolitik* of East Germany in particular performed an anti-West propaganda role. A conference on cultural war damage was held in Weimar in April 1946 to discuss not only a three-year plan for restoration but also the 'democratisation' of conservation in the Soviet-controlled area, as opposed to the non-democratic conservation policy across the border.[59] What a democratic conservation policy might consist of was not specified. The opposing ideologies of the developing western and eastern Europes structured and found uses for the process of cultural reconstruction.

In East Germany, initially known as the *Ostzone*, the care of historic monuments was the responsibility of the newly-named *Deutsche Zentralverwaltung für Volksbildung* ('German Central Administration for National Education'). Here there was little agonising over the correct style in which to restore such buildings. In the former East Berlin, an area which had contained many of the city's grandest historic monuments, the policy was to rebuild exact copies of what were in many cases complete ruins. The State Opera on Unter den Linden, for example, reappeared in a close approximation of its former self in the 1950s, as did the Altes Museum, the Humboldt University (formerly the Friedrich-Wilhelm-University) with its library, the Zeughaus and the Brandenburg Gate, which was given a new 'quadriga', made on the authority of plaster models and photographs. Even the Unter den Linden lime trees were replanted after the war.

Berlin architecture received relatively early attention, this being the showcase for the new East German state and its cultural policies. Progress was often faster here than in the West, although the areas just behind the impressive 'new' monuments of Unter den Linden were left as wasteland. The most significant historic monuments of other East German cities were also rebuilt, mostly from the 1950s onwards, from the cathedrals of Halberstadt and Magdeburg to Walter Gropius' Bauhaus building in Dessau. Not all important buildings were attended to immediately: in Dresden, work was started on the palatial Zwinger art gallery as early as 1946, but the restoration of other buildings, such as Semper's neo-Renaissance Opera (1837), was not completed until the 1980s, while work has only just begun on others, including the Residenz and the Frauenkirche. The condition of the latter and the possibility of reconstruction were discussed soon after the war in the journal *Die Kunstpflege*:

The Frauenkirche resembles a classical ruin in the extent of its destruction. Only the skeletons of the choir and the north staircase remain standing. But since there exist large scale plans and details of the whole church, . . . in theory at least the reconstruction of the Frauenkirche one day should not be characterised as impossible.[60]

'One day' has become more than sixty years later, as the completion of the restored Frauenkirche is currently planned for 2006. This most symbolic church is just one example of non-reconstruction in East Germany, where many signs of war damage in the form of abandoned ruins are still visible – although it should be added that as late as the 1970s, some areas of West German cities such as Frankfurt still bore some signs of damage, usually in the form of cleared but undeveloped plots of land in the city centres. In the East this was partly a funding problem, but also partly ideological: ruined monuments bombed by the Allies stood as evidence of the barbarity of the evil West. It is interesting that the post-Communist authorities have authorised the reconstruction of the Frauenkirche, no longer needing that particular symbolism but needing a means to encourage tourism instead. The site of the Frauenkirche is now a work-in-progress to be visited, with plans and representations of the past and future structure on show next to the piles of numbered stones, and nearby stalls selling souvenirs such as watches containing a piece of the original church. The British government have contributed a replacement gold cross and orb for the top of the dome, installed on 13 February 2000, the fifty-fifth anniversary of the bombing of Dresden.

East German restoration was also carried out with the aim of claiming 'true' German culture for this side of the border. Restoration priorities in Weimar are interesting in this connection: immediately after the war the Soviet military government rapidly repaired and rebuilt the damaged houses of Schiller and Goethe there. The West German Goethehaus in Frankfurt was being restored at the same time, with the 1949 two-hundredth anniversary of Goethe's birth in mind – an example of the battle for the cultural soul of Germany. This was a race that the East Germans won, as the restoration of their Goethehaus was completed in 1949, in time for the anniversary celebrations, not having been as badly damaged as the Frankfurt house. The preface to a 1959 official publication celebrating the East German restoration achievement made the following claims:

This publication presents the work carried out on these important cultural sites, the property of the German people and thus an inalienable part of our socialist German national culture. The efforts of our state's conservation experts are a clear expression of the positive relationship between our nation and the humanist tradition ... This text illustrates the state of German art and culture on the tenth anniversary of the German Democratic Republic, achieved by the labour of the working people.[61]

The subtext here, not very far beneath the surface, is the essentially un-German nature of *Kultur* in West Germany, hopelessly corrupted by capitalism and the influence of America. The East German position on who was to blame for the ruination of their cities is significant here: primarily to blame were the Nazis and Fascism, followed by the capitalist-imperialist *Bombenterror* of the uncultured West, which continued to control West Germany. By contrast, the heroes of the immediate postwar period in this account were the Soviet soldiers 'who, educated to respect the culture of their own and other nations, ensured the safety of historic monuments'.[62] This piece of postwar cultural propaganda included before-and-after photographs of damaged-then-restored monuments to demonstrate the restorative prowess of the East German system; the Dresden Frauenkirche does not appear in the selection.

EUROPEAN RECONSTRUCTION

If during the war both sides affirmed their belief that the correct and honourable treatment of works of art and architecture in wartime is one of the recognised attributes of the civilised nation and that mistreatment of culture is a sign of barbarism and inhumanity, after the war it was the Allied nations who confidently claimed their particularly civilised status with regard to culture. Respect for historic monuments seems indeed to have been of more interest to Britain and America after the conflict than during. During the war, the fate of historic monuments was primarily the concern of propagandists and those working in the art world, art historians and curators. For those concerned with directing military strategy, culture was of relatively minor interest – a factor which needed to be taken account of for publicity reasons but which never took priority over military objectives. As discussed in Chapter 3, the Allies took care to project an image of cultural concern, particularly during the invasion of Normandy, but their much advertised cultural protection activities took place after the damage had been done. Regrets took the place of precautions and cultural responsibilities were assumed only in the wake of the destruction. The following quotation on the subject of responsibility is from a 1949 Unesco survey of cultural damage:

There is an even greater test we face: the justification of our record in the past war. We justify our own destruction of libraries, museums and laboratories by how we reconstruct during the years that lie ahead. By being the victors we have won the right and the responsibility for determining the nature of the peace. Our air-raids will leave nothing but bitterness, if we neglect and withdraw from the ruins we have caused. We differ not one whit from the barbarians . . . if we can face unmoved the rubble of Caen, St Lo and Falaise . . . We will justify our bombing of Leipzig by rebuilding Warsaw first, then with the citizens of Warsaw rebuild the city of Leipzig.[63]

Interesting here is the assumption that to be considered as non-barbarian it is enough to rebuild after causing damage and that such damage can be justified at all. Cultural destruction provoked some especially convoluted rationalisations on the part of the Allies, always after the event. The most overt official concern had been over the case of Dresden, in the last phase of the conflict, by which time few German cities remained intact.

The damage having been done, the caring and cultured face of the Allies was emphasised in postwar expressions of the importance of cultural reconstruction. Great significance was suddenly attached to this consequence of war and to the problems of monument restoration in the postwar period, on paper at least, if not immediately in practice. The Director-General of Unesco, the wing of the United Nations established in 1946 to raise funds for the rehabilitation of museums, libraries, archives and universities, regretted that the war had 'blasted away the physical underpinnings of civilization in more than a dozen lands . . . [and] educational and cultural reconstruction in the war-devastated countries is more than just a humanitarian need . . . War cut off the mental food supplies of millions'.[64] Optimism was expressed that aid for cultural reconstruction would encourage the populace to rebuild their lives and their countries, with a small amount of this 'inessential' rebuilding motivating a more general revival. A particularly important role was earmarked for museums:

Museums are . . . exceptionally well qualified to foster international understanding. They illustrate each nations' originality and diversity and, simultaneously, the higher unity of art which knows no frontiers and expresses the aspirations of all men toward a finer civilization. Their significance is not limited by language differences, and their methods as well as their treasures have universal appeal.[65]

Thus the reconstruction of a museum could be at the same time a symbol and an engine of peace. It was hoped that the more the thoughts of the populace could be focused on art, the less likely they would be to start another war – a curious optimism, given the recent events. Much hope was pinned on the educational effect of the reconstruction process itself, with the recognition of the irreplaceable nature of works of art and of the sheer material difficulty of rebuilding discouraging a repeat performance.

Unesco's activities did not, however, extend to the actual funding of historic monument reconstruction projects, despite early intentions that this should be one of the organisation's tasks. A proposal for a 'tourist tax' to raise money for cultural reconstruction was rejected and no other major source of finance found. It was eventually decided – under pressure from the Americans – that Unesco could not afford to involve itself in the rebuilding of particular war damaged monuments and that it should restrict its involvement to the establishment of an 'International Centre for the Preservation and Restoration of Cultural Property' in Rome, leaving to individual countries themselves the responsibility for finding the necessary funds for practical reconstruction. This proved a disappointment to many member states who had envisaged a more direct relationship between the United Nations' cultural wing and the devastated historic cities of Europe. In the event, it was the smaller scale business of re-equipping scientific laboratories and libraries which Unesco involved itself in, not the much larger scale rebuilding of whole towns.[66]

If culture in general gained a startlingly increased importance for governments after the war, this was nothing to match the significance suddenly attached to a specifically European culture. The wartime attempts of Nazi propaganda to claim European culture for themselves were discussed in Chapter 3 – this was a European culture characterised as valiantly resisting the foreign, uncivilised Anglo-American threat from the air. After the war American and British commentators adopted their own version of this cultural pan-Europeanism, as did German writers. Books with titles such as *Dämonie der Zerstörung* (1948) and *Lost Treasures of Europe* (1946) supplied lists of damaged historic monuments in all European countries – the latter covered Britain, France, Italy, Germany, and Russia.[67] The message was that 'we have all suffered and we have all transgressed', a shared experience. One American position was to emphasise the cultural links between Europe and America, as Henry La Farge does in the introduction to *Lost Treasures of Europe*:

No matter what her particular contributions are and have been to the civilization and culture of the modern world, America has her own cultural roots deep in the traditions of Europe . . . The effects on our modern structure of society of the democratic ideas, the philosophy and art of

Greece, the political and legal organizations of Rome, and the civic, religious, and artistic developments in Italy, France and Germany during the Middle Ages and the Renaissance are too patent to need further elaboration. Time and time again during the two and a half centuries of our national existence, our political and intellectual leaders as well as our Average American have crossed the seas to make intimate, firsthand contacts with the surviving evidence of past culture.[68]

This portrayal of the Average American clearly contrasted with the version that appeared in Nazi propaganda, that is, the ignorant invader from the land of sky-scrapers and refrigerators. The author did acknowledge that the sense of loss experienced by 'real' Europeans was much greater than that suffered by Americans, but was keen to stress the shared sympathy that stemmed from a common cultural heritage. This was a sentiment wholeheartedly adopted by German commentators too, partly out of a need for American support for the funding of reconstruction projects. This was Paul Clemen's 1946 plea for aid:

Today the whole of Europe and her culture stands trembling and moved by the wounds that this war has left behind – in the whole of Europe. Should we not – we who bear these wounds and who have inflicted them in the course of the war – try to heal them . . . together?[69]

A common heritage suggested a shared guilt and a joint responsibility. The postwar ideal of a European unity founded on common economic concerns is well-known. The European Coal and Steel Community was founded in 1951 to pool resources and production of these two commodities in Germany, France, the Benelux countries and Italy, with the aim of preventing further conflicts, as coal and steel are essential for the waging of war. These political and economic ideals were the basis for what has now developed into the European Union. Less well-known are the contemporary ideas on the role that cultural unity could play in the development of a new and peaceful Europe. The problem, as expressed by the Unesco Director General in 1948, was 'how to transcend nationalism in the field . . . of culture'.[70] A mutually supportive, rather than a competitive, attitude was the postwar aim of organisations such as Unesco, and it was even suggested that states should offer financial support for the cultural reconstruction of other nations – as cross-border damage was all too possible, why should the rebuilding of war damaged historic monuments remain a purely national concern?[71]

This internationalisation of responsibility for monument conservation was the logical conclusion to the argument that historic
monuments were the 'common heritage of mankind', although not
a conclusion that was much supported in practice.

The appeal to a common European culture, to be recognised by
all European nations, was a convenient neutral territory in which
to initiate some form of postwar reconciliation between Germany
and her neighbours. This was an abstract 'territory', not demarcated
by geographical or political frontiers, a zone beyond the concerns
of conflicting and competing nationalities. On cultural ground,
even a Frenchman could be concerned about the condition of a
German historic monument, and vice versa, a sentiment expressed
in 1946 by Georg Lill with an apt reference to similar events during
World War One: 'Anyone who feels deeply about art feels the same
piercing pain when hearing that the cathedral of Reims or the
cathedral of Cologne has been destroyed'.[72] There was optimism
about the healing effects of Allied help with the restoration of
historic monuments – if the Germans could observe some cultural
concern on the part of their former enemies, co-operation with the
occupying military governments might be encouraged, and the
political and social rehabilitation of the country might be accelerated.
One American MFA & A officer, writing of the positive reaction to
cultural aid work such as helping to find materials for emergency
repairs for the Dom in Aachen, concluded: 'Was there, perhaps, in
this mutual confidence and common interest, the germ of something
that might be made to work for world peace at least as effectively as
the disciplinary measures upon which we now rest so much
faith?'.[73] While close co-operation and reconciliation on a political
level might have been inappropriate so soon after the war, the
process could at least begin on a carefully depoliticised patch of
cultural ground.

One commentator went further in predicting that the cultural
sphere was the only area in which Germany could retain any international respect in the postwar period: 'No more power politics
or world trade for Germany. One thing remains to us: not just the
memory that we were a cultural nation of European and world significance, no, more the fact that we still are'.[74] This was something
not entirely under the control of the occupying armies, an aspect of
'new' German society that could be funded by the Marshall Plan
but not completely determined by it, where Germany could keep
some degree of autonomy and self-respect.

For the issue of cultural war damage and postwar cultural

reconstruction to remain 'depoliticised', certain attitudes towards the damage had to be maintained by both sides. A tactful silence on questions of guilt and blame for the destruction was required from the Germans and indeed there were no postwar publications criticising the Allies for the culturally destructive policy of area bombing, just as there had been few in post-liberation France.[75] In German language art historical publications the damage was attributed to 'the war' or to 'the recent events' – the 1949 edition of the Baedeker guide to Stuttgart describes the damage to its former tourist attractions but does not dwell on how it occurred. Even where those who caused the destruction were named, this was simply stated, without the addition of a judgment. This lack of reaction in West Germany contrasted with postwar East German criticism of Allied destruction – here it should be noted that the East Germans were not dependent on America and the Marshall Plan for the funding of reconstruction. The military occupation of the Western zones was also an issue here, since the American, British and French governments controlled all aspects of postwar German life, including the publication of books. This control extended to art history books: conservation official Georg Lill's 1946 *Um Bayerns Kulturbauten. Zerstörung und Wiederaufbau* ('On Bavaria's Cultural Buildings. Destruction and Reconstruction') was issued with 'Military Government Information Control License Number US-E-117' (stated in English inside the front cover of this German language book). The Allies themselves, keeping their part in the cultural neutrality pact, were required to demonstrate a steady interest in the reconstruction of the former enemy's historic monuments. As discussed above, this was done, albeit somewhat unenthusiastically after the initial wave of discoveries of paintings in mines was over.

One jarring note was the initial exclusion of Germany from Unesco – ex-Axis countries were not granted automatic membership to the international cultural club and, while Italy and Austria were admitted in 1947, Polish objections to German membership meant that a Unesco office was only established in Stuttgart in 1948. This also meant the absence of Germany from initial surveys of Europe-wide cultural damage published by Unesco: the postwar needs of museums, libraries and universities in many European countries were covered, but the condition of cultural institutions in Germany were omitted.[76] As these reports were designed to attract funding for cultural and educational reconstruction projects, the exclusion of Germany was not simply a matter of etiquette. The victorious Allies assumed the right to define the entry requirements for the new postwar European cultural alliance and beneath the diplomatic surface lay the not entirely neutral judgement that Germany cities had 'deserved' the destruction of their historic monuments. By contrast, it was assumed that Britain, France, Belgium and Holland and Italy had not deserved the cultural war damage on their territory and therefore had more right to compensation and sympathy. The new West Germany was not in a position to protest, and concentrated instead on cultivating the notion of *die Stunde Null* – the zero hour – where the old culpable Germany stopped and a fresh society and nation began. A destroyed historic city centre could stand as a very concrete symbol of starting from scratch, an architectural tabula rasa.

It was not only governments and international organisations who took an interest in war damaged architecture. Away from the political connotations of postwar historic monument reconstruction, the remains of cultural war damage were being dealt with on a less overtly political level in architectural and tourist guides to the western European countries affected. These publications, often the continuation of series existing before the war, had to decide whether to acknowledge the damage in their postwar editions or to continue as though the historic monuments that were the focus of their texts had not been touched by the recent conflict. The recent violent alterations to their subject matter demanded explanation and rationalisation. Of architectural history reference books issued or reissued in the postwar period, the curious refusal of Nikolaus Pevsner's *An Outline of European Architecture* to refer to the recent war damage has already been discussed in the Introduction. Pevsner's more detailed building-by-building 1952 guide to London in his *Buildings of England* series did address the issue of war damaged architecture, with only the following proviso: 'Nothing is supposed to be included which is not visible. . . . As a rule I try not to mention what has disappeared completely, but give its due to what is only damaged'.[77] Other publications of this kind were also prepared to acknowledge the damage to and occasional disappearance of the object of their studies, albeit with a similar reluctance to delete the ruins from the text completely. This was the approach of Georg Dehio's *Handbuch der Deutschen Kunstdenkmäler*, the comprehensive architectural survey originally published at the beginning of the twentieth century, and reworked by Ernst Gall. Gall's 1950 edition on the historic monuments of the Hessen region (including Frankfurt and Kassel) was the first postwar version of the series to appear and adopted the following strategy for dealing with the fact of war damage: the original entries for ruined monuments were kept, but the sign of the cross was added to indicate their 'death'. Any information on reconstruction so far was also included, thus showing a certain optimism that the wartime destruction was merely a temporary disruption of the normal, continuous history of these buildings. The section on Kassel contains many cross signs and few indications of rebuilding, and would be considerably shorter without the retained detailed descriptions of non-existent architecture.[78] The following year's new edition covering Mainz was equally upbeat: 'The greater part of the *Altstadt* was destroyed by air raids in 1942 and 1945. Reconstruction is making great strides. Nevertheless, Mainz still has much to offer the attentive and thoughtful observer'.[79] A more backward-looking edition was the 1952 survey of *Deutschordensland Preussen* – the prewar name for the area around Gdansk – which had been ready for publication in 1944 but rendered redundant by Germany's loss of this territory.[80] It was decided to issue the book without alteration, an architectural memory of prewar Germany and her former historic monuments.

For a tourist guide-book this mournful memorial role would have been inappropriate, and guides from the postwar period were firmly upbeat in tone, focusing on new attractions for visitors, instead of damaged old sights. By 1949, optimism about the future of the war-damaged German cities was at last possible. The Baedeker guide of that year to Stuttgart managed to recommend at least some sights for the tourist, even though most of the conventional attractions had been destroyed. Despite the incomplete nature of the restoration work, the guide-book's emphasis was all on the great efforts made to improve the city: 'Immediately after the end of the war reconstruction of the city was started by Oberbürgermeister... Klett and pushed forward with untiring diligence and Swabian tenacity'.[81] The implied self-sufficiency and regional pride made Stuttgart seem almost independent, hardly a German city at all. The attractive – and relatively undamaged – modern areas of the city, on the outskirts and in the suburbs, were recommended instead of the *Altstadt*, and twentieth-century attractions such as cinemas, theatres, dance halls, swimming-pools and restaurants were listed as worth visiting, in place of Gothic churches, Renaissance squares and Baroque palaces. Stuttgart was presented as the new, progressive face of redeveloping Germany, with plenty to offer the tourist, including accommodation: 'The number of beds indicated fluctuates according to the progressive rebuilding of the hotels'.[82] As for the general attractiveness of the town centre, there are suspiciously frequent references to the beauty of the surrounding countryside and of the attractive view that the tourist could obtain of the city centre by driving out at night to the hills, but the overall impression is of reconstruction and improvement, of not looking back to the pre-war or the wartime Stuttgart but to the future.

The first postwar English-language edition of the Baedeker guide to London, published in 1951, was perhaps overly positive about the effects of Luftwaffe bombing on the capital's historic monuments, confidently asserting in an entry on St Paul's Cathedral that 'The German air attacks of the Second World War have cleared of buildings a vast area to the North and East of the cathedral, so that the beauty of the exterior can now be better appreciated. Amid this destruction St Paul's survived . . .'.[83] The Baedeker series had suffered an image problem in Britain since the wartime association of its name with the deliberate destruction of historic monuments – 'Baedeker raid' even appeared in the Oxford Dictionary – and, as late as 1966, was still prefacing its guides with avowals that Baedeker was devoted to their appreciation: '. . . Baedeker took no active part in a campaign to destroy these buildings and art treasures which he and his forefathers, for nearly a century, had been at such pains to describe and evaluate'.[84] Again, the guide to London concentrated on new monuments, rather than on recently ruined architecture.

Similar optimism can be detected in the 1949 *Guide Bleu* to Rouen: 'Despite the serious damage caused by the 1939–1945 war, Rouen has retained its status of *ville d'art*'.[85] Here the emphasis was not so much on the complete renewal of the city, but on the elements of the pre-war town that had been preserved and which were gradually returning to their original appearance – guides to French cities perhaps had less need to erase the recent past from memory, as the war damage to historic monuments could in no way be said to be their fault. In the case of Rouen, the plan of the architect and town planner Greber was to rebuild 'a town worthy of its past'.[86] As in the Baedeker guides, an attempt is made to achieve the normal tone of a tourist guide, with some unavoidable post-war-damage remarks: 'Because of repairs in progress to the cathedral, only the north transept and a part of the side aisle . . . can be visited. Nevertheless we describe below the interior as it was before the damage'.[87] With a thorough restoration confidently expected, there was no need to ignore the past.

These tourist guide books also indicate a shared expectation that the tourists would return after the damage and in one case specifically because of the damage: the 1946 *Guide Bleu* to Normandy was subtitled 'Tourist Destinations, the Battlefield Pilgrimage'. While so many cities in western Europe had been altered for the worse by enemy, or sometimes Allied bombing, the impression given by the postwar editions of long established guides is that they were still worth visiting, having retained their essential characters, despite the unusual appearance of their principal sights. Indeed, tourism between nations formerly at war was seen as a possible means of promoting understanding of and sympathy for other countries, with an appreciation of their historic cities and monuments, ruined or otherwise, encouraging European instead of national sympathies, an idea more recently revived by the European Union.

Notes

1. From Kesselring's testimony in *Trial of the Major War Criminals before the International Military Tribunal, Nuremberg*, Vol. IX, Proceedings 8 March–23 March 1946, pp. 178–9.
2. Ibid., p. 190.
3. Interrogation of Göring, ibid., p. 330.
4. Britain received $3,176 million, France $2,706 million and West Germany $1,389 million.
5. This figure is given in a 1958 book published by the Bonn Bundesminister für Vertriebene, Flüchtlinge und Kriegsgeschädigte, *Dokumente Deutscher Kriegsschäden*, Band I, p. X.
6. See Alexander Link, 'Zerstörung und Wiederaufbau' in Keim and Link (eds), *Leben in den Trümmern. Mainz 1945 bis 1948*, pp. 16–17.
7. See for example the essay 'Hoffentlich kein Heldenlied', reproduced in Ranke (ed.), *August Sander. Die Zerstörung Kölns. Photographien 1945–46*. The photographs are mostly of ruined historic monuments, but Böll's text tells of different concerns.
8. Discussed in an article 'La reconstruction des immeubles d'habitation sinistrés', in *Urbanisme*, nos. 5–6, 1950, pp. 22–4.
9. On the postwar housing situation in Britain see Addison, *Now the War is Over. A Social History of Britain 1945–51*, Chapter 3 'A Home of Our Own', pp. 55–85.
10. This despite the fact that planning permission had been given (in 1952). See Thomas, *Coventry Cathedral*, p. 109.
11. See the *Report of the American Commission for the Protection and Salvage of Artistic and Historic Monuments in War Areas*, Section 2. Germany and Austria, pp. 153–4.
12. See Cairncross, *The Price of War. British Policy on German Reparations 1941–1949*, p. 10.
13. Gollancz, *In Darkest Germany*, p. 84 (from the chapter entitled 'The Planning of Ruin').
14. This figure is given by Woolley in *A Record of the Work done by the Military Authorities for the Protection of the Treasures of Art and History in War Areas*, p. 57.
15. Rorimer, *Survival*, pp. 136–7.

16. Details of some of these organisations are given in the *Report of the American Commission for the Protection and Salvage of Artistic and Historic Monuments in War Areas.*

17. Woolley, *A Record of the Work done by the Military Authorities for the Protection of the Treasures of Art and History in War Areas*, pp. 8–9.

18. This episode is discussed in the *Report of the American Commission for the Protection and Salvage of Artistic and Historic Monuments in War Areas*, Section 2 on Germany and Austria, pp. 149–50.

19. See Adenauer's *Memoirs 1945–1953*, pp. 23–4.

20. See the *College Art Journal*, January 1946, vol. 5, no. 2, 'German Paintings in the National Gallery: Official Statement', pp. 75–7, and 'German Painting in the National Gallery: a Protest', pp. 78–82.

21. Clemen, *Rheinische Baudenkmäler und ihr Schicksal. Ein Aufruf an die Rheinländer*, p. 21. Clemen had, of course, already written on First World War architectural damage and reconstruction.

22. The consequences of this problem are described in Metternich's introduction to the *Jahrbuch der rheinischen Denkmalpflege in Nord-Rheinland*, XIX Jahrgang, 1951, special edition on 'Die Baudenkmäler in Nord-Rheinland. Kriegsschaden und Wiederaufbau', p. XIV.

23. Ibid., entry on Cologne, with text by editor Heinz Peters, p. 290.

24. This figure is given in the entry for Aachen in 'Berichte und Verzeichnisse über die Kunstzerstörungen in Deutschland', in *Die Kunstpflege*, no. 1, dated 1947 but published spring 1948, p. 103.

25. On Canterbury see Williamson, *Though the Streets Burn*, p. 306.

26. From a table of estimated costs and completed work in Leymarie, *Art Museums in Need*, p. 12. The slow pace of rebuilding of museums and galleries across western Europe was summarised as follows in 1949: '. . . the reconstruction of museums is proceeding rapidly in Poland and Italy, slowly in France and England, at an average pace in Belgium and Holland, very slowly indeed in Germany' (from Gille-Delafon, 'The Reconstruction of Art Museums', in *Museum*, Vol. II, No. 2, 1949, pp. 72–5.)

27. On the new Coventry Cathedral see *The Times* supplement of 25 May 1962, which includes details on how funding for the construction was raised and an article by the architect Basil Spence, 'Again the Phoenix has Risen'.

28. R. Tavernier, 'Pierres précieuses d'autrefois', in *Urbanisme*, nos. 105–6, 1945, p. 135.

29. The quotation is from Sartre's article 'Paris sous l'occupation', published in *La France Libre*, vol. IX, no. 49, 15 November 1944, pp. 9–18.

30. Methuen, *Normandy Diary*, p. 17.

31. Ibid., also p. 110.

32. See Léon, *La Vie des monuments français. Destruction. Restauration*, pp. 530ff.

33. From the foreword by the editor, Georg Lill, in *Die Kunstpflege*, no. 1, 1947, p. 7 (the journal was known as *Deutsche Kunst und Denkmalpflege* before the war).

34. See Chastel and Babelon, 'La notion de patrimoine' in *Revue de l'art*, No. 49, 1980.

35. The story is told in Thomas, *Coventry Cathedral*, p. 74.

36. From Watson and Abercrombie, *A Plan for Plymouth. The Report prepared for the City Council*, published in 1943, p.16.

37. The remains of Charles Church – the outer walls and west tower – are

now surrounded by a busy roundabout, without pedestrian access, making a visit to this war memorial a hazardous business.

38. Letter to *The Times*, 15 August 1944, 'Ruined City Churches'.

39. From Richards and Summerson (eds), *The Bombed Buildings of Britain*, p. 8.

40. Ibid., p. 7.

41. From letters to *The Times* of 19 August 1944 (from W. L. Munday of Plymouth) and 24 August 1944 (from Gilbert Ledward) respectively.

42. From Clemen, *Rheinische Baudenkmäler und ihr Schicksal. Ein Aufruf an die Rheinländer*, p. 13.

43. On the French policy of preserving some signs of war damage, see the article by Emile Brunet (an architect involved in post-World War One restoration of cathedrals), 'La Restauration de la cathédrale de Soissons', in *Bulletin Monumental*, 1928, pp. 65–99. The same view was expressed after the Second World War by Roberto Pane in an article on 'The restoration of historic buildings after the war', in *Museum*, Vol. III, No. 1, 1950, pp. 78–89.

44. Clemen, *Rheinische Baudenkmäler und ihr Schicksal. Ein Aufruf an die Rheinländer*, p. 37.

45. 'Fragen des Wiederaufbaus in München', in *Kunstchronik*, Heft 9, September 1949, pp. 169–70.

46. On some of the new techniques and materials used in the reconstruction of historic monuments, see Pane, 'The restoration of historic monuments after the war', in *Museum*, Vol. III, No.1, 1950, pp. 78–89.

47. Essays representing the various contemporary points of view are collected in *Kirchen in Trümmern. Was wird aus den Kölner Kirchen?* (edited by the Gesellschaft für christliche Kultur, 1948).

48. The issue was discussed by H. K. Zimmerman in an article 'Wiederaufbau des Frankfurter Goethehauses?' in *Die Kunstpflege*, no. 1, 1947, pp. 51–4. See also the catalogue to the more recent travelling Goethe Institute exhibition *Das Frankfurter Goethe-Haus*, 1999 (arranged to coincide with the 250th anniversary of Goethe's birth).

49. See Mulzer, *Der Wiederaufbau der Altstadt von Nürnberg 1945 bis 1970*.

50. Editorial in *Urbanisme*, nos. 103–4, 1945, p. 2.

51. The exhibition was held from November 1945 to January 1946 in the then Gare des Invalides. See *Urbanisme*, nos. 105–6, 1945.

52. The 1941 issues of *Urbanisme* spread the modernist word on reconstruction and published plans for eventual action.

53. Le Corbusier, *Destin de Paris*, p. 57.

54. Le Corbusier, *La Charte d'Athènes*, paragraphs 66 and 70.

55. Lods, quoted in Keim and Link (eds.), *Leben in den Trümmern. Mainz 1945 bis 1948*, p. 27.

56. Quoted ibid., p. 29.

57. Ibid., p. 29. See also Oppenheim, *Die städtebauliche Entwicklung der Stadt Mainz*, 1948, and *Kultur und Wissenschaft im rheinischen Raum*, 1949.

58. As stated in the preface to Götz, *Schicksale deutscher Baudenkmale im zweiten Weltkrieg*, Band 1.

59. See the article by Strauß, 'Denkmalpflege in der Ostzone. Problemstellung und erste Arbeit', in *Die Kunstpflege*, no.1, dated 1947 but published spring 1948, pp. 79–86.

60. See the entry on Dresden in 'Berichte und Verzeichnisse über die Kunstzerstörungen in Deutschland', ibid., p. 120.

61. From Achilles, *Zehn Jahre Denkmalpflege in der Deutschen Demokratischen Republik*, p. 5.

62. Ibid., p. 7.
63. From Barry, *Libraries in Need*, published by Unesco in 1949.
64. Jaime Torres Bodet, quoted in the Unesco publication by Leymarie, *Art Museums in Need*, foreword.
65. Ibid., p. 15.
66. The gradual exclusion of actual reconstruction from the Unesco brief is recorded in early *Reports of the Director General on the Activities of the Organization* – see in particular those of 1948 and 1952. The 'tourist tax' proposal is discussed in an archive document Unesco/CUA/122, dated 28 June 1963, on the 'Study of Measures for the Preservation of Monuments through the Establishment of an International Fund or by Any Other Appropriate Means'. For a general history of Unesco's early policies, see the study by Jan Opocensky, *The Beginnings of Unesco 1942–1948* (typescript).
67. Alexander Randa's *Dämonie der Zerstörung* was published in Zurich and Henry La Farge's *Lost Treasures of Europe* in New York and London.
68. La Farge, *Lost Treasures of Europe*, pp. 7–8.
69. Clemen, *Rheinische Baudenkmäler und ihr Schicksal. Ein Aufruf an die Rheinländer*, pp. 20–1.
70. Unesco, *Report of the Director General on the Activities of the Organization in 1948*, p. 26.
71. See the *Report of the Director General on the Activities of the Organization in 1949*, section on the 'Historical Monuments Division of the Department of Cultural Activities', pp. 60–1.
72. Lill, *Um Bayerns Kulturbauten. Zerstörung und Wiederaufbau*, p. 20.
73. From Hancock, 'Experiences of a Monuments Officer in Germany', in *College Art Journal*, Vol. V, no. 3, March 1946, pp. 271–311, this quote p. 311.
74. Lill, *Um Bayerns Kulturbauten. Zerstörung und Wiederaufbau*, p. 32.
75. It was not until the early 1960s that the first critical approaches to Second World War bombing began to appear in Germany, for example Hans Rumpf's *Das war der Bombenkrieg. Deutsche Städte im Feuersturm* (1961).
76. See for instance the 1948 report on *Universities in Need* and those compiled by Leymarie, *Art Museums in Need* (1949) and Barry, *Libraries in Need* (1949).
77. Pevsner, *The Buildings of England. London*, 1952 edition, pp. 11–12.
78. See Dehio and Gall, *Handbuch der Deutschen Kunstdenkmäler. Hessen, Vol. I, Nord*, entry on Kassel, pp. 2–16.
79. Dehio and Gall, *Handbuch der Deutschen Kunstdenkmäler. Pfalz und Rheinhessen*, entry on Mainz, pp. 1–50.
80. Dehio and Gall, *Handbuch der Deutschen Kunstdenkmäler. Deutschordensland Preußen*.
81. *Stuttgart und Umgebung*, p. 30. This English translation was published to attract British and American visitors.
82. Ibid., p. 6.
83. Baedeker, *London and its Environs*, 1951 edition, p. 120.
84. Baedeker, *Great Britain, Volume I, Southern England and East Anglia*, 1966 edition, preface, p. vi.
85. Les Guides Bleu, *Rouen*, 1949, p. 3.
86. Ibid., p. 9.
87. Ibid., p. 21.

Conclusion

Physical reminders of the architectural destruction of the Second World War have mostly faded now, the reconstruction of historic monuments and cities now being largely complete, albeit in altered form. Historic monuments in western Europe were inadequately protected, bombed and bombarded with little effort made to avoid them, their consequent ruins then used for propaganda purposes and a mutual exchange of 'barbarian'-style insults between Germany and the Allies, then only very slowly rebuilt, being as little of a priority in practice in postwar Europe as during the conflict – and all this for the second time in the twentieth century, all of these misuses of historic monuments having already been a feature of the First World War. But more than fifty years later the material signs of this episode in the history of the buildings have blended into the fabric of rebuilt towns, although the information is there for those who care to look in the form of commemorative plaques on rebuilt monuments in the midst of redesigned city centres, from Coventry and Plymouth, to Caen and Rouen, to Cologne and Munich, and the occasional ruined church preserved as a war memorial. Apart from the Frauenkirche in Dresden, perhaps the best place for the war damage tourist to find an evocation of extensive architectural destruction is the 'Mitte' district of Berlin, where the 1950s reconstructions of historic monuments on Unter den Linden have aged convincingly, in contrast to the architectural gaps on Wilhelmstrasse, where empty plots and apartment blocks have replaced the destroyed government ministries. But besides these physical traces, there are other lasting effects of twentieth-century cultural war damage to take into the twenty-first century.

The idea of a common European culture promoted with such enthusiasm in the immediate postwar period has survived well beyond the initial burst of anti-nationalist feeling. It is an idea that has appealed most strongly to governments, then as now, who have seen in the notion of European community at a cultural level the means to promote that of political and economic union. A commitment to the promotion of the 'flowering' of a specifically European culture was included as Article 128 of the Maastricht Treaty on European Union (1992). The most recent cultural programme proposed by the European Commission, entitled 'Culture 2000' and intended to run until 2004, gives the following rationale for its existence:

... the acceleration of European integration, with the decision to introduce the euro and the decision ... to start the enlargement process which will eventually lead to a 26-country Union. Faced with this prospect, cultural action must help express a European citizenship based on a knowledge and mutual comprehension of European cultures and an awareness of the features common to such cultures.[1]

Related, if rather nebulous, concepts such as 'cultural co-operation', 'cultural action' and 'a cultural area common to the European people' pepper this document, even the notion of 'cultural rights', whereby the European citizen is said to have a right to the preservation of a separate cultural identity, under the protective umbrella of a common Europeanness. A precise definition of exactly what a purely European culture might consist of appears nowhere in the official literature, but a great official faith in the power of culture to smooth over differences on an international level is demonstrated here, following on in the tradition established with institutions such as Unesco and the Council of Europe (founded in 1949) after the Second World War.[2]

In practice, this hoped-for cultural union has been attempted through a variety of 'cultural actions'. In the specific field of historic monument conservation for instance, 1975 was designated 'European Architectural Heritage Year', an initiative of the Council of Europe joined by the (then) European Community to encourage an interest in architecture and its preservation on the part of both governments and citizens.[3] More recently there has been the Raphael programme, established to contribute funds to historic monument restoration projects across Europe. Besides physical improvements to the buildings, Raphael was also intended to promote public access to 'the European cultural heritage', funding signposting and websites to enable the cultural tourist to find and understand the monuments.[4] Perhaps the most visible cultural project funded by the European Union is the European City of Culture programme, which was launched in 1985 and is still electing cities as temporary cultural capitals of Europe, a year during which events are planned to attract cultural tourists and to impress upon them the specifically European nature of the monuments and historic cities they are visiting.[5] The cultural deficit caused by the architectural destruction of the Second World War is now corrected by this resolute intergovernmental emphasis on preservation.

Despite these efforts to spread the word about a common European heritage, it is uncertain whether the European citizen has received the message. One problem with the cultural programmes described above identified by the European Commission itself is that the public does not seem to be aware of the efforts made on their behalf, due to a lack of publicity of the projects funded for their cultural well-being. They are consequently ignorant of the 'cultural dimension ... to furthering European integration' and perceive the European Union as a purely economic – and possibly sinister – political arrangement, with no cultural cushion to soften the blows of the introduction of the euro, for instance.[6] The European citizen's continuing lack of awareness of a common cultural heritage is related to another problem with the institutional approach to promoting culture: the commitment to the idea of European culture is not matched by adequate funding. The budget for culture is relatively small: the 1997–2000 Raphael programme was allocated 30 million ecu (the pre-euro currency), while the proposed budget for the 'Culture 2000' programme is 167 million euro for the period 2000–2004.[7] The latter figure in particular may seem a substantial sum of money but must cover the whole of Europe and a large number of projects besides the conservation of historic monuments and cities for five years. The problem is a familiar one – the symbolic value and glossy appeal of the cultural sphere is useful for propaganda purposes, in peacetime as during war, but there is great reluctance to pay for its upkeep. The European institutions have correctly identified the idea of a Europe-wide common culture as one of the more attractive and accessible elements of their overall project, but leave most of the costs of culture on the ground to the individual member states – who may want to take the credit for preserving their cultural heritage themselves, rather than passing it to the European Union.

Another response of the international community to the destruction of art and architecture during the Second World War was to revise the international law that had so thoroughly failed to protect cultural property in wartime, too weakly worded to deter transgression on all sides. In 1954 new measures were introduced for the protection of art and architecture during wartime, in the form of a new Hague Convention – the first since 1907 – entitled the 'Hague Convention for the Protection of Cultural Property in the Event of Armed Conflict'. This treaty, drafted under the aegis of Unesco, was agreed and signed in 1954 by all the major European powers, the United States and the Soviet Union (although the process of ratification by individual governments took rather longer) and is still in force today.[8] It was the first such treaty to be devoted entirely to the safeguarding of historic monuments and mobile works of art in wartime, previous Hague Conventions having condensed provisions for culture into a few inadequate and overlooked articles.

The 1954 Convention was intended to develop the international legal protection for art and architecture significantly and its more innovatory articles demonstrate some progress made on the unsatisfactory 1907 version. The treaty opens with the following declaration of its ambitions:

The High Contracting Parties, Recognising that cultural property has suffered grave damage during recent armed conflicts and that, by reason of the developments in the technique of warfare, it is in increasing danger of destruction; Being convinced that damage to cultural property belonging to any people whatsoever means damage to the cultural heritage of all mankind, since each people makes its contribution to the culture of the world; . . . Have agreed upon the following provisions.[9]

It is not at all obvious, however, how a greater degree of protection would be achieved on the basis of this treaty. Article 1 defines the term 'cultural property' in the same way as earlier treaties, as historic monuments, public and private art collections, libraries and archives, and adds to this list 'centres containing monuments', that is areas in which large amounts of cultural property are located, such as historic city centres – a response to the nature of Second World War bombing. Article 3 introduces a new requirement: 'The High Contracting Parties undertake to prepare in time of peace for the safeguarding of cultural property situated within their own territory against the foreseeable effects of armed conflict'. A more pragmatic approach is adopted here towards the wartime threat to art and architecture, in that countries are given more responsibility for the survival of their own cultural property and are encouraged to expect and to prepare for damage, instead of relying upon the honourable behaviour of their enemies, then complaining when this does not materialise. Another new measure appears in Article 4, paragraph 1: 'The High Contracting Parties undertake to respect cultural property situated within their own territory as well as within the territory of other High Contracting Parties by refraining from any use of the property and its immediate surroundings . . . for purposes which are likely to expose it to destruction or damage in the event of armed conflict . . .'. Unfortunately, while both these articles would have at least made illegal certain World War One abuses of historic monuments – the use of cathedral towers as observation posts for instance – neither seem relevant to the pre-vention of damage caused by area bombing, the principle method used in World War Two. The prudent placing of sandbags and the distancing of military installations from historic monuments had proved no protection against the indiscriminate bombing of city centres, making these supposedly improved legal provisions out-dated even by 1939–45 standards, let alone those of the nuclear age.

The weaknesses of the 1954 Convention were discussed at a 1962 conference for participating countries, including the reappearance of the traditional 'except in case of military necessity' let-out clause in Article 4, paragraph 2, which stated that a country was permitted to exploit its own historic monuments for military purposes in these circumstances. This was at least a more restricted application than in the 1907 Convention, which also allowed bombardment of the enemy's monuments 'in case of military necessity', but still left undefined the precise nature of this necessity, leaving room for abuses.[10] Conference delegates recommended that this should be replaced with a more concrete regulation, not open to interpretation, although it was recognised that the establishment of absolutely 'uniform and universally valid rules' in this area was impossible.[11] Against this last point, it might be argued that the whole purpose of having such rules at all was to affirm the 'absolute' or universally acknowledged value of historic monuments and the unmitigable unjustifiability of failure to protect or avoid damaging them in wartime. The post-Second World War ruins of so many monuments and historic cities in western Europe were testimony to the rela-tivist approach of 'only wrong in certain circumstances', where these circumstances were defined to suit the needs and conscience of whoever was doing the damage. The conference concluded with the adoption of the following pessimistic resolution: '. . . in the present state of armaments production technique, the most reliable guarantee for preserving cultural property and, hence, for achieving the aims of the Convention, lies in general and complete disarmament under effective international control'.[12] Thus expert opinion on the principal international treaty protecting art and architecture in wartime judged that the only way to avoid cultural war damage was not to have wars.

If the protection measures for architecture contained in the 1954 Hague Convention seem inadequate on paper, they have also been proved so in practice in more recent conflicts on European soil. In the former Yugoslavia the treaty has been found to have no more preventive, or indeed punitive, power than the 1907 Convention. The following assessment of the treaty in action was made in 1991 during the conflict in Bosnia, at the Annual Conference on Museum Security: 'This is the first time that the Hague Convention is being applied in a real war in Europe. Its weakness is seen in its slowness and the series of formal procedures which obstruct necessary rapid action'.[13] Many historic monuments were used as weapons and ammunition stores or barracks, rather than being protected, and many were targeted, regardless of military necessity. On this evidence, the protection of art and architecture in armed conflict was no more a priority during this recent war than during the earlier wars of the twentieth century, and neither international law nor the protestations of the sanctity, immunity and neutrality of cultural property have, it seems, prevented its destruction and theft. As one commentator expressed it: 'The appropriate flags have been flown (both of the Hague Convention and of Unesco); but these do not repel shells unless they are backed up by action by the international community'.[14]

A study of the law as it applied to the situation in Bosnia concluded that the law, as established in the 1954 Hague Convention, had been broken and that consequently those responsible for cultural war crimes should eventually be brought before the International Criminal Tribunal for the Former Yugoslavia in The Hague.[15] This after-the-event judiciary role would seem to be the only practical function for the 1954 Convention as it stands, given its lack of preventive power. No indictments have been made as yet for illegal cultural war damage and whether the Tribunal has the will or the resources to investigate this category of war crime seems unlikely, throwing doubt on even the punitive function of the Convention.[16] Discussions have been held on how the 1954 treaty might achieve a more actively preventive function, although attention has focused on the development of more effective methods of damage limitation in the event of an attack on cultural property, and on the publication of a manual advising on these methods, rather than on deterring such attacks in the first place.[17] A similar manual was produced after the architectural destruction of the Second World War, indicating the lack of policy progress made since then.[18] This is a disappointing state of affairs following the centenary of the first international laws protecting works of art in wartime, as contained in the Hague Convention of 1899.

Despite all moral debate and establishment of legal protection measures, cultural property was and is regularly sacrificed to military strategy, regardless of a frequently reiterated devotion to its preservation on the part of most governments. A fundamental vagueness surrounding the precise value to be attributed to art becomes apparent as soon as a conflict arises between the stated policy of unconditional protection and the often opposing demands arising from a situation of armed conflict. Historic monuments can be of central importance to the life of a country, of incalculable value, lying at the very heart of national culture (if a nation's cathedrals are being bombed by the enemy), or can be expendable, an ultimately superfluous manifestation of non-essential creativity (if a nation's forces are bombing the cathedrals of its enemy).

The often taken-for-granted belief in a universal respect for art is subject to the most fundamental of tests during a war: if a genuine importance were placed on the continuing existence of historic monuments and cultural property in general, how could their destruction be justified? And if it can be justified – or certain parties make strenuous efforts to do so – what does this tell us about the value traditionally placed on art? Given the value commonly attached to what is today called cultural heritage, a nation which declared a lack of interest in the preservation of art and architecture would risk being judged uncivilised. During the Second World War this unspoken rule was placed under great pressure. While an official support for the ideal of the 'sanctity' of art was maintained by both the Allies and Germany, in the press and in propaganda publications in particular, little was done on either side to avoid damage to and destruction of the cultural property of the enemy, quite apart from the cases of active targeting. The avoidance of cultural damage was not in practice a universal priority, even if generally professed as such. This may be interpreted as pragmatism or, more negatively, as neglect; what is interesting is the effort put into maintenance of the official position of the great importance of art, especially after the damage was done.

Notes

1. From the European Commission document *First European Community Framework Programme in Support of Culture, 2000–2004*, 98/0169 (COD), dated 6 May 1998, p. 3.
2. The impulse has been supported with a range of postwar international charters and treaties intended to protect historic monuments. On the European level there is the 'Convention for the Protection of the Architectural Heritage of Europe' (1985), and the 'European Convention on the Protection of the Archaeological Heritage' (1992); applying world-wide are the 'Charter of Venice – International Charter for the Conservation and Restoration of Historic Monuments and Towns' (1964), and the 'Unesco World Heritage Convention Concerning the Protection of the World Cultural and Natural Heritage' (1972).
3. On the commitment of the European Community to this initiative see for instance the *Official Journal of the European Communities*, No. L21/23, 28 January 1975 and No. C156/27–28, 10 December 1974.
4. For the period 1997–2000, around 200 historic monuments received funds for conservation and publicity – see ibid., pp. 7–8. On the scope of the Raphael programme, see the *Official Journal of the European Communities*, No. C219, 18 July 1997.
5. A notable success within this programme was the year devoted to Glasgow (1990) which re-established the city as a tourist destination. In 1999 Weimar was the European City of Culture and in 2000 the title is shared between nine cities across Europe, some in countries which are not yet part of the European Union: Avignon, Bergen, Bologna, Brussels, Kraków, Helsinki, Prague, Reykjavik and Santiago de Compostela.
6. On this point, see the *First European Community Framework Programme in Support of Culture*, p. 5.
7. Ibid., pp. 7–8 and p. 16. The document contains a breakdown of the costs.
8. Ratification is the essential step of transferring the content of international treaties into the laws of individual countries. By 1962, states which had signed the 1954 treaty but had not yet ratified it and thus become fully party to the Convention included Britain, the United States and West Germany. East Germany ratified only in 1974.
9. The full text is included in International Committee of the Red Cross, *International Law Concerning the Conduct of Hostilities. Collection of Hague Conventions and Some Other Treaties.*
10. The title of the conference, held at Unesco House in Paris 16–25 July 1962, was 'First Meeting of the High Contracting Parties to the Convention for the Protection of Cultural Property in the Event of Armed Conflict'. The proceedings are recorded in an archive document Unesco/CUA/120. On the military necessity issue, see para. 19.
11. Ibid., paras. 12 & 13.
12. Ibid., para. 22.
13. The Conference was held in Vienna, October 1991. The quotation is from a paper on 'Present Conditions in Museums and Galleries in Croatia', published in *Informatica Museologica* 1991, 1–4 (XXII), Zagreb 1992. The former Yugoslavia ratified the 1954 Convention as early as 1956.
14. Council of Europe, Doc. 6756, *Information Report on the destruction by war of the cultural heritage in Croatia and Bosnia-Herzegovina*, 2 February 1993, pp. 9–10. The 1999 conflict in Kosovo is too recent for

there to be any assessment of cultural damage there, but some reports of deliberate misuse and targeting of historic monuments have been made – see for instance the reports 'Bomb blasts new Serbian cathedral' and 'Churches symbols of occupation' in *The Independent* of 2 August 1999.

15. Patrick J. Boylan, *Review of the Convention for the Protection of Cultural Property in the Event of Armed Conflict (The Hague Convention of 1954)*, Unesco 1994. The United Nations International Criminal Tribunal for the Former Yugoslavia was established in November 1993, to deal with crimes committed in the former Yugoslavia since 1991. On the suggestion that it should prosecute cultural crimes, see Council of Europe, Doc. 6999, *Fourth Information Report on war damage to the cultural heritage in Croatia and Bosnia-Herzegovina*, 19 January 1994, pp. 27–8. See also Council of Europe, Doc. 7401, *Opinion on the situation in some parts of the former Yugoslavia*, 26 September 1995.

16. The many indictments of the Bosnian-Serb leadership include, however, that of 'the systematic infliction of damage and destruction on both Muslim and Roman Catholic sacred sites' – see United Nations General Assembly, Security Council, *Report of the International Tribunal for the Prosecution of Persons Responsible for Serious Violations of International Humanitarian Law Committed in the Territory of the Former Yugoslavia Since 1991*, 23 August 1995, paras. 59–62; see also International Criminal Tribunal for the Former Yugoslavia, Press Release 25 July 1995, *Indictment: Radovan Karadzic and Ratko Mladic*, paras. 19, 30–1, 38–9. The violation of the laws and customs of war referred to so far has been the destruction of places of worship, not of cultural property – although churches can, of course, be both and it is interesting to note which aspect of the buildings has been chosen for prosecution purposes.

17. In October 1992 a joint meeting was held on this issue in the Hague between representatives of Unesco and Icomos (International Council on Monuments and Sites). See Council of Europe, Doc. 6869, *Second Information Report on war damage to the cultural heritage in Croatia and Bosnia-Herzegovina*, 17 July 1993, p. 21.

18. Lavachery & Noblecourt, *Les Techniques de protection des biens culturels en cas de conflit armé*, published by Unesco in 1954.

Bibliography

Achilles, Leopold (ed., Im Auftrag des Ministeriums für Kultur der Deutschen Demokratischen Republik) (1959), *Zehn Jahre Denkmalpflege in der Deutschen Demokratischen Republik*, Leipzig: Seemann Buch- und Kunstverlag

Addison, Paul (1985), *Now the War is Over. A Social History of Britain 1945–51*, London: Jonathan Cape

Adenauer, Konrad (1966), *Memoirs 1945–53* (trans. Beate Ruhm von Oppen), London: Weidenfeld and Nicolson

Akinsha, Konstantin and Grigorii Kozlov (1995), *Beautiful Loot: the Soviet Plunder of Europe's Art Treasures*, New York: Random House

Akinsha, Konstantin and Grigorii Kozlov (1995), *Stolen Treasure: the Hunt for the World's Lost Masterpieces*, London: Weidenfeld and Nicholson

Alexandre, Arsène (1918), *Les Monuments français détruits par l'Allemagne*, Paris and Nancy

Andrews, Julian (ed.) (1980), *Sutherland: The Wartime Drawings*, London: Sotheby Parke Bernet Publications

Anthony-Thouret, Pierre (1923), *Le Crime de Reims après le crime de Louvain*, Paris

Baedeker, Karl (1949), *Stuttgart und Umgebung*, Stuttgart: Frank'sche Verlagshandlung

Baedeker, Karl (1951), *Handbook for Travellers. London and its Environs*, London: Allen and Unwin

Baedeker, Karl (1961), *Handbook for Travellers. Cologne and Bonn with Environs*, London: Allen and Unwin

Baedeker, Karl (1966), *Handbook for Travellers. Great Britain. Volume I: Southern England and East Anglia*, London: Allen and Unwin

Balfour, Michael (1979), *Propaganda in War 1939–1945. Organisations, Policies and Publics in Britain and Germany*, London: Routledge and Kegan Paul

Barry, Joseph (1949), *Libraries in Need*, Paris: Unesco

Bartov, Omer (1985), *The Eastern Front 1941–45. German Troops and the Barbarisation of Warfare*, London: Macmillan

Bell, George (1946), *The Church and Humanity (1939–1946)*, London: Longmans, Green and Co.

Beseler, Hartwig and Niels Gutschow (1988), *Kriegsschicksale deutscher Architektur. Verluste – Schäden – Wiederaufbau*, 2 vols, Neumünster: Karl Wachholtz Verlag

Best, Geoffrey (1983), 'The Bishop and the Bomber', *History Today*, September 1983, pp. 28–32

Best, Geoffrey (1994), *War and Law Since 1945*, Oxford: Clarendon Press

Betjemen, John (1944), *John Piper*, Harmondsworth, Middlesex: Penguin Books

Boelcke, Willi A. (ed.) (1967), *'Wollt Ihr den totalen Krieg?' Die geheimen Goebbels-Konferenzen 1939–1943*, Stuttgart: Deutsche Verlags-Anstalt (published in an English translation (trans. by Ewald Osers) with the title *The Secret Conferences of Dr. Goebbels. The Nazi Propaganda War 1939–43*, New York: Dutton and Co. 1970)

Böll, Heinrich, 'Hoffentlich kein Heldenlied' in Ranke, Winfried (1985), *August Sander. Die Zerstörung Kölns. Photographien 1945–46*, Munich: Schirmer/Mosel

Bonn, Bundesminister für Vertriebene, Flüchtlinge und Kriegsgeschädigte (1960), *Dokumente deutscher Kriegsschäden. Evakuierte – Kriegssachgeschädigte – Währungsgeschädigte. Die geschichtliche und rechtliche Entwicklung. Beiheft I: Aus den Tagen des Luftkrieges und des Wiederaufbaues: Erlebnis und Erfahrungsberichte*

Bouret-Aubertot, J. (1923), *Les Bombardements Aériens*, Paris

Botting, Douglas (1985), *In the Ruins of the Reich*, London: Allen and Unwin

Boylan, Patrick J. (1994), *Review of the Convention for the Protection of Cultural Property in the Event of Armed Conflict (The Hague Convention of 1954)*, Paris: Unesco

Briggs, Martin S. (1952), *Goths and Vandals. A Study of the Destruction, Neglect and Preservation of Historical Buildings in England*, London: Constable Publisher

British Committee on the Preservation and Restoration of Works of Art, Archives and Other Material in Enemy Hands (1945), *Works of Art in Italy. Losses and Survivals in the War, Vol. 1 – South of Bologna*, London: HMSO

British Committee on the Preservation and Restoration of Works of Art, Archives and Other Material in Enemy Hands (1946), *Works of Art in Italy. Losses and Survivals in the War, Vol. 2 – North of Bologna*, London: HMSO

British Committee on the Preservation and Restoration of Works of Art, Archives and Other Material in Enemy Hands (1946), *Works of Art in Germany (British Zone of Occupation). Losses and Survivals in the War*, London: HMSO

British Museum (1939), *Air Raid Precautions in Museums, Picture Galleries and Libraries*, London: British Museum

Brunet, Emile (1928), 'La Restauration de la cathédrale de Soissons', in *Bulletin monumentale*, 1928, pp. 64–99

Cairncross, Alec (1986), *The Price of War. British Policy on German Reparations 1941–1949*, Oxford: Basil Blackwell Ltd

Calder, Angus (1991), *The Myth of the Blitz*, London: Jonathan Cape

Campbell, Louise (1996), *Coventry Cathedral. Art and Architecture in Post-war Britain*, Oxford: Clarendon Press

Carpentier, Paul (1916), *Les Lois de la guerre continentale*, Paris

Cassou, Jean (1947), *Le Pillage par les Allemands des oeuvres d'art et des bibliothèques appartenant à des Juifs en France*, Paris: Editions du Centre de Documentation Juive Contemporaine

Chastel, André and J.-P. Babelon, 'La notion de patrimoine', in *Revue de l'art*, no. 49, 1980

Chambry, L. (1915), *The Truth About Louvain*, London

Churchill, Winston S. (1941), *Speeches and Addresses. Into Battle...*, London: Cassell

Churchill, Winston S. (1943), *The End of the Beginning. War Speeches 1942*, London: Cassell

Churchill, Winston S. (1944), *Onwards to Victory. War Speeches 1943*, London: Cassell

Clemen, Paul (1914), 'Unser Schutz der Kunstdenkmäler im Kriege', *Internationale Monatsschrift für Wissenschaft, Kunst und Technik*, Band IX, Heft 5, 1 December 1914, pp. 303–16

Clemen, Paul and Cornelius Gurlitt (1916), *Die Klosterbauten der Cisterzienser in Belgien*, Berlin

Clemen, Paul (ed.) (1919), *Kunstschutz im Kriege. Berichte über den Zustand der Kunstdenkmäler auf den verschiedenen Kriegsschauplätzen und über die deutschen und österreichischen Maßnahmen zu ihrer Erhaltung, Rettung, Erforschung*, Leipzig: E. A. Seemann Verlag

Clemen, Paul (1946), *Rheinische Baudenkmäler und ihr Schicksal. Ein Aufruf and die Rheinländer*, Düsseldorf: Schwann

Collier, Basil (1947), *The Defence of the United Kingdom*, London: HMSO

Commission des crimes de guerre en Belgique (1946), *Les Crimes de guerre commis lors de l'invasion du territoire national – Mai 1940 – La Destruction de la Bibliothèque de Louvain*, Brussels: Ministère de la Justice

Conférence de Bruxelles (1874), *Actes de la Conférence de Bruxelles, 1874*, Brussels

Cooper, Matthew (1981), *The German Air Force 1933–1945. An Anatomy of Failure*, London, New York and Sydney: Jane's

Council of Europe, Doc. 6904 (1993), *Third Information Report on war damage to the cultural heritage in Croatia and Bosnia-Herzegovina*, presented by the Committee on Culture and Education, Strasbourg, 20 September 1993 (the first Information Report on this subject was issued 2 February 1993 and the ninth and last Report on 19 January 1996)

Council of Europe, Doc. 7401 (1995), *Opinion on the situation in some parts of the former Yugoslavia*, Strasbourg 26 September 1995

Craig, Gordon A. (1978), *Germany 1866–1945*, Oxford: Clarendon Press

Darcel, Alfred, 'Les Musées, les arts et les artistes pendant le siège de Paris', *Gazette des Beaux-Arts*, 2e période, tome IV, 1 October 1871, pp. 285–306 and 1 November 1871, pp. 414–29

Darcel, Alfred, 'Les Musées, les arts et les artistes pendant la Commune', *Gazette des Beaux-Arts*, 2e période, tome V, 1872, pp. 41–65, 140–58, 210–29, 398–418 and 479–90

Dayot, Armand (1901), *L'Invasion, le Siège 1870, la Commune 1871, d'après des peintures, gravures, photographies, sculptures, médailles, autographes, objets du temps*, Paris

Dehio, Georg and Ernst Gall (1950), *Handbuch der Deutschen Kunstdenkmäler: Nördliches und Südliches Hessen*, 2 vols., Munich and Berlin: Deutscher Kunstverlag

Dehio, Georg and Ernst Gall (1951), *Handbuch der Deutschen Kunstdenkmäler: Pfalz und Rheinhessen*, Munich and Berlin: Deutscher Kunstverlag

Dehio, Georg and Ernst Gall (1952), *Handbuch der Deutschen Kunst-denkmäler: Deutschordensland Preußen*, Munich and Berlin: Deutscher Kunstverlag

Dickens, Arthur Geoffrey (1947), *Lübeck Diary*, London: Gollancz

Diefendorf, Jeffry M. (ed.) (1990), *Rebuilding Europe's Bombed Cities*, London: Macmillan

Diefendorf, Jeffry M. (1993), *In the Wake of War. The Reconstruction of German Cities after World War II*, Oxford: Oxford University Press

Durth, Werner and Niels Gutschow (1988), *Träume in Trümmern. Planungen zum Wiederaufbau zerstörter Städte im Westen Deutschlands 1940–1950*, Braunschweig/Wiesbaden

European Commission (1998), *First European Community Framework Programme in Support of Culture (2000–2004)*, Brussels

Feliciano, Hector (1995), *Le Musée disparu*, Paris: Austral

Fischbach, G. (1871), *Le Siège et le bombardement de Strasbourg*, Paris

Foss, Brian (1991), 'Message and Medium: Government Patronage, National Identity and National Culture in Britain 1939–45', *The Oxford Art Journal*, vol. 14, no. 2 1991, pp. 52–72

Frankland, Noble (1965), *The Bombing Offensive against Germany. Outlines and Perspectives*, London: Faber and Faber

Frankland, Noble (1970), *Bomber Offensive. The Devastation of Europe*, London: Macdonald and Co.

Gamboni, Dario (1997), *The Destruction of Art. Iconoclasm and Vandalism since the French Revolution*, London: Reaktion Books

Garlake, Margaret (1998), *New Art New World. British Art in Postwar Society*, London and Newhaven: Yale University Press

Garner, James W. (1920), *International Law and the World War* (2 vols), London and New York

Garrett, Stephen A. (1993), *Ethics and Air Power in World War II. The British Bombing of German Cities*, London: Macmillan

Gesellschaft für christliche Kultur (1948), *Kirchen in Trümmern. Zwölf Vorträge zum Thema: Was wird aus den Kölner Kirchen?*, Cologne

Gille-Delafon, S. (1949), 'The Reconstruction of Art Museums', in *Museum*, vol. II, no. 2, pp. 72–5

Goebbels, Joseph (1943), *Das Eherne Herz. Reden und Aufsätze aus den Jahren 1941–42*, Munich: Zentralverlag der NSDAP/Franz Eher

Goebbels, Joseph (1944), *Der Steile Aufstieg. Reden und Aufsätze aus den Jahren 1942–43*, Munich: Zentralverlag der NSDAP/Franz Eher

Goebbels, Joseph (ed. Rolf Hochhuth) (1977), *Tagebücher 1945. Die letzten Aufzeichnungen*, Hamburg: Hoffmann und Campe Verlag

Goethe Institute (1999), *Das Frankfurter Goethe-Haus*

Gollancz, Victor (1947), *In Darkest Germany*, London: Gollancz

Gosset, André and Lecomte, Paul (1946), *Caen pendant la bataille*, Caen: Ozanne et Cie

Götz, Eckhardt (ed.) (1978), *Schicksale deutscher Baudenkmale im zweiten Weltkrieg. Eine Dokumentation der Schäden und Totalverluste auf dem Gebiet der Deutschen Demokratischen Republik*, 2 vols, Berlin (DDR): Henschelverlag, Munich: Verlag C. H. Beck

Grautoff, Otto (ed.) (1915), *Die Kunstverwaltung in Frankreich und Deutschland*, Bern: Verlag Max Drechsel

Green, S. M. (n.d.), *The Story of the Exeter Blitz*, Exeter: A. Wheaton and Co. Ltd

Les Guides Bleus (1949), *Rouen*, Paris: Hachette

Les Guides Bleus (1956), *Normandie*, Paris: Hachette

Hagemann, Walter (1948), *Publizistik im Dritten Reich. Ein Beitrag zur Methodik der Massenführung*, Hamburg: Hansischer Gildenverlag

Hampe, Erich (1963), *Der Zivile Luftschutz im Zweiten Weltkrieg. Dokumentation und Erfahrungsberichte über Aufbau und Einsatz*, Frankfurt am Main: Bernard und Graefe Verlag

Hancock, Walker (1946), 'Experiences of A Monuments Officer in Germany' in *College Art Journal*, vol. V, no. 3, pp. 271–311

Handfest, Irene (1985), *Der Luftkrieg in Nürnberg. Quellen des Stadtarchivs zum 2.Januar 1945*, Nuremberg: Stadtarchiv Nürnberg

Harclerode, Peter and Brendan Pittaway (1999), *The Lost Masters: the Looting of Europe's Treasurehouses*, London: Gollancz

Harries, Meirion and Susie (1983), *The War Artists. British Official War Art of the Twentieth Century*, London: Michael Joseph, in association with the Imperial War Museum and the Tate Gallery

Harris, Arthur (1947), *Bomber Offensive*, London: Collins

Harris, Arthur (1995), *Despatch on War Operations 23rd February 1942 to 8th May 1945*, London: Frank Cass

Hautecoeur, Louis (1948), *Les Beaux-Arts en France, passé et avenir*, Paris: Picard

Hogan, Michael J. (1987), *The Marshall Plan. America, Britain and the reconstruction of Western Europe, 1947–1952*, Cambridge: Cambridge University Press

Hogg, Ian V. (1992), *The Encyclopedia of Weaponry*, London: Quarto Publishing

Horne, Alistair (1965), *The Fall of Paris. The Siege and the Commune 1870–1871*, London: Macmillan

Horne, Alistair (1969), *To Lose a Battle. France 1940*, London: Macmillan

Howard, Michael (1961), *The Franco-Prussian War: the German Invasion of France 1870–1871*, London: Hart-Davis

Howard, Michael (ed.) (1979), *Restraints on War. Studies in the Limitation of Armed Conflict*, Oxford: Oxford University Press

Howard, Richard Thomas (1941), *The Story of the Destruction of Coventry Cathedral, November 14th, 1940*, Gloucester: British Publishing Co.

Howard, Richard Thomas (1962), *Ruined and Rebuilt. The Story of Coventry Cathedral 1939–1962*, Coventry: Coventry Cathedral Council

Hubatsch, Walther (1962), *Hitlers Weisungen für die Kriegsführung 1939–1945. Dokumente des Oberkommandos der Wehrmacht*, Frankfurt am Main

Iklé, Fred Charles (1958), *The Social Impact of Bomb Destruction*, Norman: University of Oklahoma Press 1958

International Committee of the Red Cross (1989), *International Law Concerning the Conduct of Hostilities. Collection of Hague Conventions and some other Treaties*, Geneva: Red Cross

Irving, David J. (1963), *The Destruction of Dresden*, London: William Kimber and Co. Ltd

Irving, David J. (1963), *Und Deutschlands Städte starben nicht. Ein Dokumentarbericht*, Zurich: Schweizer Druck- und Verlagshaus AG

Jankowski, Stanislaw, 'Warsaw: Destruction, Secret Town Planning 1939–1944 and Postwar Reconstruction' in Diefendorf, Jeffry M. (ed.) (1990), *Rebuilding Europe's Bombed Cities*, London: Macmillan

Keegan, John (1982), *Six Armies in Normandy*, London: Cape
Keegan, John (1995), *The Battle for History. Re-fighting World War Two*, London: Hutchinson
Keim, Anton Maria and Alexander Link (eds) (1985), *Leben in den Trümmern. Mainz 1945 bis 1948*, Mainz: Mainz Edition
Kent, William (1947), *The Lost Treasures of London*, London: Phoenix House Ltd
Kessler, Leo (1979), *The Great York Air Raid. The Baedeker Bombing Attack on York, April 29th, 1942*, Clapham: Dalesman Books
Kettenacker, Lothar (1997), *Germany since 1945*, Oxford: Oxford University Press
Kirwin, Gerald (1985), 'Allied Bombing and Nazi Domestic Propaganda', *European History Quarterly*, vol. 15, no. 3, July 1985, pp. 341–62
Kris, Ernst and Hans Speier (1944), *German Radio Propaganda. Report on Home Broadcasts during the War*, New York and London: Oxford University Press
La Farge, Henry (1946), *Lost Treasures of Europe*, London: Batsford Ltd and New York: Pantheon Books Ltd
Lambourne, Nicola (1999), 'Production versus Destruction: Art, World War I and Art History' in *Art History*, vol. 22, no. 3, September 1999, pp. 347–63
Landrieux, Maurice (1919), *La Cathédrale de Reims. Un Crime Allemand*, Paris
Lane, Barbara Miller (1968), *Architecture and Politics in Germany 1918–1945*, Cambridge, MA: Harvard University Press
Larsson, L. O., *Die Neugestaltung der Reichshauptstadt. Speers General-bebauungsplan für Berlin*
Lavachery, H. and A. Noblecourt (1954), *Les Techniques de protection des biens culturels en cas de conflit armé*, Paris: Unesco
Le Corbusier (1941), *La Charte d'Athènes*, Paris: Plon
Le Corbusier (1941), *Destin de Paris*, Paris: Editions Fernand Sorlot
Léon, Paul (1917), *Les Monuments historiques, conservation, restauration*, Paris: Picard
Léon, Paul (1951), *La Vie des monuments français, destruction, restauration*, Paris: Picard
Léon, Paul (1955), '1939–1955. Les Monuments' in *Les Monuments his-toriques de la France*, January–March 1955, pp. 3–8
Leymarie, Jean (1949), *Art Museums in Need*, Paris: Unesco
Lill, Georg (1946), *Um Bayerns Kulturbauten. Zerstörung und Wiederaufbau*, Munich: Drei-Fichten-Verlag
Lill, Georg (1948), *Zerstörte Kunst in Bayern*, Munich: Verlag Schnell und Steiner
Link, Alexander, 'Zerstörung und Wiederaufbau' in Keim, Anton Maria and Link (eds) (1985), *Leben in den Trümmern. Mainz 1945 bis 1948*, Mainz: Mainz Edition, pp. 13–32
Lochner, Louis P. (ed. and trans.) (1948), *The Goebbels Diaries 1942–1943*, New York: Doubleday
Longmate, Norman (1985), *Hitler's Rockets. The Story of the V-2s*, London: Hutchinson
MacDonagh, Michael (1935), *In London during the Great War. The Diary of a Journalist*, London: Eyre and Spottiswoode
McLaine, Ian (1979), *Ministry of Morale. Home Front Morale and the*

Ministry of Information in World War II, London: Allen and Unwin

Marchand, Alfred (1871), *Le Siège de Strasbourg 1870 – la bibliothèque – la cathédrale*, Paris

Matthews, W. R. (ed.) (1945), *Bombed Churches as War Memorials*, Cheam: The Architectural Press

Maurois, André (1947), *Rouen dévasté*, Rouen: Société normande des amis du livre

Mellor, David, Gill Saunders and Patrick Wright (1990), *Recording Britain. A Pictorial Domesday of Pre-War Britain*, Newton Abbot and London: David and Charles, in association with the Victoria and Albert Museum

Methuen, Lord (Paul Ayshford) (1952), *Normandy Diary. Being a Record of Survivals and Losses of Historical Monuments in North-Western France, together with those in the Island of Walcheren and in that Part of Belgium traversed by 21st Army Group in 1944–45*, London: Robert Hale Ltd

Michelin et Cie/Michelin Tyre Co. (1917), *The Marne Battlefields 1914. An Illustrated History and Guide*, Clermont-Ferrand and London

Michelin et Cie/Michelin Tyre Co. (1919), *Soissons Before and During the War*, Clermont-Ferrand and London

Morison, Frank (1937), *War on Great Cities. A Study of the Facts*, London: Faber and Faber

Morton, J. B. (1942), *War Pictures by British Artists. No. 2 Blitz*, London, New York and Toronto: Oxford University Press

Mulzer, Erich (1972), *Der Wiederaufbau der Altstadt von Nürnberg 1945 bis 1970*, Erlangen: Erlangen Geographische Arbeiten

Müntz, E. (1872), 'Les Monuments d'art détruits à Strasbourg' in *Gazette des Beaux-Arts*, 1872, pp. 349–60

Murray, Williamson (1985), *Luftwaffe. Strategy for Defeat 1933–1945*, London: Allen and Unwin

Narracott, A. H. (1945), *Air Power in War*, London: Frederick Muller Ltd

Nash, D. B. (1980), *Imperial German Army Handbook 1914–1918*, London: Ian Allen Ltd

National Buildings Record (1942), *First Annual Report for the period ending April 12th 1942*

National Buildings Record (1943), *Second Annual Report for the period ending April 12th 1943*

National Gallery, London (1942), *War Pictures at the National Gallery*, exhibition catalogue with an introduction by Eric Newton

National Gallery, London (1943), *Rebuilding Britain*, exhibition catalogue

National Gallery, London (1944), *War Pictures at the National Gallery*, exhibition catalogue

National Gallery, London (1944), *National Buildings Record Photographs*, exhibition catalogue

Neu, Heinrich (1958), 'Die Verluste an Kulturgut in Deutschland durch den zweiten Weltkrieg', in *Dokumente Deutscher Kriegsschäden*, Band I, Bonn: Bundesminister für Vertriebene, Flüchtlinge und Kriegsgeschädigte

Newton, Eric (ed.) (1945), *War Through Artists' Eyes. Paintings and Drawings by British War Artists*, London: John Murray

Nicholas, Lynn H. (1994), *The Rape of Europa. The Fate of Europe's Art Treasures in the Third Reich*, New York: Alfred A. Knopf

Nothomb, Pierre (1915), *Les Barbares en Belgique*, Paris

Office International des Musées (1939), *La Protection des monuments et oeuvres d'art en temps de guerre*, Paris: Office International des Musées

Official Journal of the European Communities, no. C 219, vol. 40, 18 July 1997, 'Call for proposals for events and dissemination initiatives of a European dimension in favour of the preservation and increased awareness of European cultural heritage'

Pane, Roberto (1950), 'The Restoration of Historic Buildings After the War', in *Museum*, vol. III, no. 1, pp. 78–89

Pevsner, Nikolaus (1942 and later editions), *An Outline of European Architecture*, Harmondsworth, Middlesex: Penguin Books

Pevsner, Nikolaus and Bridget Cherry (1989), *The Buildings of England, London, Volume I. The Cities of London and Westminster*, Harmondsworth, Middlesex: Penguin Books

Priestley, J. B. (1940), *Postscripts*, London: Heineman

Randa, Alexander (1948), *Dämonie der Zerstörung*, Zurich: Thomas Verlag

Ranke, Winfried (1985), *August Sander. Die Zerstörung Kölns. Photographien 1945–46*, Munich: Schirmer/Mosel

Rappaport, P. (1945), *Der Wiederaufbau der deutschen Städte. Leitgedanken*, Essen-Steele: Verlag Willi Webels

Réau, Louis (1959), *Histoire du Vandalisme. Les Monuments détruits de l'art français* (2 vols), Paris: Hachette

Report of the American Commission for the Protection and Salvage of Artistic and Historic Monuments in War Areas (1946), Washington

Report of the Commission of Jurists (1923), The Hague

Rhodes, Anthony (1976), *Propaganda. The Art of Persuasion: World War II*, New York and London: Chelsea House

Richards, J. M. and John Summerson (eds) (1947), *The Bombed Buildings of Britain*, 2nd edn (1st edn 1942), London: The Architectural Press

Rodemann, Karl (ed.) (1951), *Das Berliner Schloss und sein Untergang. Ein Bildbericht über die Zerstörung Berliner Kunstdenkmäler*, Berlin: Tauber Verlag

Rorimer, James J. (1950), *Survival. The Salvage and Protection of Art in War*, New York: Abelard Press

Ross, Marvin C. (1946), 'The Kunstschutz in Occupied France' in *College Art Journal*, May 1946, pp. 336–52

Rostand, André (1948), *Monuments meurtris du Cotentin libéré*, Coutances

Rothnie, Niall (1992), *The Baedeker Blitz. Hitler's Attack on Britain's Historic Cities*, London: Ian Allen Ltd

Roubier, Jean and Marcel Aubert (1946), *Rouen*, Paris: Fayard

Roubier, Jean and Louis Réau (1946), *Caen*, Paris: Fayard

Royal Commission on the Historical Monuments of England (1991), *50 Years of the National Buildings Record 1941–1991*, introduction by Sir John Summerson, Beckenham: Trigon Press

Royal Institute of British Architects (1943), *Towards a New Britain*, London: R.I.B.A.

Royaume de Belgique, Ministère de la Justice, Commission des Crimes de guerre (1946), *Les Crimes de guerre commis lors de l'invasion du territoire national – Mai 1940 – La destruction de la Bibliothèque de Louvain*, Liège

Royer, Jean (1941), 'Reconstruction' in *Urbanisme*, October–November 1941, pp. 64–77

Royse, M. W. (1928), *Aerial Bombardment and the International Regulation of Warfare*, New York: Harold Vinal Ltd

Rumpf, Hans (1961), *Das war der Bombenkrieg. Deutsche Städte im Feuersturm. Ein Dokumentarbericht*, Oldenburg and Hamburg: Gerhard Stalling Verlag

Sartre, Jean-Paul (1944), 'Paris sous l'occupation' in *La France Libre*, vol. IX, no. 49, 15 November 1944, pp. 9–18

Sauvage, R. N. (1945), 'Etat des monuments de Caen, détruits, ruinés ou endommagés par les bombardements de 1944', *Bulletin de la Société des Antiquaires de Normandie*, vol. XLIX, 1942–5, pp. 507–17

Sauvage, R. N. (1949), *Les Destructions de 1944 dans le Calvados*, Caen

Schnéegans, A. (1871), *La Guerre en Alsace – Strasbourg*, Paris and Neuchâtel

Schröer, Alois (1951), *Der Hohe Dom zu Münster. Sein Stirb und Werde in der Not unserer Zeit*, Münster: Regensbergsche Verlagsbuchhandlung

Seydewitz, Max (1956), *Die unbesiegbare Stadt. Zerstörung und Wiederaufbau von Dresden*, 3rd edn, Berlin: Kongress-Verlag

Sharp, Thomas (1946), *Exeter Phoenix*, Exeter: Exeter City Council

Shirer, William L. (1941), *Berlin Diary 1934–1941*, London: Hamish Hamilton

Shirer, William L. (1947), *End of a Berlin Diary*, New York: Alfred A. Knopf

Shirer, William L. (1970), *The Collapse of the Third Republic. An Inquiry into the Fall of France in 1940*, London: Heineman and Secker and Warburg

Sous-Secrétariat d'Etat des Beaux-Arts (1915), *Les Allemands destructeurs de cathédrales et de trésors du passé*, Paris

Spaight, J. M. (1924), *Air Power and War Rights*, London: Longmans, Green and Co.

Spaight, J. M. (1930), *Air Power and the Cities*, London: Longmans, Green and Co.

Spaight, J. M. (1941), *The Battle of Britain, 1940*, London: Geoffrey Bles

Spaight, J. M. (1944), *Bombing Vindicated*, London: Geoffrey Bles

Speer, Albert (1943), *Neue deutsche Baukunst*, Prague: Volk und Reich Verlag

Speer, Albert (1969), *Erinnerungen*, Berlin: Propyläen Verlag

Spence, Basil (1962), *Phoenix at Coventry. The Building of a Cathedral*, London: Geoffrey Bles

Spender, Stephen (Introduction by) (1943), *War Pictures by British Artists. Second Series No. 4 Air Raids*, London, New York and Toronto: Oxford University Press

Steinbeck, John (1942), *Bombs Away. The Story of a Bomber Team*, New York: Viking Press

Strauss, Gerhard (1947), 'Denkmalpflege in der Ostzone. Problemstellung und erste Arbeit' in *Die Kunstpflege*, no. 1, 1947, pp. 79–86

Taittinger, Pierre (1948), . . . *Et Paris ne fut pas détruit*, Paris: Elan

Tate Gallery, London (1982), *Graham Sutherland*, exhibition catalogue

Tate Gallery, London (1983), *John Piper*, exhibition catalogue

Tavernier, R. (1945), 'Pierres précieuses d'autrefois' in *Urbanisme*, nos. 105–6

Taylor, Brandon and Wilfried van der Will (1990), *The Nazification of Art, Design, Music, Architecture and Film*, Winchester: Winchester School of Art

Taylor, Fred (trans. and ed.) (1982), *The Goebbels Diaries 1939–1941*, London: Hamish Hamilton

Taylor, John (1992), 'London's Latest "Immortal" – the Statue to Sir Arthur Harris of Bomber Command', *Kritische Berichte*, vol. XX 3, 1992, pp. 96–102

Taylor, Telford (1993), *The Anatomy of the Nuremberg Trials. A Personal Memoir*, London: Bloomsbury

Thomas, Hugh (1977), *The Spanish Civil War*, 3rd ed., London: Hamish Hamilton

Thomas, John (1987), *Coventry Cathedral*, London: Unwin Hyman

Treue, Wilhelm (1957), *Kunstraub – Über die Schicksale von Kunstwerken in Krieg, Revolution und Frieden*, Düsseldorf

Trevor-Roper, H. R. (1964), *Hitler's War Directives 1939–1945*, London: Sidgwick and Jackson

Trial of the Major War Criminals before the International Military Tribunal, Nuremberg 14 November 1945 – 1 October 1946, Vol. IX, Nuremberg 1947

Trimm, Timothée (1871), *Les Ruines de Paris – chronique de Paris brulé – description des monuments, palais, maisons incendiées, scènes de dévastation, état actuel des ruines*, Paris

Troost, Gerdy (1943), *Das Bauen im neuen Reich*, Bayreuth

Trost, Klara (1950), *Zerstörte Kostbarkeiten von liebgeworden Werken deutscher Baukunst*, Frankfurt am Main: Verlag August Lutzeyen

Unesco (1947), *Voici l'Unesco. Activité de l'Unesco pendant les premiers mois de son existence*, Paris: Unesco

Unesco (1947), *The Book of Needs of Fifteen War-Devastated Countries in Education, Science and Culture*, Vol. I, Paris: Unesco

Unesco (1948), *Universities in Need*, Paris: Unesco

Unesco (1948), *Report of the Director General on the Activities of the Organization in 1948*, Paris: Unesco

Unesco (1949), *Report of the Director General on the Activities of the Organization in 1949*, Paris: Unesco

Unesco (1952), *Report of the Director General on the Activities of the Organization in 1952*, Paris: Unesco

Unesco (1955), *Report of the Director General on the Activities of the Organization in 1954*, Paris: Unesco

Unesco (1985), *Conventions and Recommendations of Unesco concerning the protection of the cultural heritage*, Paris: Unesco

United Nations General Assembly, Security Council (1995), *Report of the International Tribunal for the Prosecution of Persons Responsible for Serious Violations of International Humanitarian Law Committed in the Territory of the Former Yugoslavia Since 1991*, 23 August 1995

United States Strategic Bombing Survey (1945), *Area Studies Division Report No. 7. A Detailed Study of the Effects of Bombing on Lübeck, Germany*, typescript dated 27 October 1945

United States Strategic Bombing Survey (1945), *Military Analysis Division Report No. 4. Description of Royal Air Force Bombing*, typescript dated 3 November 1945

United States Strategic Bombing Survey (1947), *Morale Division Report. The Effects of Strategic Bombing on German Morale*, 2 vols, Washington: US Government Printing Office (dates of Survey: March–July 1945)

Vachon, Marius (1882), *Strasbourg, les musées, les bibliothèques et la cathédrale. L'Art pendant la guerre de 1870–71*, Paris

Vachon, Marius (1915), *Les Villes martyres de France et de Belgique*, Paris

Valland, Rose (1997), *Le Front de l'art. Défense des collections françaises*

1939–1945, Paris: Editions de la Réunion des musées nationaux (originally published 1961)

Végh, Julius von (1915), *Die Bilderstürmer. Eine Kulturgeschichtliche Studie*, Strasbourg: Heitz and Mindel

Verrier, Jean (1940), 'Les Monuments historiques atteints par la guerre', *Bulletin Monumental*, vol. XCIX, 1940, pp. 239–60

Verrier, Jean (1947), *Les Dommages de guerre aux édifices classés parmi les Monuments Historiques et inscrits à l'Inventaire Supplémentaire*, Paris: Société Française d'Architecture

Vetter, Ferdinand (1915), 'La Croix d'or. Protection des monuments artistiques et historiques en temps de guerre' in *Journal de Genève*, 11 May 1915

Vetter, Ferdinand (1917), *Friede dem Kunstwerk! Zwischenstaatliche Sicherung der Kunstdenkmäler im Kriege als Weg zum künftigen dauerhaften Frieden*, Olten

Vincent, Jean (1943), *La Reconstruction des villes et des immeubles sinistrés après la guerre de 1940*, Paris: Bishop et fils

Voss, K. (1946), *Lübeck, wie es war*, Lübeck

Warnke, Martin (ed.) (1977), *Bildersturm. Die Zerstörung des Kunstwerks*, Frankfurt am Main: Syndikat

Watson, J. Paton and Patrick Abercrombie (1943), *A Plan for Plymouth. The Report Prepared for the City Council*, Plymouth: Underhill Ltd

Watt, Donald C., 'Restraints on War in the Air Before 1945' in Howard, Michael (ed.) (1979), *Restraints on War. Studies in the Limitation of Armed Conflict*, Oxford: OUP

Webster, Sir Charles and Noble Frankland (1961), *The Strategic Air Offensive Against Germany 1939–1945*, 4 vols, London: HMSO

Weimar 1999 – European City of Culture Corporation (1997), *Weimar 99. Cultural Capital of Europe*, Weimar

Werner, Anton von (1913), *Erlebnisse und Eindrücke*, Berlin

Williamson, Catherine E. (1949), *Though the Streets Burn*, London: Headey Brothers

Wimhurst, Claude (1942), *The Bombardment of Bath*, Bath: The Mendip Press

Wolff Metternich, Franz Graf (1944), *Die Denkmalpflege in Frankreich*, Berlin: Deutscher Kunstverlag

Wolff Metternich, Franz Graf (1951), 'Die Baudenkmäler in Nord-Rheinland. Kriegsschaden und Wiederaufbau' in *Jahrbuch der rheinischen Denkmalpflege in Nord-Rheinland*, XIX Jahrgang, 1951

Woolley, Sir Leonard (1945), 'The Preservation of Historical Architecture in the War Zones', *Journal of the Royal Institute of British Architects*, Vol. 53, December 1945, pp. 35–42.

Woolley, Sir Leonard (1947), *A Record of the Work Done by the Military Authorities for the Protection of the Treasures of Art and History in War Areas*, London: HMSO

Worringer, Wilhelm (1914), 'Die Kathedrale in Reims' in *Kunst und Künstler*, November 1914, pp. 85–90

Zimmerman, H. K. (1947), 'Wiederaufbau des Frankfurter Goethehauses?' in *Die Kunstpflege*, no. 1, 1947, pp. 51–4

Newspapers and Journals consulted

College Art Journal
The Connoisseur
Frankfurter Zeitung
Horizon
Jahrbuch der rheinischen Denkmalpflege in Nord-Rheinland
Kunstchronik
Die Kunstpflege
La France Libre
Les Monuments historiques de la France
Museum
Official Journal of the European Communities
The Times
Urbanisme
Völkischer Beobachter

Archive sources

Paris, Archives de la Bibliothèque du Patrimoine:
Dossier 1565, Reims Cathedral, 1914–1918 damage and postwar restoration
Dossier 1587, Reims Cathedral, statuary, 1914–1918 damage and postwar restoration
Dossier 103, Soissons Cathedral, 1914–1918 damage and postwar restoration
Dossier 96, St Quentin, Collégiale, 1914–1918 damage and postwar restoration
London, Imperial War Museum, Department of Art, Second World War Artists Archive
File GP/55/51 John Piper 1940–1950
File GP/55/57 Graham Sutherland 1940–1950
Unesco archive documents
Unesco/CUA/120, First Meeting of the High Contracting Parties to the Convention for the Protection of Cultural Property in the Event of Armed Conflict, Unesco House, Paris, 16–25 July 1962
Unesco/CUA/122, Study of Measures for the Preservation of Monuments through the Establishment of an International Fund or by Any Other Appropriate Means, Paris, 28 June 1963
Inactive Correspondence Files, Series 1946/1956, France: Historic Monuments 069: 72 A 064 (44) "49"
Jan Opocensky (1949–50), *The Beginnings of Unesco 1942–1948*, 2 vols, typescript.

Index

Numbers in *italic* refer to illustrations.

amazon.co.uk

www.amazon.co.uk

c/o Marston Gate
Ridgmont
MK43 0XP BEDFORD
United Kingdom, UK

Delivered to:
Bruce Jerram
24 Grosvernor Road
Belvedere, KENT DA17 5JY
United Kingdom, GB

Invoice/Receipt for

Your order of 7 December, 2001

Order ID 026-9160565-5934835

Invoice number ghcy15217
7 December, 2001

Qty	Item	Bin	Description	Our Price	VAT Rate	Total Price
1	War Damage in Western Europe Nicola Lambourne 0748612858 Happy Birthday Bruce Love from Roger and Jill	(P–2–E56C103)	Paperback			

amazon.co.uk™

At Amazon.co.uk, we want you to be delighted every time you shop with us. Occasionally though, we know you may want to return items, so below is our returns policy.

For books:

Our "no quibbles" guarantee means that if for any reason you are unhappy with your purchase you can return it to us in its original condition, within 30 days, and we will issue a full refund for the price you paid for the item.

For all other items:

We accept the return of all other items only if they are unopened and in their original condition. If you return goods, as detailed, within 30 days, we will issue a full refund for the price you paid for the item.

To return an item:

To return an item, please fill out the back of this delivery slip giving the reason for the return, wrap the package securely and send the package to the address below. In the case of a defective product, please provide a full description of the fault in the space provided and return the defective item in its original box (if any), with all warranty cards, licenses, manuals and accessories. Then send the package to the address below.

Amazon.co.uk
Returns Department
Ridgmont
BEDFORD
MK43 0ZA
United Kingdom

For your protection we recommend that you use a recorded-delivery service.

Detective items:

You can always return items if they are defective. Please note we only accept returns of items that have been opened if they are defective. Please see "To return an item" below for details of how to return defective items to us.

Delivery charges, gift wrapping and other services

If you are returning an item because of error on our part or because it is defective, we will be happy to refund the delivery charges incurred in sending the item to you and your costs in returning it to us. Otherwise you will be responsible for those charges and the costs of any other services provided to you in connection with your purchase, for example gift wrapping.

rights.

Problems, Questions, Suggestions?

If you have any questions regarding this order, please contact us via:

Non-UK Residents Phone: +44 20 8636 9451
UK Residents **ONLY** Phone: 0800 279 6620
Non-UK Residents Fax: +44 20 8636 9401
UK Residents **ONLY** Fax: 0800 279 6630
E-mail: orders@amazon.co.uk

Reason for Return:

_____

_____

_____

_____

Thanks for shopping at Amazon.co.uk!
http://www.amazon.co.uk

1980/ghcy15217/–1–/1RL/1RMH/1695/std–uk–dom/1392965/1207–10:57/1208–00:00

VAT Number, GB 727 2558 21